A Curriculum Model for Individuals with Severe Learning and Behavior Disorders

A Curriculum Model for Individuals with Severe Learning and Behavior Disorders

By
Linda Rumanoff Simonson, M.A.
Benhaven School/Community for Autistic
and Neurologically Impaired Individuals
New Haven, Connecticut

University Park Press
Baltimore

UNIVERSITY PARK PRESS
International Publishers in Science, Medicine, and Education
233 East Redwood Street
Baltimore, Maryland 21202

Copyright © 1979 by University Park Press.

Composed by University Park Press, Typesetting Division.
Manufactured in the United States of America by
The Maple Press Company.

All rights, including that of translation into other languages, reserved. Photomechanical reproduction (photocopy, microcopy) of this book or parts thereof without special permission of the publisher is prohibited.

Library of Congress Cataloging in Publication Data
Simonson, Linda Rumanoff.
A curriculum model for individuals with severe learning and behavior disorders.

Bibliography: p.
Includes index.
1. Mentally handicapped children — Education.
2. Learning disabilities. 3. Problem children — Education. 4. Autism. I. Title.
LC4601.R83   371.9'2   79-13332
ISBN 0-8391-1322-6

Contents

Preface vii

Part I **INTRODUCTION TO THE CURRICULUM MODEL**

    1 **Autism** Some Facts and Theories 3
    2 **The Curriculum Model** An Overview 11
    3 **Considerations in Using a Functional Curriculum** 23
    4 **Principles of Effective Teaching** 29

Part II **IMPLEMENTING THE CURRICULUM UNITS**

    5 **Curriculum Unit Selection and Adaptation** 41
    6 **Implementing the Work Activity Area of a Curriculum Unit** 49
    7 **Implementing the Language Skills Area of a Curriculum Unit** 67
    8 **Implementing the Reading Skills Area of a Curriculum Unit** 105
    9 **Implementing the Number Skills Area of a Curriculum Unit** 145
    10 **Implementing the Supplementary Skills Area of a Curriculum Unit** 173
    11 **Integrating Curriculum Units** 175

Part III **PREPARATION AND ASSESSMENT WITHIN THE CURRICULUM MODEL**

    12 **Introducing the Curriculum** Teacher and Materials Preparation 179
    13 **Evaluating a Program and Monitoring Progress** 189
    14 **Developing Your Own Curriculum Units** 211
    15 **Evaluation and Conclusion** 215

Part IV **APPENDICES** THE CURRICULUM UNITS

    Appendix A **Table-Setting Curriculum** 225

Appendix B	**Blackboard-Cleaning Curriculum**	241
Appendix C	**Bed-Making Curriculum**	255
Appendix D	**Toothbrushing Curriculum**	269
Appendix E	**Sandwich-Making Curriculum**	287

References 301
Index 305

Preface

Teaching the handicapped learner, regardless of the severity or scope of his handicap, is aptly termed *special* education. The learner has special needs that must be recognized, special strengths that must be utilized, and special problems that must be identified. The individual with learning and behavior disorders requires, then, a very special-ized program of training.

As a teacher of individuals with severe learning and behavior disorders, I was faced with the awesome questions of what to teach and how to teach most effectively. I was fortunate to teach within a school with experienced professionals, who not only shared what they had learned about effective teaching, but also provided me with a basic philosophy that contributed to the methods and content in this curriculum model. My answer to the dilemma of what to teach persons with severe handicaps in learning and behavior developed in part from this philosophy and in part in response to the needs and abilities of the students with whom I have worked for the past eight years. It is my hope and belief that this curriculum model will serve as a valuable tool and provide effective programs for educating those individuals who demonstrate the most severe learning and behavior problems. I hope that the teaching methods presented here, and the examples of how to identify and attack a wide variety of difficulties, will aid and encourage educators to continue efforts to develop effective approaches, techniques, and suitable curricula for individuals with severe learning and behavior disorders.

I would like to thank the students of Benhaven, who taught me how to teach by showing me how they learn. For the opportunity to learn from her, the students, and the staff, I thank Dr. Amy Lettick, the founder and director of Benhaven. The following people have provided me with models of professional skill and talent, as well as with encouragement throughout the years: Larry and Robin Wood, Inger Connery, Sylvia Medalie, and, in those first "groping" years, David Freschi. I gratefully thank all those who have worked in my classroom and have contributed so much to the effectiveness of the curriculum through their patience, energy, and skill. A word of thanks, also, to Marianne Pearsall, for the hours of tedious typing. Finally, it is with love and appreciation that I acknowledge my family and friends, whose support, interest, and encouragement sustained me and stimulated my efforts to make this curriculum available to others.

*To S.M.S.,
whose faith and love
make anything possible*

Part I

Introduction to the Curriculum Model

1

AUTISM
Some Facts and Theories

The curriculum model discussed in this book was designed at Benhaven, a school/community for autistic and brain-damaged persons, and developed in response to the need for a meaningful and effective curriculum. Because it has been implemented in a classroom for individuals diagnosed as autistic, it seems appropriate to preface the introduction of the curriculum with a discussion of the behavioral characteristics, etiological theories, and treatment procedures associated with infantile autism.

Early infantile autism was first identified in 1943 by Leo Kanner, who diagnosed 11 atypical children with the following common characteristics: social withdrawal and an inability to establish affective relationships, mutism or abnormal language, obsession with the preservation of sameness in the environment, bizarre mannerisms and monotonous, repetitive play habits, and wild, undirected behavior. Kanner thought that these children were of normal or higher intelligence, but recent literature has indicated that intelligence, when measurable, can range from normal to deficient in autistic children. In his studies of autistic children, Rimland (1964) found infantile autism to be more prevalent among males than females (4 to 1), and half of those studied were diagnosed as nonverbal autistic.

Some of the behavior characteristics of infantile autism may be apparent within the first weeks of infancy. The infant may show none of the usual anticipatory responses to being picked up, appear not to react to noise, or show signs of discomfort when held. Mothers describe their children either as having been exceptionally good, demanding little attention and seldom crying, or as having cried inconsolably most of the time. Infants may show no response to their mothers, no normal smiling response, or late (if any) cooing. Between the ages of 6 months and 1 year, the child may engage in head banging, demonstrate irregular developmental sequences (e.g., late sitting, early standing, late walking), and react peculiarly to sensory stimulation.

By the age of 2 to 3 years, the child may be hyperactive or sluggish, engage in peculiar mannerisms, demonstrate unusual motility patterns (e.g., walking on toes, rocking), show little or no interest in toys (except to use them in a repetitive, inappropriate manner), have no communicative speech, and appear indifferent to human contact and seem socially aloof. Parents may be "used" as objects for the satisfaction of the child's needs. For instance, the child may take a parent's hand and direct it toward an object that he wants.

By the age of 4 to 5 years, the child may still demonstrate no speech or very unusual speech in which he repeats things said immediately (echolalia) or at a later time (delayed echolalia). Usually, verbal autistic children misuse pronouns or do not use them at all. Language development by age 5 is seen by most professionals as a factor in the child's prognosis for general intellectual and social development; those who have developed language by 5 years of age are viewed as having a more favorable prognosis. Usually, if language is present, it is very literal and atonal, with a strangely detached quality as if it were memorized. Such language disturbances are similar to those seen in children with developmental aphasia, but aphasics do not exhibit some of the behavioral characteristics associated with autism and usually demonstrate a capacity to relate through gesture and expression.

Ornitz (1973) described the various deviations from normal development as disturbances of motility, developmental rate, perception, relating, and language. The motility disturbances include stereotyped mannerisms that are so similar in all austistic children that they do not seem entirely voluntary. The developmental rate of autistic children is so uneven and irregular that they may demonstrate some very special abilities (for example, memorizing entire operas in Italian) while showing other serious cognitive defects. In general, disturbances of perception seem to be caused by "an impaired ability to make discriminations without feedback from motor responses" (Ornitz, 1973, p. 26). Children may also appear unresponsive to stimuli or exhibit exaggerated responses to stimuli. They may be overselective in responding to only one component of a stimulus complex. Given auditory and tactile stimuli simultaneously, a child may respond to only one of the stimuli. For example, a teacher may verbally direct a child (physically able and with normal hearing) to pick up an object (for example, a shoe). If the child does not pick up the object in response to the spoken word "shoe," the teacher may take the child's hand and help him to pick it up while saying "shoe." The child may pick up the shoe on command repeatedly with the teacher's physical prompt (tactile stimulus) and spoken word (auditory stimulus), but may be unable to perform that simple action in response to the spoken auditory stimulus alone. An overselective response to the tactile stimulus, so that the child "misses" the provided auditory stimulus, might be one explanation for this.

As they grow older, the 10% to 15% of autistic children who develop language usually demonstrate improved social relations, but they still may seem odd, eccentric, and immature. Their speech usually sounds deliberate and stiff, and they lack spontaneity in language, play, and social interaction. The other 85% to 90% do not develop language, are extremely limited in communication, lack any understanding of abstract concepts, and demonstrate severe behavioral disturbances, such as aggression or self-abuse (Cohen and Caparulo, 1975). It is primarily for these most severely handicapped individuals, for whom appropriate curricula are unavailable, that the curriculum presented in this book was developed.

CAUSES

There has been much controversy surrounding the cause or causes of autism, centering on the issue of psychogenic versus organic causes. Research has not yet conclusively supported either view.

During the 1940s and 1950s, psychodynamic and psychoanalytic theories were popular. Psychoanalysts blamed parents as cold, unloving individuals, whose children withdrew in response to their actions, attitudes, or unconscious feelings (Cohen and Caparulo, 1975). Kanner was not as extreme as other psychoanalysts in blaming parents for the disorder, although to a degree he viewed parents as causative agents. He postulated that a constitutional predisposition in the child interacts with parental characteristics and attitudes to cause the primarily affective disorder, and he described these parents as an intellectual and emotionally cold group (1973). Bruno Bettelheim, outspoken psychoanalyst and director of the Sonia Shankman Orthogenic School for autistic and emotionally disturbed children in Chicago, sees the primary disorder in autism as a severe disturbance or absence of the child's concept of self (Bettelheim, 1967). According to Bettelheim, autism is a voluntary withdrawal from the world; mutism is a symbol of that withdrawal and a defense against further emotional pain. The misuse of pronouns is interpreted by Bettelheim and other psychoanalysts as evidence of the child's lack of ego; the autistic child's different "strivings of self" have been blocked or severely interfered with during the critical stages of development. The instruments of this interference with ego development are the unloving parents, especially the frustrating mother. In Bettelheim's words, the initial cause of withdrawal is

> ...the child's correct interpretation of the negative emotions with which the most significant figures in his environment approach him. This, in turn, evokes rage in the child until he begins — as even mature persons do — to interpret the world in the image of his anger (1967, p. 66).

Others disagree with Bettelheim's reasoning that the autistic child's misuse of pronouns is evidence of a disturbed ego or sense of self. It may be seen as an inability to correctly use a rather abstract concept, a view which may be supported by the fact that many verbal autistic children have no difficulty using proper names to refer to themselves or others.

Current research rejects the extreme psychodynamic viewpoint of Bettelheim and others. A review of studies by Ornitz (1973) does not confirm that parents are cold, aloof, or have any other emotional or personality characteristics that predispose their child to the disorder. They appear to be like any other group of parents of normal or handicapped children. Any noted disturbances might be caused by the hardships of raising a difficult child or the guilt involved in having a disturbed child. There are no significant differences in parental or family characteristics or socioeconomic background. In a study of 150 autistic children and their parents, Schopler (1973) found no evidence to support the theory of parents as causative agents. Such a theory only adds to guilt and is therefore destructive. As a group, the parents studied evidenced no more than the normal range of adjustment problems and interpersonal difficulties, with the exception that they were the parents of severely difficult and unusual children (Schopler, 1973).

The concept that autism may have an organic base is supported by current research. In studies of twins, there is 100% concordance; that is, if one twin is autistic, the other twin also is atypical (Cohen, 1975). Many autistic children have abnormal or borderline abnormal brain wave patterns. Twenty-five percent of a well followed group developed seizures (grand mal or psychomotor) between the ages of 11 and 19 years, after having normal EEGs at earlier ages (Cohen, 1975). The uniform clinical picture all over the world, regardless of socioeconomic background, also points to an inborn disorder. In biochemical research, studies have shown that abnormalities in central nervous system functioning produce stereotypic behavior, hyperactivity, disorganization, and other characteristics associated with autism. Autism occurs in association with brain damage, metabolic disturbances, and infectious diseases, such as congenital rubella.

Some neurophysiological studies relating the sleep cycle and amounts of REM (rapid eye movement) sleep have shown that REM activity is reduced in autistic children to a frequency similar to infants, implying, perhaps, a maturational defect in the brain stem (Ornitz, 1973). According to Ornitz (1973), autism is "a behavioral and emotional disorder based on some kind of organic brain impairment and is not of psychogenic origin" (p. 42).

Rutter and Bartok (Oppenheim, 1974) suggest that the primary disorder of autism is the language and cognitive defect and that ". . . the social and behavioral anomalies arise as secondary consequences.... [T]he consistent failure to find deviant factors in the environmental situation suggests that the language/cognitive impairment is the main factor involved in the pathogenesis of autism" (p. 29).

Donald Cohen of the Yale Child Study Center is conducting research into a biochemical basis for the disturbance, exploring the integrative activity of the central nervous system through a study and comparison of syndromes very similar to autism that are associated with metabolic disturbances and other types of brain damage (Cohen, Shaywitz, Johnson, and Bowers, 1974). Part of that research involves monitoring the physiological and biochemical activity of children, normal and atypical, as they engage in specific kinds of activities that require varying degrees of attention and involve different cognitive and motor functions. Benhaven students have participated and are currently participating in this research. Cohen is also exploring the effects of various drugs on the biochemical activity of the central nervous system. At this time, Cohen's research looks promising, although no conclusive evidence has been produced as yet.

The most likely answer to the question of causation is that etiologies are multidetermined. Based on the repetitiveness of autistic characteristics in autistic children, family studies, tentative results of research, and the author's personal observations, evaluations, and interactions with autistic children and their families, the theories and research into organic factors seem to be the most plausible and convincing.

TREATMENT

Before presenting several treatment approaches that are used with autistic individuals, the importance of intensive evaluations and careful diagnosis must be stressed. This is especially true because autism may co-exist with mental retardation, numerous organic brain syndromes, and a variety of seizure disorders. Many organic diseases present symptoms similar to those associated with infantile autism. Therefore, a careful, differential diagnosis must be made, including an assessment of the child's disabilities and competencies, in order to implement the most appropriate intervention procedure for that individual.

Psychoanalytic therapy as a treatment presumes a psychogenic cause for autism. Bettelheim's and other psychoanalysts' conception of autism as a voluntary withdrawal is inconsistent with current research data, as are assertions that the autistic disorder can be reversed through a caregiver's good intentions and a permissive, loving environment. Bettelheim reports success in several of his books (*The Empty Fortress,* 1967; *A Home for the Heart,* gives neither baseline data nor the criteria by which a successful ... defined (Schopler and Rutter, 1976).

Another factor limiting the usefulness of psychotherapy is the cognitive and/or language functioning of the child. A nonverbal, autistic child functioning on a retarded level would gain little from a session with a psychotherapist. Even if a nonverbal method of therapy were used, such as nondirective play therapy, the very nature of the autistic child's play (inappropriate, monotonous, repetitive) would seem to limit any significant progress. If the goals of therapy are ego growth, strengthening a concept of self, and gaining insight and understanding into the world of reality vis-à-vis oneself, then an assumption must be made as to the autistic child's cognitive potential for achieving these goals through a nondirective and primarily verbal therapy. Furthermore, psychotherapy is expensive.

> ...Up to recently it was generally believed that education could do little or nothing for these children and that the medical, specifically psychiatric, profession must assume major or total treatment responsibility.... Clinics rejected them as untreatable. Private psychiatric treatment was too expensive for most families.... At the beginning we believed that our teachers should play a permissive and relatively unstructured "therapeutic" role that permitted their children the freedom to ventilate hostilities, aggressions, and primitive drives until basic intrapsychic conflicts were "worked through" and resolved... We realized what each child needs is his own personal prescription of training and education based on a psycho-educational assessment of his unique patterns of behavior and levels of functioning (Fenichel, 1966, p. 69).

An approach used by both special educators and psychologists is behavior modification. Behavioral techniques can be used to teach skills, shape appropriate behavior, and eliminate inappropriate behavior. These techniques can be used in most any setting when the people using them have been properly trained. Behavioral programs that are carefully and consistently carried out can make a person more manageable and reduce the amount of self-destructive and undesirable behavior. Appropriate behavior is crucial to adapting to any living, learning, or employment situation.

Parental counseling should be an integral part of any treatment program. Counseling should be supportive of the parent rather than guilt producing, and should provide constructive suggestions on how to better manage the child. The parents can be trained to work with their child effectively, to make him more manageable, and to teach him important skills. It is also important that the programs that are begun in one setting (e.g., school) are carried out in the home. Another benefit of parent-training programs is that the parents can view themselves as active participants in their child's growth.

Medication can be helpful in partially controlling some behaviors that interfere with learning and living. For instance, certain drugs have been effective in reducing hyperactivity, irritability, violent outbursts, and over-responsiveness. Medication is most useful as an adjunct to another treatment procedure, such as special education. Any medication must be administered properly, closely monitored, and prescribed only after a thorough medical, neurological, and psychoeducational evaluation and assessment.

Special medication treatments, such as megavitamin therapy, are available. In megavitamin therapy, the administration of vitamins in specific combinations is prescribed. However, studies on this treatment have yielded no supportive results, as yet.

Carl Delacato, a neurologist at the Institutes for the Achievement of Human Potential in Philadelphia, co-directs a treatment program for the neurologically impaired, techniques of which are used with autistic individuals. The treatment is based on the theory that autistic persons have not experienced the normal developmental sequence, which in turn has adversely affected their neurological organization. As a major part of treatment, Delacato (1974) prescribes individualized programs of "patterning" exercises designed to restructure and develop the organization of the brain. However, in the absence of either baseline data or specific results, the effectiveness of his programs is under question.

Proponents of the biological hypotheses advocate remedial education, that is, an educational program within a highly structured environment as the single most effective form of help available. Good special education is "the indicated approach" (Oppenheim, 1974). Once the child is placed in a school/treatment setting that offers an educational program geared to his needs, the "...behavioral anomalies begin to recede and lessen in severity" (Oppenheim, 1974, p. 29).

Despert, in the foreword to Lorna Wing's *Autistic Children* (1972), states, "Therapy in the case of autism must come from outside education rather than interpretation of inner life" (p. vii).

When programs are geared to individual disabilities and strengths, special education, as treatment, can achieve academic, social, and behavior changes. Speech therapy and instruction in sign language can facilitate communication for the language-impaired child. Systematic training in athletics, recreational skills, and gross motor activities can foster a sense of competence, some body awareness, and the opportunity and structure within which to work and play with peers.

The importance of vocational training cannot be overestimated. Good vocational programs give an autistic person useful and salable skills, some degree of self-support, a sense of competence, and an acceptable, productive role in society. There is a "need for research in curricula for vocational education, such as those being developed in Benhaven, in New Haven, Connecticut" (Cohen and Caparulo, 1975, p. 6). In 1973, Benhaven developed a prevocational training project to determine the value of prevocational training for 16 autistic and/or neurologically impaired children. Instruction in self-care, service and maintenance, and production-assembly tasks went on for a 10-month period. Each child was initially evaluated in the performance of each task to determine baselines and the level at which to begin training. Results of the project were encouraging: each of the 16 children progressed in every task; autistic and neurologically impaired children can benefit from prevocational training and *can* be taught to perform gainful activities (Freschi, 1973).

The indicated treatment program for autistic individuals has been succinctly described by Donald Cohen:

> While remaining appropriately and judiciously optimistic about further understanding of the biology of development, we should keep in mind that what can be offered to most children with severe developmental disturbances today are good special education, thoughtful behavior modification, and humane care. For the vast majority of children with autism in the United States today, even these basic needs are not satisfied (1975, p. 36).

At present, a special education approach, involving vocational training and behavior management, is the only effective alternative to institutionalization.

2
THE CURRICULUM MODEL
An Overview

The chapters of this book discuss the components of a curriculum model[1] for individuals with severe learning and behavior disorders. Developed in response to a need for a meaningful, effective curriculum, the curriculum is based on principles and methods growing out of the teaching experience itself, as well as prominent learning theories and teaching approaches. The term *teaching experience* describes an ongoing incorporative process in which each observation and interaction with students (in all areas of a school, on a bus, on an outing, and in all matters of everyday living in a residential setting) contributes to the continual modification and refinement of the teacher's approach to teaching. The teaching experience involves contact and communication with other educators, professionals, parents, and siblings, and the sharing of their experiences, knowledge, and insights. The process of learning through teaching becomes concrete each time a student's response (or lack of one) makes it necessary to alter, or add a new section to, the curriculum model.

It is difficult to propose a final form for the curriculum, knowing that it must be revised to suit individual student/teaching needs in order to be used appropriately. However, the success of students achieving curriculum objectives, slowly but steadily, indicates that the curriculum model presented in Part IV can serve as the basis for a meaningful and effective educational experience for many of our so-called uneducables. The "educational credibility" of the curriculum is further supported by a framework of

---

[1] The format of the curriculum model, composed of five main units, is presented in Part IV, Appendices A to E. Each unit focuses upon a particular activity, or work skill (table setting, blackboard cleaning, bed making, toothbrushing, and sandwich making), which is the focal developmental objective of the unit. Related skill areas of language, reading, numbers, and supplementary (e.g., fine motor) skills are also taught in each curriculum unit. The reader may find it useful to frequently refer to the appendices for further elaboration as particular aspects of the curriculum are discussed.

educational and learning theories, supported by many professionals and current studies in the field of special education, within which the curriculum has been developed. Therefore, before the curriculum itself is presented, a discussion of some of its basic features and the theories and principles that have influenced and supported its development is appropriate.

PRINCIPLES AND THEORIES BEHIND THE CURRICULUM

The curriculum is based on a behavioral approach to teaching. In a broader sense, it applies widely accepted learning theories to the process of instruction. The theories of Pavlov, Thorndike, Hull, Skinner, Guthrie, Hebb, and Piaget can be applied to any teaching situation. Some of these theories, when translated into practical educational terms, suggest principles for more effective teaching. The following six principles are extremely important in teaching exceptional children and are basic to the curriculum (Bugelski, 1964):

1. *Practice and repetition improve retention; overlearning and relearning material are both efficient and effective (Thorndike).* For the learning-disabled individual, repetition and overlearning are critical to acquiring most any skill. The curriculum is designed so that all of the skill areas (e.g., language, reading, numbers) reinforce each other. The same materials and vocabulary are used in each skill area to provide built-in repetition and practice of concepts and skills.
2. *Learning is continuous and cumulative (Hull).* An approach that presents material in a structured series of steps, as has been adopted in this curriculum, allows all new learning to be built upon previously learned material.
3. *When the learner is preoccupied with something else, the learning process is impeded (Hull). The learner must be ready and "available" to learn (Thorndike).* One of the implications of these statements applies particularly to persons with learning and behavioral disturbances, who often engage in behaviors incompatible with learning or who demonstrate resistance to instruction. This resistance may range from throwing materials or attempting to leave the situation to not attending to the teacher or the materials. Therefore, it is essential that the teacher establish control and work to eliminate any behaviors that may interfere with learning.
4. *Teaching new behaviors, or modifying, shaping, or eliminating existing behaviors, is most effective when desired and undesired behaviors or responses are first identified (Skinner).* Using reinforcers that are rewarding to the learner, whether primary (e.g., food) or secondary

(e.g., praise), and being consistent in both demands on and responses to the learner largely determine effectiveness.

5. *A task is simplified for the learner and the teacher if it is broken down into its finest units for specific instruction (Guthrie). The learner's chances for success are increased when he is taught a higher level operation after he has demonstrated that he can perform the background (prerequisite) operations (Hebb, Piaget).* The format of the curriculum is a series of instructional objectives for specific skill areas, with each skill broken down sequentially into its simplest components. The learner proceeds at his own pace, moving to a more complex level of a task only after demonstrating success at the previous, simpler levels.

6. *The task of learning is made easier and more pleasant if the teacher arranges for the learner to be successful at the activity to be learned. It is inefficient teaching to let the learner leave the situation with an incorrect response (Guthrie).* Generally a person with a learning disability has a history of failure; he is easily frustrated and alienated by the learning situation. An incremental approach, with a series of small successes, can increase the likelihood of further achievement. In addition, learners tend to remember the last item or response in a sequence; therefore it is more efficient for the learner to leave a task situation with a correct response. In order for the learner to make the correct response, and thus maximize the learning opportunity, a nonverbal cue can be provided (e.g., pointing to the correct response item) or the learner can be physically manipulated to make the appropriate response. Teaching is more effective if the learning situation itself is a positive experience.

Support for the basic features of the curriculum can be found within special education literature. The curriculum is highly structured, easily individualized, and prescriptive, and it teaches primarily functional skills. Within each unit of the curriculum, the teacher determines what specific educational goals are appropriate for a particular learner. Ebersole, Kephart, and Ebersole (1968) describe the essential features of a curriculum for the handicapped learner:

1. Methods are adapted to individual needs, strengths, and weaknesses
2. Emphasis is placed on concrete techniques
3. Objectives are a series of well planned learning steps
4. A variety of methods that reinforce one another are used
5. The curriculum is varied and interrelated

In addition, they stress the importance of a highly structured educational program, consistency in teaching, redirecting the learner to the task (physically if necessary), and avoiding teaching at the learner's frustration level. Strauss and Lehtinen, in the classic *The Brain-Injured Child* (1947), recommend a highly structured environment with individualized instruction and the use of materials that demonstrate a process and make it concrete. Myklebust and Johnson (1967) emphasize the need for thorough initial and ongoing psychoeducational evaluations as part of any educational program in order to direct remediation toward individual strengths and weaknesses. Carl Fenichel, former director of the League School for Severely Disturbed Children in Brooklyn, advocates a highly structured learning environment with a "reality-oriented" curriculum involving "living-playing-learning experiences and activities that offer continuity, stability, security, and a sense of achievement" (1966, p. 14).

Rosalind Oppenheim, mother of an autistic child, teacher, and Director of the Rimland School for Autistic Children in Evanston, Illinois, states, "...It should be understood that the curriculum must be individually tailored for each child, and designed to ameliorate or compensate for his specific functional and development deficiencies" (1974, p. 33). Oppenheim also emphasizes the importance of establishing control of the learning situation. She suggests containing the child in the learning situation and following through on any command given. If the child does not perform as directed, the teacher physically directs him to make the appropriate response (e.g., moves his hands). To accomplish this, Oppenheim recommends selecting activities through which the teacher can lead the child. Amy Lettick, mother of an autistic child, teacher, and director of Benhaven, a school/community for autistic and brain-damaged persons in New Haven, Connecticut, expresses a more philosophical aspect of the teacher-control issue:

> We believe that learning for the handicapped is not always pleasant for either the child or the teacher. However, we feel that the ultimate pleasure that comes as a result of overcoming or circumventing a handicap is worth the transitory distress that may sometimes accompany the learning process. [1972, p. 5]

The word *structure* appears repeatedly in discussions of educational programs for the severely handicapped learner. The specific lesson or task to be learned must be highly structured. Lettick (1972) describes structuring a lesson as arranging "...a particular learning experience in an orderly, sequentially sound, well-organized manner with full awareness of and control over all the various aspects of the situation" (p. 56). Oppenheim (1974) recommends a task analysis approach to teaching:

> In many instances, the successful teaching of these skills to autistic children will require a task analysis approach; prior to teaching of a specific skill, the teacher should prepare her lesson plan backwards, analyzing the task step by step all

the way back to its basic beginning. Then it can be taught to the child in this logical, sequential progression of small fundamental steps. [pp. 58-59]

These principles of teaching the individual with learning and behavioral disorders are evident in the format and content of the curriculum.

BEHAVIORAL APPROACH

The severity of the disturbances of those individuals for whom the curriculum was originally developed demanded an approach that is highly organized, consistent, and easily monitored for effectiveness. In general, the term *behavioral approach* describes the principles and methods of teaching, the format and design of the curriculum, and the use of evaluation procedures, as well as techniques, to modify behavior. It does not necessarily mean M&Ms for correct responses or time-out for inappropriate behavior. Properly used, a behavioral approach demands a high degree of professional judgment. The teacher must use all his skills to determine realistic expectations, appropriate demands, and effective teaching techniques in designing and implementing a program that will maximize the individual's potential for learning. Various methods should be considered, tried, and carefully monitored and documented to determine the effectiveness of, and the need for, changes in programming.

Study should begin with a discussion of a behavioral approach to behavior problems within the learning situation. The following concepts should be considered: 1) control must be established by the teacher, 2) if the learner is able to perform the required task, then the teacher must complete the activity, 3) once initial resistance is overcome, the learner can enjoy learning, 4) many inappropriate behaviors can be reduced or eliminated through the learning situation itself, and 5) no amount of learning is worth the effort if the individual goes into a public school or workshop setting and screams, kicks, bangs his head, or throws materials. Within the classrooms at Benhaven, an individual's behaviors are first identified as interfering or noninterfering with the performance of activities. The behaviors that interfere with learning are considered "priorities"; they must be eliminated or reduced so that learning can take place.

Often, the curriculum itself is the method used to eliminate these interfering behaviors and to increase appropriate on-task behaviors. When a learner is engaging in inappropriate actions that are not dangerous to himself or others, these behaviors are most often ignored while the learner is redirected to the task and praised for appropriate responses. The manner in which the learner is redirected is thoughtfully determined for each particular learner. If a calm, quiet, verbal redirection is most effective, it is used.

With some individuals, a nonverbal redirection — either pointing to the task materials or physically manipulating the individual, calmly and matter-of-factly, so that he performs the task — works best. For others, altering inappropriate behaviors requires a redirection delivered in a calm, firm, but stern manner.

Most inappropriate behaviors that occur in a task situation are successfully eliminated by redirecting attention to the task and providing consistent, positive responses to appropriate behaviors. It is sometimes necessary to remove or restrain a student when aggressive behavior threatens his or others' safety. However, the individual should be brought back to the task situation as quickly as possible, although the task may need to be modified to enable him to respond easily and at a steady pace. For example, if a learner is hitting an object (or person), his hand may be restrained while the teacher directs him through a rote, repetitive task requiring him to use his other hand. This provides him (and the teacher) with a positive alternative to the aggression and may help him to work out of the episode. Most often, these severely handicapped individuals can give no reason for their behavior and may not accept reasoning or comfort at the time. One merely prolongs the episode and confuses and frustrates the individual by asking "Why?" or "What's wrong?" If there is an ascertainable "why" in the environment or within the individual (e.g., discomfort, illness), a good teacher will attempt to identify it and deal with it. Furthermore, there are certain behaviors that are unacceptable regardless of cause, so that our primary efforts should be to modify these behaviors in order, perhaps, to keep the individual from a locked ward in an institution.

I have not found it necessary to set up complex contingencies within the classroom. However, I would not hesitate to develop an appropriate contingency program when it seems warranted. For instance, D., an 18-year-old girl with a psycholinguistic age of 5 years, 11 months (as measured on the Illinois Test of Psycholinguistic Abilities), often became violent during lessons. She would scream, hit, kick, scratch, bite, pull hair, throw materials, and use objects as weapons. She was observed in a variety of situations, and no pattern or reason for these behaviors could be identified. Teachers responded in many ways: they tried to calm her verbally and/or physically, they reprimanded her, they rewarded her for appropriate behaviors and took away rewards for negative behavior, they restrained her, they forced her through activities, they ignored the behaviors when possible, and they encouraged her to verbalize her feelings. It was apparent that a consistent program was needed in order to protect D. and others from injury and to make D. "available" for learning.

Meetings were held among D.'s teachers to discuss D. and develop an appropriate behavior program. Teachers were able to identify several possible factors contributing to the likelihood of aggressive episodes. These included both auditory and visual distractions in the classroom (general noise level, amount of movement, and number of others in classroom), confusion regarding verbal directions given to her (when directions were stated in several different ways or repeated several times), D.'s apparently low frustration tolerance, and fear of failure. It was also agreed that D. responded well to praise, if delivered briefly and consistently, with neither unnecessary language nor too much excitement. In addition, reprimands and emotional responses to her aggression appeared to increase the intensity and duration of episodes. In view of these considerations, teachers seated D. in a corner, removed from the center of classroom activity. Lessons were reviewed and modified to ensure realistic expectations consistent with D.'s abilities, and directions were restated using very consistent, concrete language.

The program itself is a simple contingency whereby D.'s lessons are broken down into five 5-minute segments. She carries a booklet with her to each class, with a page for each day and five squares for each class period. D. earns a star (placed in each square) for completion of work within each 5-minute segment and a candy for five stars (25 minutes of good working behavior). The chances of successful completion are maximized by breaking the lesson into small, brief segments. There is, of course, a consistent procedure for dealing with any aggression that occurs; the "offending part" (e.g., hand, foot) is tied calmly and matter-of-factly and untied after several minutes of good working behavior (lessons may need to be temporarily modified so they do not require the use of the tied limb, e.g., an activity involving a verbal response). In addition a star is lost for aggressive behavior, but this is not mentioned until the end of the 25-minute period. This method has reduced episodes of aggression significantly and is neither a complicated nor difficult program to maintain.

Many studies in recent literature support the success of behavioral methods in teaching a variety of skills, modifying behavior, and training parents to work with their children effectively within the home (Ferster, 1961; Lovaas, 1966; Bijou and Baer, 1967; Nolen, Kunzelmann, and Haring, 1967; Hewett, 1968; Graziano, 1970; Lovaas et al., 1973). Critics of behavioral methods often point out that behavior changes last only as long as the specific program is carried out. In some cases this may be a valid criticism, but an important part of designing a good behavioral program is considering whether behavior change can be easily maintained within the environment and whether effective fade-out procedures can be implemented. When possible and appropriate, a good program design is one that is most natural both within the environment and for the people carrying it out. In this way, the program can be easily maintained and behavior change easily sustained.

Based on readings and experience with the severely handicapped in the classroom and in the home, a thoughtfully and carefully used behavioral program is the most appropriate approach to learning in view of the handicapped individual's cognitive and social disabilities. The behavioral approach is the most effective in achieving academic, behavioral, and social objectives, and the most humane in that the individual becomes more competent, more in control, and more successful in school, in the workshop, and at home.

CURRICULUM DESIGN

Design and format of this curriculum are behavioral. Each unit contains a work activity (e.g., table setting) and related language, reading, numbers, and supplementary (including fine motor) skill areas. Within each of the skill areas, instructional objectives are stated (e.g., "Learner will set one place setting when provided with the appropriate objects and verbal direction, 'Set the table' "). By specifying instructional objectives, the teacher knows exactly what he is to teach at a particular level (determined by the learner's performance). He knows what the learner is to learn and how the learner will demonstrate that he has learned it. The teacher must find creative and effective ways of achieving each objective, but, when the learner has achieved a goal and successfully learned the material, the explicitly stated corresponding objective is easily identified. The person teaching may affect how the material is taught or the rate of learning, but what is to be learned and the criteria for success remain consistent, regardless of who is teaching or who is learning. The key is to set up objectives that are valid for any individual learning the particular task or skill. Then, all the teacher must do is initially evaluate a learner's performance and begin teaching him at the appropriate level.

Careful evaluation procedures are necessary in order to test various teaching methods for effectiveness, monitor what is learned and the rate of acquisition, and identify any factors that may affect learning. These procedures may take no more than one or two minutes during teaching. A simple evaluation procedure is to record correct and incorrect responses on a task or the number of teacher interventions needed for the learner to adequately perform the task. A few minutes during a lesson may be set aside for testing or for a certain number of trials to be recorded (e.g., the first 10 trials of a task). There are many practical benefits to keeping data on each learning objective. It enables the teacher to obtain a clear picture of the progress of the student. Based on this information, the teacher can modify lessons or objectives, add new material, or make any other indicated changes and monitor their effects. It is helpful for purposes of communication to other staff members, professionals, parents, or a school board to base reports on reliable, informative data.

The curriculum is task centered; that is, each curriculum unit involves different skill areas (e.g., language, reading, numbers) within a specific activity. The content of the different skill areas is more meaningful and familiar to the learner because it is related to a concrete activity that he can perform. Since the material within the different skill areas focuses upon the same activity, it is systematically repeated and reinforced. Support for teacher control of the learning situation is another advantage of a task-centered curriculum. The task of establishing control over the learning situation and the learner's behaviors is made easier because the teacher can, if necessary, put a learner through an activity that requires primarily motor responses. A very practical benefit of a task-centered curriculum is that, if the learner learns nothing else, at least he will have learned to perform a functional task (e.g., making a bed, setting a table, or brushing his teeth).

Many available curricula are skill centered rather than task centered. They are geared toward training specific processes, such as visual perception, language, or fine motor skills. Frostig (1972) developed a program based on the theory that training in visual-perceptual exercises enhances development in language, sensorimotor functions, higher thought processes, integrative abilities, and social and emotional growth. However, a study of this theory found that training visual-perceptual abilities using currently available programs had no positive effect on reading and possibly no effect on visual perception (Hammill, 1972). Hammill reviewed 12 studies that dealt with the relationship of visual perception to reading. These studies showed no practical relationship between visual perception and reading. Hammill then reviewed 25 intervention studies, conducted since 1960, that dealt with the effects of visual perception training on reading skills. In 21 of the 25 studies, the author concluded that "concomitant improvement in reading cannot be expected as a result of systematic visual-motor training" (Hammill, 1972, p. 43).

This review of the research suggests that perhaps visual-perceptual processes are not trainable through any existing programs. A review of 38 studies of attempts to train children from varying populations in psycholinguistic skills suggests that most psycholinguistic dimensions, as measured by the Illinois Test of Psycholinguistic Abilities (ITPA), are either untrainable or highly resistant to stimulation (Hammill and Larsen, 1974). The evidence supports a curriculum in which the material to be learned is taught directly; if the goal is to read, the learner is taught to read rather than to trace lines.

Another feature of the task-centered curriculum is that each activity to be taught is subjected to a task analysis. Tasks are broken down into small, sequential components to be learned, so that each step is a prerequisite to the next. Instruction for each learner begins at a level appropriate to his abilities and proceeds at the learner's own pace. Each step of the task is stated as an instructional objective, making explicit exactly what is to be learned. Any task that can be broken down into small, teachable units in a logical hierarchy from the simplest steps to the more complex should be able to be taught. Furthermore, many so-called uneducables can learn to perform a variety of tasks and can benefit from accompanying academic skills, which may help them to function more competently and independently in their environment, when taught through a sequential progression of skills.

My primary objective in teaching severely handicapped individuals is to teach them skills that will help them live more useful, independent, and pleasant lives. The achievement of social growth and some degree of control over behavioral disturbances are implicit goals within the more general long term objective. The curriculum provides a structured, easily individualized, clear, and consistent program, geared toward the achievement of behavioral, work-oriented, and academic goals. It differs from existing programs in that it is comprehensive; each curriculum unit contains a task (work activity) and language, reading, number, and supplementary skills relating to that task.

The main impetus for its form has been a realistic appraisal of the needs and abilities of the students at Benhaven, in view of their previous limited academic achievements and their ages (most were between 15 and 22 years old). I see a 19-year-old who cannot perform more than a few activities without constant supervision, does not use language except to communicate some basic needs, and has demonstrated no reading skills other than some ability to recognize whole words. It seemed apparent that realistic and appropriate goals should be designed to help give him a chance at something better than a life of custodial care. Thus, a logical and practical approach of identifying what kinds of activities would be most useful to the handicapped individual and to those caring for him is taken in this curriculum. These activities fall into several general categories: self-care and hygiene (e.g., brushing teeth, taking a shower), activities of daily living (e.g., making a bed, setting a table), food preparation (e.g., making a sandwich), and recreational activities (e.g., playing badminton). Curriculum units from the first three of the above-mentioned categories are presented as models in the appendices in Part IV. Each curriculum unit has as its center a *work activity* (or work skill) from one of these categories (e.g., table setting), which is broken down into performance levels in a sequence from the most simple step to the more complex steps.

Within the classroom, academic instruction is expected. Thus, after the identification of the adequate and independent performance of a particular activity as an important goal for a learner, related skill areas are introduced. In this manner, academics relevant to the activity, and therefore meaningful to the individual performing the activity, can be taught successfully. The first academic area in each curriculum unit with activity-related material is *language skills*. Behaviorally disturbed students operate on very concrete levels and do not seem to understand abstract concepts unless those concepts are concretely demonstrated. Therefore, the design of this component of the curriculum was based on the assumption that language relating to an activity with which the learner was familiar would be meaningful and more readily learned and that language used within the context of the specific activity could perhaps be generalized to other situations as well.

Reading skills is the next area that appears in each curriculum unit. Divided into word recognition skills and reading comprehension skills, the primary objective of the reading skill area is for the learner to eventually read and follow a sequence of written directions. If the learner can be taught to perform an activity in response to written directions, supervision may be eliminated or reduced. Some individuals may have great difficulty in completing an activity independently without some supervision or external cues. Written directions may provide those external cues without necessitating additional supervision.

The next area in the curriculum is *number skills,* which is divided into three skills basic to the functional use of number concepts: 1) counting, 2) numeral identification, and 3) numeral/quantity association. The mastery of simple number concepts, even if only counting 1 through 10, can be a useful skill that can expand an individual's repertoire of the kinds of tasks he can perform.

Once the necessary reading and number skills are mastered, these skills may be combined in tasks to teach *reading and number comprehension skills.*

Several objectives in the fine motor area are identified in *supplementary skills,* the final curriculum skill area. For students with the appropriate skills, the ability to identify objects and write them down or to count out a number of items and record the numeral can be used in training them to perform such tasks as taking an inventory. Other supplementary skills can be added according to individual needs and abilities.

CURRICULUM APPLICATION

All of the curriculum units teach skills that can be applied to the home situation. Living at Benhaven's residence, Northside, I have had the opportunity to implement much of the curriculum within a home environment. For example, one of the residents could correctly set a table at mealtime but did it in a rather haphazard manner. After writing out each step for him to read and follow, he now sets a table in half the time and with half the footwork. For a few of the residents who can set a table and have some reading and number skills, a written list of the number of objects needed for each meal (the number often varies) allows them to set the table without supervision. In much of the daily routine, the staff uses the instructional objectives (see the work activity levels in the work activity skill area of each curriculum unit) to teach such tasks as doing laundry, loading the dishwasher, making a bed, vacuuming, making a lunch, taking a shower, shaving, and even preparing a simple dinner for as many as 10 people. The language used for each of these activities is consistent with the language used in the classroom. It is gratifying to see a resident spontaneously use language in an appropriate situation at home, after working on it within the limits of the classroom.

In addition to the possibilities for implementing the curriculum in the home environment, many of the skills have practical applications for vocations. An individual who can independently set a table for any number of place settings could be trained to set 10 tables in a cafeteria. Many maintenance tasks (e.g., cleaning tables, sweeping, vacuuming) can be taught within the curriculum and are applicable to maintenance work on a larger scale. The curriculum units are meant to serve as *models;* nearly any task worth teaching can be taught following the principles and format of the curriculum. The curriculum is being used to teach students working on Benhaven's farm to care for the poultry, to use language related to that activity, and to follow written directions in carrying out the necessary tasks. A curriculum unit is being set up based on this model for the planting, care, and harvesting of Benhaven's 2-acre vegetable garden. The main point is that many work activities are rich in language skills and concepts that can be concretely demonstrated through the activity. Functional reading and number skills can enable the severely handicapped learner to work without constant supervision. He becomes a more competent, productive, independent, and happier individual.

3

CONSIDERATIONS IN USING A FUNCTIONAL CURRICULUM

For the teacher of severely handicapped learners, what to teach is as important and problematic a concern as how to teach. Educational programs may be largely dictated by an administrative body, or the teacher may be primarily responsible for developing appropriate programs for his students. In any case, choosing the most suitable curriculum requires careful consideration of the environment within which you teach, input from other staff members and professionals, standards set by school boards, and problems of parents or caregivers, as well as the needs and abilities of the students. A variety of curricula are available, but they may be inappropriate or inadequate for many students functioning at low levels in academic areas. Many curricula are geared toward achieving more traditional academic objectives. Others are task oriented, primarily teaching self-help skills and activities of daily living. The curriculum model presented here is described as a *functional* curriculum; it teaches both useful, practical skills and activities and the academics related to these specific activities. In deciding what type of curriculum is most appropriate, the teacher must determine a student's present level of functioning by using the available resources, as well as through observation and evaluation. In addition, the age of the student, amount of previous formal education, and long term objectives for the student must be carefully considered.

STUDENT'S AGE AND LEVEL OF FUNCTIONING

Practical issues to be considered include the age of the student and the amount of time that he has been involved in educational programs. A young student (3-11 years of age) or one who has never been in a school environment may have the potential to learn within a more traditional (albeit special) academic program. However, limitations imposed by law on most public funding for older students' formal education make such financial assistance unavailable after age 21. Thus the teacher is faced with the practical problem of teaching useful skills that will enable the individual to function better and more independently in an environment outside the classroom. The older student who has not yet demonstrated much success in educational programs (e.g., has severely limited language skills, little or no reading ability, and requires constant supervision in order to perform most tasks) can learn skills in these areas through a functional curriculum, such as that proposed by the model in this book.

Regardless of age, pertinent information about student's past involvement in educational programs should be provided to facilitate appropriate programming for a student entering a new school setting. Records of programs, previous objectives, progress, and problem areas should be carefully reviewed. Former teachers and professionals, as well as parents, also can provide the teacher with information about the student, and their perspectives and expectations for his immediate future. In fact, parental input is required by Public Law 94-142 (Education for All Handicapped Children Act).

EDUCATIONAL NEEDS

Determining a student's present level of functioning can be done through observation and evaluation. It is often helpful to discuss information with other staff members who work with the student in order to identify his strengths and weaknesses. The student's abilities and needs should be discussed in terms of both learning and behavior. Overlap is common, in that much of a student's learning (or lack of it) is dependent to some extent on his behavior. For instance, visual-perceptual abilities may be difficult to assess because of the difficulties in making a student attend to the material, or a student may throw objects when given a simple sorting task. These behaviors, regardless of cause, interfere with learning and performance. They must be eliminated or modified so that the student is available for learning. In the following chapters, methods of overcoming these kinds of problems through the curriculum are discussed.

In addition to identifying relative strengths and weaknesses in learning and behavior, the teaching, and to some extent the home environment, should be considered. Does the learning situation allow a teacher to teach individually or in small groups? Can a bathroom, kitchen, or other area(s) of the school be arranged to teach functional skills? One of the primary objectives of a functional curriculum is to teach the student skills that he can use outside the classroom. Therefore, whether parents or caregivers are willing and can be trained to implement in the home situation some of the activities taught in the classroom is also an element for consideration.

SHORT AND LONG TERM OBJECTIVES

Considering the student's age, present level of functioning, and his educational needs within and beyond the classroom, what are realistic short and long term objectives? These objectives must be identified in order to choose an appropriate curriculum. For instance, a student who demonstrates understanding of two- and three-step verbal directions, can express his needs, match visual symbols printed on cards, trace and copy printed figures, and complete an activity with minimal supervision may have potential to learn skills within a more conventional academic curriculum. His short term objectives will obviously differ from the objectives of a student who does not demonstrate any of these abilities, and his long term objectives may or may not be different depending on his age, the number of years left for formal education, and his demonstrated level of achievement within a program. For the very limited student, a functional curriculum such as the one presented in this book is probably the most suitable. For the higher functioning individual, this curriculum may be used successfully as a comprehensive program (in addition to the gross motor and vocational areas, if appropriate) or for remediation of specific areas while he is in other programs geared to his needs and abilities.

COMPREHENSIVE OR REMEDIAL USE OF THE CURRICULUM

The curriculum presented in this book includes performance objectives for work activities, language, reading, and number skills. Provision for the teaching of supplementary skills is also made. The curriculum can be used as a comprehensive program for persons with limited language skills, little or no demonstrated reading or number skills, and an inability (because of learning impairments or behavior) to perform a task without constant supervision. It also can be used to strengthen areas of weakness in a higher functioning individual. For instance, a student may demonstrate good word recognition skills, but poor comprehension. The curriculum model can be used to teach him a specific activity and vocabulary related to that activity. He can then be given simple written directions composed of that vocabulary and related to the activity that he has learned to perform and with which he is familiar. He is likely to demonstrate the ability to read and follow directions more successfully and more quickly if the learning experience has been related to a concrete activity than if he is given the more conventional and abstract comprehension tasks of reading some material and answering questions about it.

Students may be able to learn activities, such as setting a table, but have behaviors that often interfere with performance. For example, one of my students twiddles objects in his hand and taps them on walls, desks, and the floor. He will leave a task situation to run to another desk or wall and twiddle and tap. Obviously, this is not a desirable or appropriate work behavior. Using a task that involves movement and the use of objects (e.g., table setting) and that he has learned to perform correctly without instructional interventions, allows me to focus on eliminating the interfering behavior. He has demonstrated that he knows where each set of objects should be placed, so I can intervene to redirect him back to the task and away from the inappropriate behaviors. I am no longer teaching him an activity; I am using the activity to foster appropriate work behavior and independent performance.

I began by physically bringing him to the table (to be set) after he picked up each set of objects (plates, cups, etc.), firmly naming the object, and forcing his hand to the table. Gradually I moved toward him as if to bring him to the table, and named the object; I did not need to touch him. The next step was to name each object as soon as he placed the previous objects correctly, so that he had no time to perform his tapping rituals. Now, several months later, I occasionally stamp my foot once or twice as he sets the table if he begins to move away from the task. The table-setting task involves movement and object placement, and he is able to remain on-task except for an occasional attempt to move off. This is an example of using an area of the curriculum to first teach a skill and then to work through an interfering behavior. Next, we must work to generalize on-task behavior to other activities and bring the behavior under control of any supervisor. By working through other activities that he can perform with others as supervisors, the interfering behaviors are likely to be eliminated (should they recur) much faster than in the table-setting behavior program.

In using the curriculum, whether as a complete unit or in part, certain areas should be emphasized depending on individual abilities and needs. The teacher may use the student's strengths to remediate weak areas. For instance, a student may have relatively good visual perception but poor receptive language (ability to understand verbal input). One way to strengthen his ability to listen to and follow simple directions is to teach him a task that is primarily visual, such as preparing a place setting (visual configuration of objects). Using demonstration and imitation, the student learns to set a place correctly and independently. Next, the teacher may say or sign each step of the activity in the sequence that the student has been taught to perform it ("Put the placemat on the table," "Put the plate on the placemat," "Put the cup on the placemat," etc.). When the student performs each step of the activity after the teacher gives each verbal direction, the teacher may then give the directions out of the activity sequence. The student learns to wait and listen to each direction, and his familiarity with the activity allows him to pay attention to the verbal input and relate each direction to a concrete step of the activity. Ways to expand the learner's ability to listen to, and demonstrate understanding of, more varied and complex verbal directions are discussed in later chapters.

After considering the student's age, previous records of success or failure, the feasibility of implementing a functional program in, and eventually outside, the classroom, and determining his present level of functioning, you may decide to implement the curriculum as a comprehensive program or to remediate specific areas of weakness. This curriculum may also be used an an evaluative tool. You, the teacher, may test and evaluate the student on the performance objectives in various areas of the curriculum. On the basis of this evaluation, you may either decide that the curriculum is not the most suitable program or you will have a clearer picture of how best to use it to maximize learning.

4
PRINCIPLES OF EFFECTIVE TEACHING

Teaching effectively involves many factors beyond the content of the lesson. A highly structured, well organized lesson plan may fail if other factors are not considered and integrated into the teaching situation. Issues such as the environment, teacher preparation, presentation of the lesson, appropriate use of reinforcement, and ongoing evaluation are critical to the success or failure of any lesson.

ENVIRONMENT

One of the first considerations in any teaching situation is the environment. Handicapped learners are often highly distractible and hypersensitive to visual and auditory stimuli. Students often react to a verbal interaction between another teacher and student across the room or to noise from a classroom across the hall. Therefore it is important to try to limit both auditory and visual distractions as much as possible. Closing the classroom door may lessen sounds from other areas of the school and prevent the visual distraction caused by others moving around outside the classroom and past the classroom door. Within the classroom, it may be more difficult to modify environmental distractions, especially when caused by other students. It may be necessary to isolate either the student who is the source of distraction or the student with whom the teacher is working. Some classrooms are equipped with a soundproof isolation room or area, which may be used for this purpose. If no such area is available, the classroom itself can be arranged to limit both visual and auditory stimulation. Partitions, such as bookcases or shelves, may be set up around individual working areas. Desks can be arranged so that they face a wall rather than a window or other students.

Walls should be painted a neutral or pastel color, and decorations limited. Brightly colored posters or student's artwork may be cheering to the teacher and visitors but serve as convenient distractions to the handicapped learner. However, if it seems important to display such decorations, limit them to a specific area of the classroom away from work areas.

Lighting may also affect the learner's attention to tasks. Fluorescent lights seem to be especially distracting. (Some of my students would often gaze at the flickering lights; several students have even jumped up and tried to touch them.) It is important to have good lighting, but a softer light might be more suitable for any special classroom.

Seating within the classroom should be arranged to give the teacher maximum control of the students' behavior. If a student is sometimes aggressive or has difficulty remaining in his seat, a good arrangement is to seat him with his back to a wall and the desk between student and teacher. Certain activities, for example, teaching sign language, may be best taught by sitting next to the student. If you sit across from the student and present signs for imitation, remember to use your right hand if the student is to use his left, and vice versa, since the student is likely to mirror your signs. When doing a fine motor activity, it may be easier to help the student from a position in back of him.

The relative position of teacher and student may be important in establishing control in situations where the student is uncooperative. For the teacher who is smaller than the student, this may be accomplished by conducting the lesson from a standing position. Most students seem to recognize that the person standing over them has a "power" advantage.

There may be situations when the teacher must teach from a less than ideal position. For example, I have occasionally conducted lessons with a student on the floor, when attempts to get him in a more orthodox position, i.e., seated at his desk, are unsuccessful. My nonverbal message to the student is, "O.K. I can't move you or coax you, so you win on that count. However, we will work, and you will learn that you cannot control the situation entirely." Usually, we begin the lesson, or some modification of it, on the floor. However, I gradually move the materials in such a manner that he must reach for them. As he becomes more involved in the lesson, I manipulate the materials and the task closer to the desk. Eventually, he usually rises enough for me to physically force him into his seat. Often, the student gets up himself when I move to a chair and continue the lesson from a position above him. At that point, the normal lesson is resumed and my credibility as an authority figure is intact.

Some tasks, especially in the work activity skill area, require that the student move through the environment. This may not be practical if a student literally wanders from the task or is less attentive to task materials when he is not seated. It may be necessary to modify lessons so that the student is standing, but his movement is restricted. For instance, I use a small table that I can move close to a student's desk for some activities, such as setting a table, cleaning a table, or following verbal directions (e.g., "Put a fork on the table," "Put a plate on the chair," "Put a cup under the table," etc.). As the student learns to perform the activity correctly and his behavior is better controlled, movement can be gradually less restricted.

The actual work area should be free of visual distractions. Only the materials necessary for the performance of the task should be in view. In a reading lesson, I keep all but the word cards to be presented in my lap or on the floor next to my chair. As the student reads a word, the word card is turned facedown so as not to distract or confuse the learner. In a task requiring several objects, such as table setting, it may be necessary to modify the task. The teacher must observe the student to see how his performance is affected by the presence of task materials. If his errors are related to the materials, the presentation should be changed. For instance, a student may take two or three different objects at a time and have difficulty placing them in the correct positions on a placemat. Until he has learned to correctly set a place setting, the teacher might hand him each object one at a time, name each object in turn, or point to each object to be set. These modifications can be gradually eliminated as the student's performance improves.

The types of materials used in a lesson require careful consideration of a student's behaviors. Materials that are unbreakable should be used whenever possible. If a student is self-abusive or aggressive, materials that might serve as weapons should not be given to him. For those students who mouth or try to eat objects, materials must be nontoxic. Whenever possible, only paper and plastic goods should be used. Of course, even a blackboard eraser can be a dangerous weapon in someone's hands at some time. Both practicality and safety must always be considered when selecting materials.

TEACHER PREPARATION

In order to teach a lesson effectively, the teacher must be well prepared. A good teacher is familiar with lesson procedures, materials, short and long term objectives, and the use of reinforcement and evaluation procedures. When teaching individuals with severe learning and behavior disorders, the teacher must know and understand the lesson well enough to attend to the specific learning and behavior patterns and problems that may emerge during the course of the lesson. The teacher must have as much of the learning situation within his control as possible in order to respond to issues that may arise and are not under his immediate control. If a student leaps from his seat or throws materials, the teacher must respond immediately. He must appraise any new situation that the student presents and react quickly and purposefully. Having materials readily available and knowing the purpose and procedures of a lesson allow the teacher to either redirect the learner back to the task or make immediate modifications in the task, if necessary.

In a crisis situation, the teacher may have to abandon the short term lesson objectives and work toward regaining control. However, this should be a conscious decision and not a result of panic. It is up to the teacher to provide the control in a situation where the student has lost it. A very direct and often effective way to do this is by involving the student in the task at hand or in some modification of it, even if it requires physically putting him through the activity. When a student is out of control, whether throwing materials, screaming, or engaging in self-abusive or aggressive behaviors, it may be necessary to restrain or physically manipulate him in order to direct him back into the structure of a lesson. Several kinds of task modifications can be made according to the situation and the degree of severity of the student's behaviors. One important factor to keep in mind is that the student who is out of control is likely to be disorganized, disoriented, and confused. Any task in which a teacher attempts to involve the learner must be simple enough so that frustration does not compound the problems. Better control of the student may also be maintained if he is seated.

The teacher who knows and understands a lesson is better able to modify it appropriately. For instance, a lesson that involves following verbal directions may be simplified by limiting the number of directions given to repetition of one or two directions. A reading task may be simplified to the level of simple matching. If the task cannot be suitably modified, the teacher should have a simple task requiring rote, repetitive responses ready and available. As the student begins to respond correctly without physical manipulation and appears to calm down, the regular task may be resumed.

The teacher who understands the development and design of a lesson can also better determine whether inappropriate behaviors are a result of the student's frustration. Identifying possible reasons for inappropriate behaviors, poor performance, or good performance is easier when the teacher clearly understands the steps involved in teaching a lesson, and why he is teaching the lesson according to a specific procedure. The teacher who is familiar and comfortable with a given lesson is more ready and able to observe and evaluate a student's performance and to respond to difficult or new situations that may occur within the lesson.

When working with any student, it is important that the lesson proceed smoothly and steadily. The teacher should have materials prepared before beginning the lesson and within easy reach. The teacher must know the sequence of steps in the teaching procedure well enough to stay at least one step ahead of the student. It is important to keep the student actively engaged throughout the lesson, with as few interruptions in the lesson flow as possible.

Being aware of short term objectives in a lesson helps to keep the teacher on-task. It is easy to lose sight of short or long term objectives, especially when a student presents many obstacles to the achievement of these goals. The teacher must constantly observe and evaluate the student's performance in view of short and long term objectives in order to recognize the need for changes in a lesson.

PRESENTATION OF THE LESSON

In presenting a lesson to a student, I often must think of myself as an actress of sorts. Depending upon the student's learning and behavior patterns and the immediate situation, I may play the "scene" in a variety of ways. The teacher must assume a demeanor, a tone, and a style that are most effective in teaching a particular student. For example, a teacher may naturally have a very soothing, nonthreatening manner. When working with some students or in particular situations, it may be necessary to adopt a more directly authoritative style. Some students respond better to a more gentle approach with directions given very softly. Two qualities that are important in any lesson delivery are to be firm without being abrasive and to remain calm and matter-of-fact, even in difficult situations. It may be effective in certain situations to appear angry, but genuine feelings of anger and frustration often interfere with the teacher's ability to remain in control. It requires a high degree of professional skill to maintain your emotional equilibrium through the many trials involved in teaching individuals with severe learning and behavior problems, but an effective teacher always strives toward achieving a degree of emotional distance from the problems that are encountered while working with a student. This is not to say that a teacher cannot feel frustration, disappointment, anger, or fear, but that these emotions may interfere with taking appropriate, purposeful, and consistent action. I have sometimes needed to remove myself from a teaching situation in order to keep myself from reacting in a way that would hurt the student rather than help him learn. In situations in which a student's responses or lack of responses during a given lesson make the teacher feel frustrated, disappointed, or inadequate, it may be better to present a task that the student can perform and later evaluate the possible reasons for difficulty with the problem lesson. Is the student paying attention? Does he make consistent errors? Can the lesson be modified so that his chances for success are improved? Does he appear to understand what he is supposed to do? Is his behavior interfering with learning? If the problem appears to be behavioral, what consistent responses can you make to modify or eliminate those behaviors? Are the trouble behaviors, perhaps, a result of the student's frustration with the task?

Another situation in which a teacher may become angry or afraid is when a student actually hurts, or attempts to hurt, himself, another student, or the teacher. A purposeful, planned procedure should be worked out so the teacher's responses are guided by a consistent method rather than by emotion. Again, I have had to remove myself from interactions with students so that someone who was not directly involved (another staff person) could implement a given behavioral procedure. The important thing is to recognize the point at which you have stopped being an effective teacher and become vulnerable to very normal and powerful emotions. In order to teach most effectively, an enormous amount of personal stability and confidence in any approach you are carrying out is required. You can only acquire this confidence by systematically trying different approaches, guided by your knowledge of the student and the objectives that you are striving to achieve. Here again, discussions with other staff members and professionals and consistent methods of monitoring any teaching situation or behavioral procedures may help you to determine the most appropriate methods for dealing with a student's learning and behavior problems.

Finding an effective style of teaching a particular student requires trying different approaches and being ready and willing to modify one's style. Once you have decided to deliver a lesson in a specific manner (e.g., fast paced or slow and steadily paced, loudly or softly, with verbal cues or nonverbal cues), do it consistently, give it a fair amount of time, and keep objective data on the results. Only then can you determine the success or failure of an approach, and whether and what changes might be appropriate.

In adopting an effective manner of lesson presentation, tone of voice can be a critical factor. Establishing control does not always require a loud voice or an intimidating tone. A teacher may be firm without being loud and without being negative or flat. Be aware of the message that the tone of voice conveys; I have observed teachers say "good" (and done it myself) to a student in a tone that means "bad." This often happens when a student has made several incorrect responses and then finally responds correctly. One way to avoid this is to prevent the student from making multiple errors on the same task item. Intervene to modify the task, provide an additional cue, or demonstrate the correct response before the student has responded incorrectly several times. When to intervene depends on the student; if he has demonstrated the ability to self-correct, or if incorrect responses seem to be caused by not attending, then allow him to try again. With some students, I intervene after the first error because I know they will perseverate and repeat the same error over and over again. This does not facilitate learning, and it may make the learning situation a frustrating one for both student and teacher. It is important to try to make learning pleasant when possible, and one way is to intervene before the student makes multiple errors. The teacher should sound pleased when the student performs well, although it is not necessary (and often undesirable) to become overexcited and verbally overstimulate the student.

Another important factor in presenting a lesson is the pace of the lesson. A steady pace is always desirable, and this is facilitated by knowing the lesson procedures and having materials prepared and readily available. I have found that a relatively fast paced lesson often reduces or eliminates inappropriate behaviors or wandering attention. With some students who generally move very slowly (especially those who are medicated and take any of the phenothiazines, i.e., Mellaril, Thorazine, Prolixin), increasing the pace of the lesson often quickens their responses without sacrificing accuracy. Students who demonstrate a slow processing time may perform better at a slower, steady lesson pace.

Consistency in the way a lesson is presented is vital to its effectiveness. Consistency is related to the teacher's familiarity with the lesson procedures, awareness of short and long term objectives, and use of ongoing evaluation procedures to monitor effectiveness. However, being consistent does not mean being rigid or inflexible. It means adhering to a well thought out plan of action, but being open to change any approach that is proved (by observation and data) ineffective or inefficient for any reason.

The important thing to remember is that voice, tone, lesson pace, and consistent delivery may have as much to do with the success or failure of a lesson as the quality of the lesson plan. I have seen well organized, clearly stated lesson plans literally ruined by poor presentation. I have also seen a poor lesson plan delivered so skillfully that the student learns in spite of it.

REINFORCEMENT

The use of reinforcement during a lesson deserves careful consideration. There are many categories of reinforcement, including primary, secondary, negative, and positive. In using any kind of reinforcement, consistency in application and evaluation of effect are necessary. Some general issues of concern are the effect you wish to have, what changes in learning and/or behavior you are attempting to achieve, how easy or difficult the reinforcement program is to maintain, and what is an appropriate rate of reinforcement. I do not use primary reinforcers (e.g., food) unless other methods have been ineffective, because they are sometimes difficult to eliminate. More often during a lesson I use verbal praise (a simple "No") or a nonverbal response (facial expression, gesture) to foster appropriate responses and behavior. In extreme situations, it may be necessary to physically restrain a student who is acting out, but I like to view this as a means of controlling the student so that the lesson may continue rather than as a negative reinforcement or punishment. Restraint may become punishment by the manner in which it is applied, calmly and matter-of-factly or in a more reprimanding fashion.

With less severe but nontheless interfering behaviors, ignoring them and redirecting the learner back to the specific task at hand may significantly reduce or eliminate inappropriate behaviors. Speeding up the pace of the lesson may also decrease the amount of off-task behavior. The important thing is to decide on an approach to a problem, whether ignoring and redirecting, reprimanding, isolating, or giving concrete rewards, and implement it consistently and systematically with appropriate measures of evaluation.

In using verbal reinforcement, or when providing feedback to a student, consider the amount of stimulation that is provided and its effect on the student. Some students become overexcited, distracted, or confused by too much verbal input. The repetition of the word "No" may likely frustrate the student (and the teacher). Nonverbal feedback is often a more desirable means of communicating, whether a response is correct or incorrect. For example, during a reading lesson I often turn a card facedown after a student gives a correct response, or continue to hold it up if a response is incorrect. The student quickly learns that if I am still holding the card he must try again. If he is incorrect on his second attempt, I provide a cue or the correct response for imitation. The student does not need to hear "No," and the session is more pleasant for both of us. It is important to consider if the student benefits from verbal stimulation through reinforcement, by providing feedback, or in directing the lesson. If it is either unnecessary or interfering with the learning process or the flow of the lesson, the amount of verbal input should be appropriately modified.

The types of cues and interventions the teacher provides during a lesson are important in maximizing learning. Instructional and supervisory interventions may be physical, verbal, or nonverbal. The teacher must determine through observation and evaluation what intervention procedures will be most effective and when to fade them out so that the learner is working independently. It is usually best to use the least amount of intervention to achieve the desired effect, so the learner does not become dependent on external cues. If a nonverbal cue, such as stamping the floor, clapping your hands, or tapping the desk, succeeds in getting the student's attention so that he performs a given task correctly, then this should be used rather than a nonverbal direction. A nonverbal direction differs from a nonverbal cue in that it can refer specifically to a task item, e.g., pointing to an object or word rather than merely getting a student's attention to the task. A more drastic intervention is to nonverbally demonstrate a step of an activity or a response so the learner can imitate it. If one of these procedures is not enough, it may be necessary to physically manipulate the learner through all or part of a task.

Verbal interventions (cues, directions) may differ in the amount of direction they provide. A verbal cue, such as "Look" or "Read it" or "What do you do next?", may be sufficient to get the learner to respond correctly. Sometimes the initial sound of a word cues the learner to the correct response. If not, it may be necessary to provide a verbal direction that tells the student what to do or how to perform a task (e.g., "Put the plate on the placemat"). The important issues are determining appropriate intervention procedures, using them consistently, and carefully monitoring performance so that the specific intervention is faded out and eliminated as soon as the student demonstrates that it is no longer necessary.

ONGOING EVALUATION

A tool that is necessary and helpful in reviewing the appropriateness and effectiveness of a lesson is the evaluation procedure. Any evaluation procedure should be as clear and simple as possible in order to be easily implemented. It should be an integral part of any lesson plan, so that progress and the need for changes are consistently monitored. The teacher must be as familiar with the evaluation process as with the lesson procedure itself. The teacher must know what is being evaluated and be able to record data quickly and easily. There are many possible ways to record progress in a lesson, but clarity and simplicity are necessary features so that formal evaluation does not interfere with the lesson presentation. As much time should be taken to learn and to teach evaluation methods as needed so that it becomes almost mechanical. Achievement, or the lack of it, cannot be effectively and efficiently monitored without some degree of formal, objective evaluation measures. Suggestions for simple methods of evaluating the performance objectives within the curriculum are presented in Chapter 13.

The principles that have been presented here for consideration — the environment, teacher preparation, various aspects of the lesson delivery, including reinforcement, and evaluation — are important elements of any teaching situation. These factors are critical to the success or failure of any efforts to maximize opportunities for growth in the individual with severe learning and behavior disorders.

Part II

Implementing the Curriculum Units

5
CURRICULUM UNIT SELECTION AND ADAPTATION

CONSIDERATIONS IN CHOOSING THE MOST SUITABLE CURRICULUM UNIT

Careful consideration of a learner's present level of functioning and his needs and abilities may indicate that a functional curriculum, such as the one proposed in this book, is appropriate either as a comprehensive program for a learner or as part of his total educational program. The teacher then must decide with which curriculum unit to begin.

The practical considerations are many: What activity or activities can be most easily implemented within the classroom or school environment? Is there a bed, a bathroom, or a kitchen within the teaching setting? Are laundry facilities available? What kinds of activities does the student perform at home or would the parents like him to learn? Can the student brush his teeth adequately? Can he prepare a simple lunch for himself? Does he know how to make a bed properly or set a table? If the student participates in a vocational program, what related activities can he do or learn to do within the classroom?

Activities in the self-care area, home or grounds maintenance, kitchen skills, and recreational areas can be easily adapted as a basis for the curriculum units. (Methods for developing curriculum units are discussed in Chapter 14.) In terms of a student's work activity skills, there may be a specific area in need of development, such as self-care. If a student's primary needs are in the language or reading skill areas, an activity especially rich in vocabulary or language concepts might be most appropriate. Certain activities might help the student in particular areas at school. For instance, several of my students are learning to paint walls and furniture in the vocational area of the school. Those who have difficulty with the vertical stroking motion are working on washing a blackboard, using a similar up and down motion with a sponge.

A student's interests are another consideration. If he is interested in food, as are most students, simple food preparation may be an activity with which to begin. For the student who enjoys water play a maintenance activity, such as blackboard washing or sink cleaning, might be appropriate. However, any activity in which the student is particularly interested may be overstimulating or provide too much temptation to engage in inappropriate behaviors. Nevertheless, with careful teacher supervision, the activity still might be valuable in fostering appropriate work behaviors and self-control.

The student's strengths and weaknesses, both learning and behavioral, should be reviewed. A student who demonstrates good visual perception and the ability to duplicate visual patterns (e.g., with blocks or objects) might be able to learn an activity involving primarily those skills (e.g., table setting) fairly quickly. A student with good gross motor skills may more readily learn an activity requiring gross movements and coordination, such as a maintenance activity. A work activity that involves areas in which a student demonstrates weaknesses may also be selected for instruction by the teacher. The performance objectives in the various skill areas of the curriculum are broken down into small, concrete, teachable steps (or activity levels), and can be further broken down into more manageable components, if necessary. The teacher can therefore concentrate efforts upon acquisition or remediation of very specific skills. Each curriculum unit suggests supportive activities that can be integrated into the program to reinforce areas of weakness. For example, visual memory skills may be developed during lessons designed for that purpose (see Chapter 7) while the student learns to use those skills in performing steps of an activity requiring them (e.g., table setting).

In considering behaviors, the teacher may decide to confront a specific behavior or may try to minimize the chances of the behavior occurring by the specific curriculum unit he chooses. If a student twiddles or throws objects, table setting may or may not be an appropriate activity (although materials should be paper or plastic). For the hypoactive or lethargic student, activities requiring movement through the environment and some physical effort (e.g., cleaning, maintenance activities) may or may not be suitable. Consideration of this latter aspect might also apply to the hyperactive student, for whom an activity requiring some channeling of energy may be valuable.

The model presented in this book was initiated with the table-setting activity as the basis for the curriculum in the classroom. Not only is it easy to implement (paper products, plastic objects, and a table are readily available), but all students sit and eat meals at a table as well, and thus the activity holds some meaning for all of them. It is also a very useful skill and can be implemented by most parents at home. The language involved can be as simple as "_____ on (the) table," for each appropriate object, or more complex (e.g., "Go to the kitchen," "Open the cupboard," "Get the plates," etc.). In addition to a breakdown of the work skill by activity level, 25 to 30 vocabulary words related to table setting, including common nouns, verbs, and prepositions, are identified in the language skills area section of the unit for instruction. The activity also concretely demonstrates certain concepts, for example, *left* and *right* ("Put the napkin to the *left* of the plate"). The objects used in table setting lend themselves easily to working on number skills, such as counting and getting a specific number of objects on request. Work behavior, reading, and number skills can easily be integrated into the activity as the student learns to read and follow written directions involving numbers (e.g., "Put 5 plates on the table," "Open the drawer," "Get 5 forks," etc.).

After considering the classroom situation, input from other staff and parents, students' needs and abilities, and the various skills that the different areas of a specific curriculum unit require or develop, a curriculum unit (or units) with which to begin can be selected. Once the teacher is ready to introduce the curriculum into the classroom, decisions about how best to use it with each learner and what specific skill areas should be emphasized must be made.

DEVELOPING INDIVIDUAL EDUCATIONAL PROGRAMS WITHIN THE CURRICULUM MODEL

Because the curriculum model provides performance objectives in several different skill areas (work activity, language, reading, numbers, and supplementary (e.g., fine motor)), the teacher must decide how much time to spend working on each area. Some students will benefit from the curriculum as part of their total educational program, as an adjunct to other programs, or as a remedial program for specific areas of weakness. For other students, the curriculum can serve as a more comprehensive program to develop skills in several or all of the above areas.

Determining how much classroom time to devote to each of the skill areas is directly related to the short and long term objectives that are identified as appropriate for a student. In the process of implementing parts of the program, it may be necessary or useful to revise, eliminate, or add to these objectives. Input from staff and parents also can contribute to the teacher's decisions as to which areas deserve primary attention.

A very practical consideration is the classroom situation itself. Do students spend several hours of the day in the classroom? What is the teacher/ student ratio? I have been fortunate enough to teach primarily in a classroom with a one-to-one, one-to-two, or one-to-three teacher/student ratio.

Students do not spend the whole school day in my classroom, but instead come in for one or more 30-minute periods, according to individual programming needs. However, the curriculum model can be successfully implemented in a classroom with a less desirable teacher/student ratio.

To illustrate possible ways to use the curriculum for individual educational programs, part of a classroom schedule and several student's programs are presented (see Table 1).

The schedule comprises a school day from 9:45 a.m. to 4:00 p.m., divided into 10 classroom periods. My classroom schedule is arranged so that the afternoons are relatively free, since I work with the residential staff in program planning during the afternoon. I am fortunate to have two very talented educational assistants to maintain a one-to-one teaching ratio. Note, however, that many students are working on the same activities, perhaps at different levels, so that it is possible to work in small groups. Most of the students spend one period in the classroom; some spend two or three periods. It is not always possible to cover all the activities listed within a given period; thus some lessons must be presented on alternate days.

Each student has a folder that includes a list of his short term objectives (covering a 3- to 4-month period), procedures for each lesson listed on the schedule, and charts for each lesson on which to record data. Several students work in specific areas from different curriculum units. There are three reasons for this: 1) a student may have demonstrated the ability to perform certain tasks in a curriculum unit during an initial evaluation, 2) some students are in the classroom to work on remediating specific areas, or 3) a student may have achieved some of the objectives of a specific curriculum unit. For example, G. (periods 3 and 5) works on the table-setting work activity and three of its related skill areas: language, reading, and numbers. He also has a language and reading lesson from the poultry care unit (an activity that he performs at Benhaven's farm, as part of the vocational component of his program) and a blackboard-cleaning activity lesson.

Some students have fewer activities per lesson period than others. For example, P. (period 4) spends a 30-minute period working on reading skills and number skills. On the other hand, W. (period 4) has five different lesson activities listed within one period. Each activity is not always covered every day, but W. generally needs less drilling and instruction on each activity than P. He has few interfering behaviors, and the lessons usually proceed smoothly and steadily. P. is at lower levels in reading and numbers and requires much instruction and repetition. He also engages in several inappropriate behaviors (twiddling and throwing) that sometimes interfere with the lessons.

All of the students' programs have changed and evolved with time and experience. When the curriculum was first developed and introduced into

Table 1. Applied academics schedule

Period	L.	T.	Teacher S.	M.	E. J.	G.
1 (9:45–10:15)	**A.** Table-setting curriculum work activity, Level 10 language unit Level 10, Condition G reading skills: spelling following directions		**T.** Table-setting curriculum work activity, Level 10 reading review reading skills: spelling following directions	**M.** Table-setting curriculum number skills: counting numeral/quantity association (count out objects, write numerals.)		
2 (10:15–10:45)	**O.** Table-setting curriculum work activity, Level 4 language skills: object identification following directions reading skills: reception number skills: counting				**J.** Table-setting curriculum work activity, Level 9 reading skills: following directions language skills: following verbal directions	
3 (11:00–11:30)	**M.** Table-setting curriculum language unit Level 10, Condition I language skills: following signed directions reading skills: spelling following directions		**P.** Table-setting curriculum work activity, Level 6 language unit Level 3, Condition E language skills: following verbal directions Blackboard-cleaning curriculum work activity, Level 1			**G.** Table-setting curriculum number skills: counting numeral identification numeral/quantity association Poultry care curriculum language skills reading skills

continued

Table 1 — continued

Period	Teacher			
	L.	S.		E.
		R.	W.	

4 (11:30–12:00)	W.
	Table-setting curriculum word activity, Level 10
	language unit Level 10, Condition H[a]
	Blackboard-cleaning curriculum
	language unit Level 5, Condition C
	reading skills
		R.
		Table-setting curriculum work activity, Level 6
		reading skills
		language skills:
		    following verbal directions
		number skills:
		    counting
		    numeral identification
				P.
				Table-setting curriculum
				reading skills
				number skills:
				    counting
				    numeral identification

5 (12:00–12:30)	G.
	Table-setting curriculum work activity, Level 8
	reading review
	reading skills:
	    following directions
	language skills:
	    following verbal directions
	Blackboard-cleaning curriculum work activity, Level 5
			W.
			Table-setting curriculum
			reading skills:
			    following directions
			language skills:
			    following verbal directions
			number skills:
			    counting
			    numeral/quantity association
				C.
				Blackboard-cleaning curriculum
				reading skills:
				    spelling words
				    following directions
				Bed-making curriculum
				work activity, Level 4
				language unit Level 3, Condition G

the classroom, it was necessary to evaluate students in the various skills areas. Work was begun in the table-setting curriculum unit. By testing each student, determination of the performance level at which to start instruction within the work activity was possible. All of the students were able to perform the activity at some level, so other skill areas (language, reading, numbers, and supplementary skills) were tested, and appropriate goals were identified. After working on these objectives for some time, it became evident which areas deserved more time and attention. For example, a student might have learned to verbally identify objects related to a work activity but have demonstrated problems in imitating a phrase of two or more words. More effort was then given to the particular units of the language program for the work activity that involved phrases or sentences. (Each work activity has a series of language Units, sequentially arranged from simple to more complex, that correspond to the performance Levels of the activity.) As another example, if a student is at a readiness level in reading, but can count out a number of objects with only a few errors, perhaps work in the reading skills area should encompass a larger portion of his classroom time. Sometimes while conducting a specific lesson other areas of weakness will become apparent. Supportive lessons to develop the area of deficit can then be designed and implemented.

As a learner achieves specific objectives, the curriculum provides the next step. Often a student must begin at a level of a task that is lower than the stated performance objective. For example, one of the reading objectives is to select word cards in response to the verbal (oral/signed) words. For students with no reading skills, instruction must commence at a very low level, such as matching. When the student is able to correctly match a number of words, work on selecting word cards in response to verbal words can be begun. Therefore, a student's schedule should be adjusted as he achieves objectives and as new objectives are set for him. The amount of time devoted to objectives or lessons depends on the student's needs and abilities.

Keep in mind that teaching and learning are an *ongoing and cumulative* process. As the student (and teacher) acquires new skills, his needs change. His program and schedule of learning activities should then be modified to best meet those needs.

6

IMPLEMENTING THE WORK ACTIVITY AREA OF A CURRICULUM UNIT

DETERMINING APPROPRIATE OBJECTIVES AND DESIGNING APPROPRIATE LESSONS

In implementing any of the skill areas of a curriculum unit, the teacher must first determine a student's present level of functioning. This can be accomplished through discussion with other staff members, parental input, the review of records, observation, and more formal evaluation methods.

Performance Level Evaluation

Evaluation of a student's level of performance on a work activity usually should be begun at Level 1, but a more advanced level may be appropriate if so indicated by other information about the student. Beginning with Level 1 of a work activity is usually advisable in order to learn as much as possible about the student's behaviors and style of learning. Particular behaviors may be evident when a student performs at a level below his abilities or at a level that poses difficulties for him. Observing him in both situations provides useful information for planning appropriate lessons and behavioral procedures.

If a student performs Level 1 of an activity adequately, advance to Level 2. Consider, for example, the table-setting curriculum unit (see Appendix A), presented at Level 1. At this level, the teacher presents the student with one of each appropriate object (plate, cup, bowl, napkin, fork, knife, spoon) and a placemat on which the outlines of each object have been drawn in the proper places (template). The teacher tells the student to "set the table." Observe how the student goes about the task, as well as what he does. Does he take several objects at once and place them correctly or incorrectly? If he places them incorrectly, intervene nonverbally by pointing to each object one at a time or by handing him each object. Try a verbal cue, such as "Look," if errors seem to be caused by lack of attention. Do these types of interventions improve the student's performance? If not, Level 1 is the appropriate level at which to begin, but you may have to design a lesson as a modification of the stated performance objective. As such, the levels of performance for each work activity should be viewed as objectives. The lessons, with appropriate modifications, should be considered as means of achieving the objectives.

If a student makes errors in matching the objects to the template, it may be necessary to teach the placement of each object separately. For example, design the lesson so that the student must put the plate in the correct position independently, but intervene with physical manipulation, nonverbal cues, or verbal cues to help him place the other objects correctly. Your evaluation procedures should be adjusted so that data are kept on the number of times he places the plate in the correct position within a given number of trials. When he places the plate with 100% accuracy, try the plate and another object. Continue adding each object separately, until the student can set the template independently.

While working on each object separately, putting the student through the entire task or helping him do it correctly will give him practice in setting the whole template. From time to time, perhaps once during the lesson, test the student by setting up the task as stated in Level 1. It is likely that he will achieve the objective without it being necessary to teach the placement of each object separately. By the time you are working on placing the fork (and the other objects that he has mastered) on the template, perhaps the repetition of setting the whole template correctly will have taught him where to place the remaining objects. Whether you must teach each object's position by drilling one new object at a time, or are able to work on several objects presenting difficulty at once, do not move on to Level 2 until the student performs Level 1 correctly.

The student who is able to correctly match each object to the object outlines on the template is ready for Level 2 (Learner places table-setting objects provided by teacher in correct positions *on a placemat*). The italicized part of the objective indicates an addition to, or change in, the step of the activity from the previous level. If the student makes several errors at this level, demonstrate the correct position of objects, point to the appropriate positions, or give verbal directions or cues as he performs the task. After several instructional trials, test the student's performance. If he still makes errors, Level 2 is an appropriate level at which to begin teaching.

In designing a lesson to achieve a given level of performance any information that your observations of the student's performance provide should be used. Think in terms of breaking down the particular step of the activity and identifying where the student has difficulty. The teacher must try to isolate and identify both learning and behavior problems in order to design a lesson that attacks these problems. It may be necessary to modify a given objective (level of performance) by changing the manner in which the lesson is conducted. For example, if the student makes errors at Level 2 that correction and repetition do not eliminate, try providing an extra cue (e.g., pointing to the correct position on the placemat before the student places each object). If this allows him to be successful, write it into your lesson plan. If there are seven objects to be set, systematically fade out the nonverbal directions (pointing) so that he places some of the objects correctly and independently. Keeping a record of the number of errors and the specific errors that are made allows you to direct the student on those objects with which he has difficulty.

To ensure that you are providing only the cues necessary for the student to learn the correct placement of objects, a test trial to determine his errors should be made at the beginning of the lesson. Correct the errors, and then repeat the task several times, providing the instruction and cues necessary for a correct performance. It is an important principle of effective and efficient teaching for the learner to repeatedly perform the task correctly in order to maximize learning. Unless the learner demonstrates the ability to self-correct, repeating the task several times and allowing him to make errors usually will not be beneficial. A student generally learns faster by performing the task correctly even if it requires interventions by the teacher. By doing a test trial at the beginning of the lesson, the student's progress can be evaluated and specific errors identified. The remainder of the lesson can then be directed toward eliminating those errors and improving performance. An advance to the next level of performance generally can be made after the student performs the task correctly two or three different times (e.g., during other lesson periods or on two or three consecutive days). However, progressing to the next level may be possible, even if the student does not reach this criterion, if the errors seem to be caused by specific behaviors (e.g., lack of attention) that may be worked out at higher levels of the task.

Task Modification

When working on a given level of an activity, try to modify the task to increase the student's chances of success. For instance, if he cleans a blackboard using random, haphazard strokes, try putting him through the correct motion while you provide a verbal direction (e.g., "Down, up...down, up..."). Fade out physical prompts first and, if his performance has improved, gradually eliminate the verbal directions. Decide on an approach, write it into your lesson procedure, and implement it consistently. Do not try several different instructional intervention procedures before you have given one a fair amount of time and effort to prove its effectiveness or ineffectiveness. Evaluate performance either at the beginning or at the end of the lesson, but conduct the evaluation the same way at the same time until the student's performance indicates that he is ready for, or in need of, a change.

Simplifying the Task In designing a lesson to achieve a specific objective, it may be necessary to modify the task in addition to providing interventions. Simplifying the task can be one means of modification. For example, I have a student who resisted physical manipulation through most activities. Verbal directions proved ineffective in improving his performance at Level 1 of the blackboard-cleaning activity. The haphazard manner in which he approached the job prevented him from doing it adequately. Thus, I first tried to provide guidelines by drawing 10 vertical lines, about 3 inches apart, from the top to the bottom of the blackboard. These seemed to improve his performance, but not significantly. Therefore, after several days, I placed a wooden "guide board," that was the length of the blackboard and about 6 inches wide, on the blackboard ledge about 2 inches to the right of the first vertical line in order to almost force him to use a more directed motion. When the student had washed away that line thoroughly using an up and down motion, I moved the board a few inches from the second vertical line. We continued in this manner until he had adequately cleaned all the lines from the blackboard. Approximately one week later the student was able to move the guide board himself. In two weeks, I eliminated the guide board, leaving only the lines as guides. When he was able to wash the blackboard adequately, using the vertical lines as a guide, I removed the lines. He was then performing at Level 1, with one or two verbal reminders. After about a week, we moved to Level 2, which is identical to Level 1, except that the learner cleans a larger area. This presented no new problems, and we were able to move to Level 3 in one day. Because the student demonstrated no difficulties other than the sloppy, inadequate stroke that was corrected at Level 1, we were able to proceed rapidly through the higher levels of that activity.

Sometimes a very minor adjustment in the way a task is presented can improve performance. For example, several students made the same types of errors at Level 4 of the table-setting activity. Level 4 is the first level at which the student sets more than one place setting. The student has demonstrated at Level 3 that he can place the objects in the correct positions. Level 4 requires him to take two of each object (provided by the teacher) and set two place settings side by side. Several students would consistently place two of the same object on one placemat. By simply moving the two placemats farther apart so that each setting could be more easily viewed as separate, these errors were quickly eliminated. At higher levels of the table-setting activity, it is often helpful to make sure that the student walks around the table to be set. In this way he views each individual place setting from the same position (standing in front of each) and is less likely to make errors. Again, be aware of the kinds of errors and problems that the learner demonstrates. Try providing external cues or directions, modify the task itself, or change the task situation so that the learner can perform the step(s) of the activity. Test the learner and systematically fade out interventions as he achieves the given task. Then, gradually arrange the task so that the learner performs the activity at the level of the specific performance objective.

Another example of designing the task or lesson to facilitate learning is illustrated by the sandwich-making activity. Level 1 states: *"Learner spreads sandwich filling (e.g., peanut butter, jelly, tuna salad, egg salad) evenly on a slice of bread when given a slice of bread with sandwich filling on it and a knife."* If a student has difficulty spreading, you might modify the lesson objective by providing the student with frozen bread. This eliminates tearing and simplifies spreading. From frozen bread you might progress to toast, and from toast to bread, as stated in the original wording of the performance objective.

Eliminating the Need for Judgment Some work activities that can be used as the basis for a curriculum unit require a degree of judgment. Most persons with severe learning and behavior disorders demonstrate difficulties in situations that involve a matter of judgment. A very simple example is a cleaning task. Few of my students understand the concepts of *clean* or *dirty,* or are able to determine whether they have adequately vacuumed a rug or washed a table. Therefore, it is helpful to either eliminate the necessity for judgment or exaggerate any concept requisite to making a particular determination. For instance, you might teach a learner to vacuum a rug in a highly structured, systematic fashion. The learner might always start vacuuming at a certain place, take five steps back, five steps forward and one step to the side, and so forth. By teaching him to perform the activity in a specific pattern, the need for determining the cleanliness of the area would be eliminated. To teach the concept of *clean,* you might make *dirty* very obvious by spreading sawdust over the area. As the learner learns to vacuum adequately, gradually fade out the use of sawdust and direct the learner to look for less obvious dirt.

A similar idea is used by instructors to teach some self-help skills. Hand washing, for example, may be learned more quickly by providing an extra visual cue. Washable coloring put on the learner's hands allows him to see what he is doing and why. A sticky substance lets the student feel what he is doing and recognize when his hands are clean. Another method used at Benhaven is to teach the student to perform each step of the activity, for example, brushing teeth, to the instructor's count of 10. A student brushes his bottom left teeth for a count of 10, his top left teeth for a count of 10, his bottom right teeth, and so on. Eventually many students either learn to count for themselves or at least to maintain the motion long enough (about 10 brushes) to adequately brush their teeth. Again, this removes the need for the student to make a judgment.

Considering the Sequential Arrangement Most work activities require movement through the environment, from one place to another, at some level of the activity. In the curriculum model, the steps of an activity requiring movement from place to place are taught at more advanced levels of the activity. Movement through the environment may present difficulties in behavior that are not as evident when the learner is engaged in a repetitive activity within a limited space. For example, in the blackboard-and table-cleaning activities, the learner locates materials and goes to a sink at performance Levels 3 and 5, respectively. He first learns to clean a blackboard or wash a table adequately. He must learn to go to the appropriate places, get proper materials, and, when finished, return the materials to the appropriate places. There are likely to be more distractions, and, consequently, there are more chances for loss of attention, confusion, and inappropriate behavior. Therefore, most of the activities begin with movement within an area (e.g., classroom) and expand to areas beyond it (e.g., bathroom, kitchen).

The teacher should feel free to incorporate steps from higher levels of an activity into the lower levels. With some students, and some activities, it may be more effective for the student to perform the activity as a whole, in sequential steps. In these cases, determine the level of performance for the student as the objective. For example, the bed-making activity Level 1 states: "Learner puts a bedspread properly on a bed that is otherwise made, when provided with the bedspread." This is the objective that you are trying to achieve. However, you may decide to help the learner make the entire bed, but evaluate him only on the step of the activity stated in Level 1. Although you may have to put the student through the other steps of the activity, or provide verbal and/or nonverbal cues, the learner should benefit from having performed the entire task. When you reach the step of the activity that is the learner's objective, evaluate him only on that step. Repeat the step as many times as seems appropriate. In this way, the learner practices the whole activity and performs it in the appropriate sequence of steps. When evaluation shows that he has achieved Level 1, move on to Level 2. The learner has performed that step with the teacher's help and will probably learn it relatively quickly.

There should be a cumulative effect from having gone through each step of the activity, while the particular task of a given level is worked on to achieve adequacy and independence in performance at that level. Again, the teacher can either follow the levels of performance as stated, working on each step of the activity, or put the student through several or all of the activity steps, while concentrating teaching efforts on and limiting performance evaluation to a specific level of the activity.

The levels of performance stated for each activity can be used as they are or modified as appropriate. They are presented as guidelines to help the teacher view the work activities as a sequential progression from simple to those more complex. You may consider a stated level of performance as incorporating several steps and work on each step separately. For instance, Level 4 of the bed-making activity states: *"Learner puts a blanket on the bed, tucks it in,* puts the pillow in the pillowcase and on the bed, and puts the bedspread on the bed properly, when provided with pillow, pillowcase, blanket, and bedspread." The student has mastered Levels 1, 2, and 3 so that he now must learn to put the blanket on the bed and tuck it in. If he demonstrates much difficulty with putting the blanket on the bed correctly, make this the objective. When the learner achieves this objective, work on tucking the blanket in properly. Work on both simultaneously or separately, but be aware of the learner's specific goal and evaluate his performance on that particular step.

The highest level of each work activity states that the learner will perform the given task in response to written directions. In addition, some activities, such as table setting, may involve number skills. Incorporating reading and number skills into the work activity not only provides step-by-step directions for a student who may need them to adequately complete the task but also provides an opportunity to use these skills functionally. Using written instructions with the student who has the appropriate reading skills may eliminate the need for supervision and increase independence. Further discussion of the incorporation of reading and number skills into the work activity is provided in Chapters 8 and 9.

BEHAVIORAL CONSIDERATIONS

The primary long term objective of any work activity is adequate and independent performance. In order to progress from one level to the next of any activity, the student must demonstrate the ability to perform the activity without teacher intervention. Inappropriate or off-task behaviors may interfere with achievement of independence at any level of an activity. The teacher must decide at which level of performance to work on these difficulties. Usually procedures for dealing with the behaviors are implemented at every level of the activity, as they occur. (The severity of the problem behaviors and the degree to which they interfere with performance will in part influence this implementation.) The question, then, is whether to stay at one level of an activity until the behavior is eliminated or to move on if performance is otherwise correct and adequate. Many behaviors may be incompatible with performance of an activity, and consequently their frequency of occurrence will decrease while the learner is engaged in the task. However, when behaviors that require intervention, such as twiddling objects, wandering from the task, or just not moving to the next step in the sequence independently, occur, the teacher must decide if it is expedient to stay at a level that the learner has mastered to focus efforts on the elimination of these behaviors. Issues to be considered in making this decision include the degree to which the behaviors interfere with performance, the frequency of occurrence, and the success of previous efforts to modify the behavior. Some students may always need some degree of supervision, if only a stamp of the foot or clap of the hand, to bring them back to the activity. Independent performance, then, is a long term objective toward which to strive.

If inappropriate behaviors do not significantly interfere with performance at a given level, it is probably best to progress to the next level of the activity. If, however, behaviors do significantly disrupt performance and completion of the task, the learner probably should remain at a level at which he can perform the task correctly so that the interfering behaviors can be directly confronted. For example, if a student repeatedly must be brought back physically to the task because he attempts to leave the situation, this inattentiveness should be modified before progression to the next activity level. If the behavior is not modified, it will likely continue and prevent the learner from being able to perform a work activity without ongoing supervision. Less severe or disruptive behaviors, such as lapses in attention to the task, may decrease in frequency as the learner masters more and more work activities. Behaviors that occur less regularly, such as periodic episodes of aggression or self-abuse, must be dealt with, but these behaviors may not necessarily prevent the student from progressing within a given work activity.

The teacher's presence is another factor that can interfere with the independent performance of an activity. The teacher is usually in the work area to supervise and monitor performance. This may have a direct effect on the way in which the student performs a work activity. It may be useful to have another teacher or staff person supervise the student in an activity in order to determine if there are any changes in performance or behavior. Teacher presence may also be minimized by gradually moving farther away from the student as he performs the activity or actually leaving the work area and observing the student beyond his field of vision. I usually tell a student to "tell me when you are finished" and teach him to come to me, tap me on the shoulder, and say or sign "I am finished." A student's dependence on the teacher's presence as an authority or for subtle hints of approval should not be underestimated. It is important, therefore, to be aware of your effect on the student and to try to set up situations that minimize that effect without interfering with the student's performance.

GENERALIZATION OF WORK ACTIVITY SKILLS

Generalizing a skill in any area to situations beyond that in which it was learned is a difficult task. Teaching the activity in as many situations, or approximations of situations, as possible is one method for fostering generalization. It is often desirable to work toward generalization when the student has mastered the activity within a given situation. Once a student can properly set a table with placemats, try removing the placemats and using a tablecloth. Can the student who washes a blackboard in the classroom adequately wash blackboards in any classroom? In activities that require going to a sink, can the student use the kitchen sink as well as the bathroom sink, if necessary? Is the student able to adequately clean tables of varying sizes, shapes, and surfaces? Can he make any bed, given the proper size sheets and blankets?

An important and practical aspect of task generalization is transfer of the activities the student has learned at school to his home situation. This requires training parents or caregivers and familiarizing them with the procedures that the student has learned to follow.

Generalization is often difficult to achieve. However, the likelihood of success is greatly increased if the student has learned to perform the activity correctly and independently in a specific situation. The teacher can then modify a situation gradually to incorporate elements of new situations. Teach the student to locate all the sinks in the environment, and then make the one he customarily uses unavailable. If there is more than one lavatory in the teaching environment, have him brush his teeth or wash his hands in different lavatories. You will have to be systematic in implementing these changes in order to teach the student rather than confuse him. Do not change more than one variable at a time, and do not add more changes until the student masters the activity in the modified situation. Because the student has demonstrated the ability to perform an activity adequately and independently, it should be relatively easy to identify problems that arise in new situations and to work to overcome them.

The individual who can perform work activities adequately and with a minimum of supervision has achieved some useful and practical skills. In the course of learning the activities, he has learned appropriate work behaviors that he can demonstrate in new work activities and situations. He has demonstrated that he can be productive, and, it is hoped, he will feel some degree of satisfaction in his accomplishments.

SAMPLE LESSON PROCEDURES

The following lesson procedures have been designed as basic, general procedures for every student. As discussed previously, these procedures may need to be modified to suit individual student needs and abilities. These modifications may be written into lesson procedures or specified on individual data charts for each lesson (see Chapter 13).

The objective, the necessary materials, a step-by-step teaching procedure, and an evaluation procedure are stated in each lesson. Lessons for two levels of performance of the work activities providing the basis for four of the curriculum units (table-setting (Appendix A), blackboard-cleaning (Appendix B), bed making (Appendix C), and sandwich making (Appendix E)) are presented at the end of this chapter. Note that the verbal directions (referred to as interventions) correspond to the language units for the specific levels of the work activity. Of course, you may modify the language units (e.g., "Put the fork on the napkin"), but the language should remain consistent throughout the levels of the activity and other skill areas of the curriculum unit.

At the lower levels of activities like blackboard cleaning and bed making, the teacher may teach the learner to perform the activity sequence according to the procedure for higher levels. (You may have him go through the blackboard-cleaning activity at Level 5 or the bed-making activity at Level 8, as discussed in this chapter.) Always determine an appropriate level of performance as the learner's objective, and evaluate him only on the steps of the activity described at that level of performance.

Table-Setting Curriculum — Activity Level 3

Objective: Learner places table-setting objects in correct positions on a placemat *when objects are on a shelf near the table.*

Materials: shelf, table, placemat, plate, bowl, cup, napkin, fork, knife, spoon

Procedure:
1. Put each object on the shelf in the following left to right sequence: placemat, plate, bowl, cup, napkin, fork, knife, and spoon.
2. Say/sign, "(Time to) set the table."
3. Using nonverbal or verbal cues, verbal directions, demonstration, and/or physical manipulation as needed, direct the learner to:
   Get (the) placemat.
   Put (the) placemat on (the) table.
   Get (the) plate.
   Put (the) plate on (the) table/placemat.
   Get (the) bowl.
   Put (the) bowl on (the) table/placemat.
   Get (the) cup.
   Put (the) cup on (the) table/placemat.
   Get (the) napkin.
   Put (the) napkin on (the) table/placemat.
   Get (the) fork.
   Put (the) fork on (the) table/placemat.
   Get (the) knife.
   Put (the) knife on (the) table/placemat.
   Get (the) spoon.
   Put (the) spoon on (the) table/placemat.

The above (step 3) nonverbal and verbal interventions should be faded out as soon as possible.

Evaluation procedure: Count and record the number of teacher interventions, both verbal and nonverbal, needed for the learner to complete the task adequately.

Table-Setting Curriculum — Activity Level 5

Objective: Learner places table-setting objects in correct positions on placemats *when two placemats are at angles to each other on the table* and the appropriate number of objects are on a shelf near the table.

Materials: shelf, table, two placemats, plates, bowls, cups, napkins, forks, knives, spoons

Procedure:
1. Put each set of objects on the shelf in the following left to right sequence: plates, bowls, cups, napkins, forks, knives, and spoons.
2. Put two placemats at angles to each other on the table.
3. Say/sign, "(Time to) set the table."
4. Using nonverbal or verbal cues, verbal directions, demonstration, and/or physical manipulation as needed, direct the learner to:
   Get (the) plates.
   Put (the) plates on (the) table/placemats.
   Get (the) bowls.
   Put (the) bowls on (the) table/placemats.
   Get (the) cups.
   Put (the) cups on (the) table/placemats.
   Get (the) napkins.
   Put (the napkins on (the) table/placemats.
   Get (the) forks.
   Put (the) forks on (the) table/placemats.
   Get (the) knives.
   Put (the) knives on (the) table/placemats.
   Get (the) spoons.
   Put (the) spoons on (the) table/placemats.

The above (step 4) nonverbal and verbal interventions should be faded out as soon as possible.

Evaluation procedure: Count and record the number of teacher interventions, both verbal and nonverbal, needed for the learner to complete the task adequately.

Blackboard-Cleaning Curriculum — Activity Level 1

Objective: Learner cleans a small (9 sq. ft.) blackboard when provided with a wet sponge and a tub of warm water.
Materials: blackboard, tub of warm water, sponge
Procedure:
1. Prepare materials (e.g., Fill tub with warm water, put stool, chair or desk next to blackboard).
2. Say/sign, "(Time to) clean the blackboard." (If learner has difficulty cleaning the blackboard, use a portable blackboard placed flat on his desk.)
3. Give tub of warm water and sponge to learner.
4. Using nonverbal or verbal cues, verbal directions, demonstration, and/or physical manipulation as needed, direct the learner to:
   (put the) tub down
   wet (the) sponge
   squeeze (the) sponge
   clean (the) blackboard
5. Learner cleans blackboard adequately, beginning at the left side of the blackboard, using a vertical motion, and moving across the blackboard to the right.
6. When blackboard has been cleaned adequately, learner (put(s) the) sponge in (the) tub

The above (steps 4-6) nonverbal and verbal interventions should be faded out as soon as possible.

Evaluation procedure: Count and record the number of teacher interventions, both verbal and nonverbal, needed for learner to complete the task adequately.

Blackboard-Cleaning Curriculum — Activity Level 5

Objective: Learner will get a tub and sponge from appropriate place (e.g., closet), go to a sink and fill the tub with warm water, clean a blackboard, *empty the dirty water into the sink, and return sponge and tub to appropriate place.*

Materials: blackboard, closet with tub and sponge, sink

Procedure:
1. Say/sign, "(Time to) clean the blackboard."
2. Using nonverbal or verbal cues, verbal directions, demonstrations, and/or physical manipulation as needed, direct the learner to:
Go to (the) closet.
Get (the) tub.
Get (the) sponge (*or* Get (the) tub and sponge).
Put (the) sponge in (the) tub.
Go to (the) bathroom/kitchen.
Go to (the) sink.
Turn (on) (the) cold water.
Turn (on) (the) hot water.
Put (the) water in (the) tub (*or* Fill (the) tub with water).
Turn off (the) hot water.
Turn off (the) cold water.
Get (the) tub (*or* Pick up (the) tub).
Go to (the) classroom.
Put (the) tub down.
Wet (the) sponge.
Squeeze (the) sponge.
Clean/wash (the) blackboard.
3. After the blackboard has been cleaned adequately, direct the learner, as needed, to:
Get (the) tub (*or* Pick up (the) tub).
Put (the) sponge in (the) tub.
Go to (the) bathroom/kitchen.
Go to (the) sink.
Pour (the) dirty water in (the) sink (*or* Empty (the) tub).
Put (the) sponge in (the) tub.
Go to (the) classroom *(or wherever closet is).*
Put (the) tub in (the) closet.

The above (steps 2–3) nonverbal and verbal interventions should be faded out as soon as possible.

Evaluation procedure: Count and record the number of teacher interventions, both verbal and nonverbal, needed for learner to complete the task adequately.

Bed-Making Curriculum — Activity Level 1

Objective: Learner puts a bedspread properly on a bed that is otherwise made, when provided with the bedspread.

Materials: made-up bed, bedspread (off) on shelf, chair, or bureau next to bed

Procedure:
1. Say/sign, "(Time to) make the bed."
2. Bring learner to the bed.
3. Using nonverbal or verbal cues, verbal directions, demonstration, and/or physical manipulation as needed, direct the learner to:
   Put (the) bedspread on (the) bed.
   Pull (the) bedspread over (the) pillow.

The above (step 3) nonverbal and verbal interventions should be faded out as soon as possible.

Evaluation procedure: Count and record the number of teacher interventions, both verbal and nonverbal, needed for learner to complete the task adequately.

Bed-Making Curriculum — Activity Level 6

Objective: Learner puts the bottom sheet on the bed and tucks it in, puts the top sheet on the bed and tucks it in, puts the blanket on the bed and tucks it in, puts the pillow in the pillowcase and on the bed, and puts the bedspread on the bed properly, when the bottom sheet, top sheet, pillowcase, pillow, blanket, and bedspread are provided.

Materials: unmade bed, bottom sheet, top sheet, pillow, pillowcase, blanket, bedspread on shelf, chair, or bureau next to bed

Procedure:
1. Say/sign, "(Time to) make the bed."
2. Bring learner to the bed.
3. Using nonverbal or verbal cues, verbal directions, demonstration, and/or physical manipulation as needed, direct the learner to:
   Put (the) bottom sheet on (the) bed.
   Tuck in (the) sheet.
   Put (the) top sheet on (the) bed.
   Tuck in (the) sheet.
   Put (the) blanket on (the) bed.
   Tuck in (the) blanket.
   Put (the) pillow in (the) pillowcase.
   Put (the) pillow on (the) bed.
   Put (the) bedspread on (the) bed.
   Pull (the) bedspread over (the) pillow.

The above (step 3) nonverbal and verbal interventions should be faded out as soon as possible.

Evaluation procedure: Count and record the number of teacher interventions, both verbal and nonverbal, needed for learner to complete the task adequately.

Sandwich-Making Curriculum — Activity Level 3

Objective: Learner puts proper amount of sandwich filling on a slice of bread, spreads it evenly, and covers it with a second slice of bread, when given two slices of bread, a container of sandwich filling, a spoon, and a knife.

Materials: bread, sandwich filling, spoon, knife, sandwich (cutting) board

Procedure:
1. Say/sign, "(Time to) make a sandwich."
2. Sit at a table with the appropriate materials.
3. Using nonverbal or verbal cues, verbal directions, demonstration, and/or physical manipulation as needed, direct the learner to:
   Get (the) spoon/knife.
   Get (the) *(sandwich filling)*.
   Put (the) *(sandwich filling)* on (the) bread.
   Spread (the) *(sandwich filling)*.
   Cover (the) bread (*or* Close (the) sandwich).

The above (step 3) nonverbal and verbal interventions should be faded out as soon as possible.

Evaluation procedure: Count and record the number of teacher interventions, both verbal and nonverbal, needed for learner to complete the task adequately.

Sandwich-Making Curriculum — Activity Level 6

Objective: Learner goes to appropriate place (e.g., drawer) and gets a spoon and a knife, gets two slices of bread from a loaf, puts the proper amount of sandwich filling on a slice of bread, spreads it evenly, covers it with a second slice of bread, and cuts the sandwich in half, when given a loaf of bread and a container of sandwich filling.

Materials: loaf of bread, sandwich filling, sandwich (cutting) board, knife and spoon in a drawer

Procedure:
1. Say/sign, "(Time to) make a sandwich."
2. Sit at a table with loaf of bread, sandwich board, and container of sandwich filling.
3. Using nonverbal or verbal cues, verbal directions, demonstration, and/or physical manipulation as needed, direct the learner to:
   Open (the) drawer.
   Get (the) spoon.
   Get (the) knife.   (*or* Get (the) spoon and knife).
   Close (the) drawer.
   Put (the) spoon on (the) table.
                   (*or* Put (the) spoon and knife on (the) table).
   Put (the) knife on (the) table.
   Get 2 slices (of bread).
   Get (the) spoon/knife.
   Get (the) *(sandwich filling)*.
   Put (the) *(sandwich filling)* on (the) bread.
   Spread (the) *(sandwich filling)*.
   Cover (the) bread (*or* Close (the) sandwich).
   Cut (the) sandwich.

The above (step 3) nonverbal and verbal interventions should be faded out as soon as possible.

Evaluation procedure: Count and record the number of teacher interventions, both verbal and nonverbal, needed for learner to complete task adequately.

7

IMPLEMENTING THE LANGUAGE SKILLS AREA OF A CURRICULUM UNIT

Most persons with severe learning and behavior disorders demonstrate extreme deficits in language and communication skills. Developing these skills is a difficult challenge for both teacher and student. The student's ability to understand verbal (oral or signed)[1] language and to communicate with others affects not only other areas of learning, but behavior and social development as well. It seems apparent that difficulties in processing and understanding language or the inability to communicate even simple needs make most interactions with the environment confusing and frustrating. The long term objectives of the language skills areas of the curriculum units are to improve reception and to foster expression of language in students with severely limited communication skills.

Students who receive language training through the curriculum within my classroom display a variety of communication problems. Most of them demonstrate difficulties in reception; some cannot follow the simplest one-step direction without situational cues. Others have expressive language (oral or signed) but do not use it spontaneously or use it inappropriately. Almost half of the students are nonverbal (i.e., they demonstrate no oral language), and two are deaf.

The language skills area of the curriculum is not designed to elicit speech in a nonverbal person (refer to Chapter 3 for further discussion). It is not a speech program, although vocabulary from the curriculum units may be used in articulation exercises. If the individual's age, previous records, and evaluations by language and speech therapists indicate that a speech program is appropriate, a program designed for that purpose should be implemented. However, at the same time, the student can also benefit from

---

[1]The term *verbal* is used throughout this book to refer to the perceivable expression of language, whether it be an aural perception (i.e., the hearing of speech) or a visual perception (i.e., the seeing of sign language).

language training, within the curriculum, to improve receptive language and encourage expressive communication.

Many of Benhaven's nonverbal students who receive speech training from the speech therapist are taught to understand and express language through *total communication,* which is a simultaneous presentation of oral and signed language. In this way, the student learns a means of communication (through sign), while speech is being developed. Criticisms of this method, that teaching oral and sign language to nonverbal students may inhibit the development of speech, have yet to be substantiated. Rather, combined oral and sign language training appears to encourage speech, by improving understanding of verbal input and fostering communication in general. Many of my students' programs include sessions with a language therapist in order to expand vocabulary, reinforce language skills, and develop language concepts beyond those concepts that are taught within the curriculum units.

One of the specific objectives within the curriculum is to improve the student's understanding of oral or oral and signed language, whether to enable him to follow simple directions or to teach him to understand and respond to more complex forms of communication, such as questions. In the expressive area, the curriculum's objectives are to teach the student to express (orally and/or through sign) phrases or sentences related to a specific work activity and to use the various components (vocabulary, sentence structure) in expressing appropriate language both in response to different situations and spontaneously.

RECEPTIVE IDENTIFICATION

The first performance objective in the language skills area of any of the curriculum units states: "Learner demonstrates reception of the following task-related objects, actions, areas of the environment, and descriptive words/phrases by selecting objects, performing actions, and going to areas of the environment in response to verbal directions." Procedures for teaching the student who cannot consistently select these task-related objects from a larger group of objects in response to the verbal commands are suggested below.

The easiest way to begin is by testing the learner's ability to point to, or otherwise select, task-related objects: If he cannot select the task-related objects from several different objects, can he select any of them when fewer are presented at one time? Can he select one object when two are presented at a time? First determine which objects he can select and under what conditions of presentation. A simple and usually effective way to teach a new object label is to group the new object with one or more objects that the learner consistently selects in response to the verbal labels. Say and sign (for a deaf or nonverbal student) the object label to be learned. Usually the learner will select the correct object immediately by a process of elimination. If he does not, point or move his hand toward the correct object, and repeat the verbal label. Repeat this procedure until the learner selects the correct object independently. Then try the same procedure but change the position of the various objects on the desk. Repeat the procedure until the learner consistently selects the new object, regardless of its position, relative to the other object or objects. Present the new object with several different objects and say/sign the verbal label. Can the student still select it consistently from any group of objects with which it is presented?

If the student is nonverbal, fade out the oral word to determine whether he can select the correct object in response to the sign alone. In teaching language to nonverbal students, provide oral feedback to the student after he selects the object in response to the signed word. In this way, you can first determine whether he associates the object with the sign and then reinforce the association with the oral word. Furthermore, it is important for the hearing, nonverbal individual to improve his understanding (reception) of spoken language, since most people will naturally speak to him, while he also needs to learn the signs in order to communicate expressively.

When the student consistently selects the new object in response to the oral or signed label, you may then incorporate that object into the group of objects he has previously mastered and ask for each object in random order. Until he has demonstrated the ability to select the new object in response to the verbal word, it is best not to require him to select the other objects with which it is presented. Focus his attention upon the new object or any object that he cannot select with 100% accuracy, and be sure he has learned it before saying and/or signing labels of any of the other objects with which it is presented. This will force him to attend only to the new object in relation to the others and will limit any confusion resulting from the interference of old learning with new learning (and vice versa).

What about the student who cannot select any of the objects presented because he has not learned them, because behavior is interfering, or because he does not understand what is expected of him in the task? The procedure would be very similar, but begin with only one object. Say/sign the object label, and indicate that you want the learner to pick it up by putting his hand on the object and holding out your hand. Put him through this action as many times as necessary until he automatically picks up the object when you say/sign its label.

In most teaching situations it is best to limit verbalizations to those that are necessary for the task. For example, say/sign the object word, and use a nonverbal cue (such as holding out your hand or putting the student through the desired response) to indicate how you want the student to respond. I have had students identify a "cup" as "find a cup," when the teacher precedes the object name with a verbal direction, such as "find" or "give me." If a verbal direction is necessary, make it brief and infrequent, perhaps at the beginning of the task. The student will quickly learn through repetition what he must do, and the verbal direction will eventually become unnecessary. Similarly, do not repeatedly say the learner's name to get his attention. It is just as effective and even more efficient to draw his attention directly to the task by naming the object that he is supposed to select. When the learner consistently picks up the object in response to the verbal word, present the object with a second object, but continue saying/signing only the first object.

In order to know when to add the second object or otherwise complicate the task, formally evaluate progress by performing a specific number of test trials. For this type of task, I usually do 10 test trials and record the number of correct and incorrect responses given under each set of conditions. For example, the learner must give me the object (when only one is presented) 10 times in response to the verbal word. Only then do I add the second object. I again say/sign the first object, and, after he selects it during each of the ten test trials, I may alter the conditions. Testing can be done at the beginning or end of each lesson, but it should be done at the same time during each lesson, with notation made as to whether the data were recorded before or after practice sessions. By recording at the beginning of a lesson, an opportunity is provided to immediately identify problems and work on them during the remainder of the lesson period.

To systematically complicate the task, add more objects but say/sign only the object label to be learned. Change the position of the object relative to the other objects, and test the learner. Note whether performance varies when other objects that are similar in sound, appearance, or function are presented with the object to be learned. For example, can the learner consistently select a spoon from a group of five objects that include a plate, bowl, napkin, cup? Can he still select a spoon when another utensil (e.g., fork, knife) is presented with it? When your data show that the learner can select the object consistently, regardless of the other objects with which it is presented, the position of the objects, and the number of objects, repeat the procedure with another object.

At this point, the learner may be confused by the introduction of a second object to be learned with the first object that he has already mastered. Therefore, after the student can consistently select the second object, regardless of position, when it is grouped with several other objects, include the previously learned object in the group of objects presented at one time.

Do not ask for the first object until the student consistently selects the second object in response to the verbal word when the second object is presented with the previously learned object and several others in a variety of positions. Then you may say/sign each of the two learned objects in random order, so that the learner must select each in response to the verbal command. Can the learner select each object correctly from several objects? Can he select each when only those two objects are presented at one time? Once he demonstrates that he can correctly and consistently select each object on command, repeat the procedure for each new object introduced; that is, teach the student to consistently select the specific object from a group of other objects. However, this is usually not necessary. By a process of elimination, most learners are able to select a newly introduced object when it is grouped with several "overlearned" objects.

Important considerations when designing a lesson such as this include 1) the number of objects presented at one time, 2) similarity in sound, appearance, and function, and 3) the position of the objects relative to each other. Change any variables one at a time, so you can observe where the learner breaks down and when and how he learns best. Keep accurate data for each condition (discussed below under "Language Program") of lesson presentation, so you will know when and how to change any of the variables, add new objects, and otherwise complicate or simplify the lesson so that the objective can be achieved.

EXPRESSIVE IDENTIFICATION

When the learner demonstrates reception of task-related objects, that is, the association between an object and its verbal label, training for verbal expressive identification of the objects may begin. Do not teach a learner to say/sign a word until he has demonstrated a receptive understanding of that word. For example, I do not actively teach him to say/sign "cup" until he consistently selects a cup from a group of objects in response to the oral/signed word. (*Actively* is used to distinguish purposeful teaching from instances in which many learners automatically imitate an oral or signed word when the teacher says/signs it. Often this imitation is due to echolalic language or because the learner has been trained to imitate spoken words or signs in other teaching situations.) The learner should be able to imitate a verbal model before the teacher requires him to express a word or phrase orally or through sign. Present one object at a time, say/sign the word, and correct the learner's articulation or his imitation of the sign. Observe any repeated errors of articulation, so that they may be corrected in the classroom or in sessions with a speech therapist. If a nonverbal learner has difficulty in imitating signs, perhaps practice on hand and finger imitation can be implemented in a fine motor or gross motor period as well as in the language lesson. As the learner imitates the verbal model, systematically fade it out. Gradually the learner may need only the initial sound of the word or initial finger movement in order to express the word. It may be helpful to continue some work on reception to reinforce the building of imitative and expressive skills.

When you can present a given number of task-related objects and the learner can correctly identify them orally and/or through sign, you are ready to work on more difficult areas: areas of the environment, verbs, prepositions, and other parts of speech. However, you may have to decide whether to move on, if the learner can identify the objects but does so with poor articulation or poor sign reproduction. Generally, if the student can identify and label objects, he should progress to the next level of language training. However, efforts should be made to continue to improve articulation or sign production of any expressive language that he acquires.

LANGUAGE PROGRAM

The method within the curriculum for teaching language components beyond object identification is based on a language program developed by Wilson, Goodman, and Wood (1975). It is a highly structured behavioral method that was developed primarily to teach manual language to persons without language. I follow it in a somewhat modified form, and it provides a clear, specific, and effective means of teaching verbal as well as nonverbal students. The three levels of language, *reception* (understanding), *imitation* (of a verbal model), and *expression* (speaking and/or signing), are systematically developed within a progression of "conditions," using different kinds of prompts. The various conditions, designated by letters A–K, are listed and defined in each curriculum unit (see the appendices). Conditions A–D describe reception objectives, Conditions E–G are imitation objectives, and Conditions H^a–K state objectives for expressive language. The different prompts include physical manipulation, demonstration by the teacher, verbal models, verbal cues, nonverbal cues, and situational cues.

On the receptive level, the learner is trained to perform an activity in response to verbal directions until he can do this without any interventions from the teacher (Condition C). To ensure that the learner has *learned* the language involved in the activity rather than performed a rote sequence of steps, Condition D requires him to follow the teacher's directions for performing the given activity when these verbal commands are given out of the activity sequence. In Conditions E–F, the learner is taught to express a phrase (steps of the given work activity) in imitation of the teacher's verbal model. The objective of Condition G is for the learner to imitate a verbal model (steps of the given work activity) and then perform the appropriate step that he has just verbally described. Conditions H^a-K define various conditions under which the learner expresses each step of the activity, from expressing the language after verbal cues are given to expressing the steps of the activity as another person/teacher performs them in any sequence.

Looking at the language program for any of the curriculum units, you can see that it is a step-by-step breakdown of the language involved in the work activity of that curriculum unit. The levels within the language program, called units, correspond to the level of each work activity. As an example, Level 1 of the language program for the table-setting activity is given below:

Basic	Expanded
plate on table	Put (the) plate on (the) table.
bowl on table	Put (the) bowl on (the) table.
cup on table	Put (the) cup on (the) table.
napkin on table	Put (the) napkin on (the) table.
fork on table	Put (the) fork on (the) table.
knife on table	Put (the) knife on (the) table.
spoon on table	Put (the) spoon on (the) table.

The teacher may modify the language to suit the individual (see Chapter 2). The language used should be appropriate for the steps of the activity and consistent with the different levels of that activity. The student who demonstrates the ability to say/sign a longer or more varied and specific phrase might be taught to respond to, imitate, and express language like the following:

I put the plate on the placemat.
I put the napkin on the placemat.
I put the fork on the napkin.
I put the knife on the placemat.
I put the spoon next to the knife.

The rationale behind the development and use of the language program (units and conditions) is that the student will learn the language by its repeated association with an activity that he performs. For example, he learns the meaning of the verb *put* by hearing the word (and seeing the sign, if he is nonverbal and/or deaf) before or as he performs the action of putting an object somewhere. If the student has mastered Level 1 of the table-setting activity, he will put the object on the table in response to the verbal direction. He understands the concept of putting nonverbally; now you can concentrate on associating that action with the appropriate language. The student will learn to associate the oral/signed preposition "on" with the action of putting an object on the table, placemat, or napkin. At language unit Level 10 of the table-setting curriculum, he opens and closes cupboards and drawers in response to the oral/signed commands, and eventually expresses the appropriate words as he performs those actions (Conditions G–I). At Level 11, the student must first learn to "go to the kitchen," in response to the verbal command (Conditions A–D).

In the next section variations of the language program are discussed, in which the learner uses these same objects, verbs, prepositions, places, and areas of the environment in situations other than the given activity. In this way, the language concepts are reinforced, the student demonstrates an understanding of the language involved without the situational cues of the activity, and the chances for generalization of the language are increased.

USING THE LANGUAGE CONDITIONS: A CASE EXAMPLE

The use of the conditions within the language programs of the curriculum units can be illustrated by considering a teaching sequence of reception, imitation, and expression in the table-setting curriculum at language unit Level 2 as taught to a hearing but nonverbal learner with limited receptive language. In teaching a nonverbal learner to express the language through sign, some additional steps, which are unnecessary with the student who has oral speech, must be taken. In this example, I commence by teaching the *basic language*, which is composed of simple three-word repetitive phrases:

>plate on table (*or* plate on placemat)
>bowl on table/placemat
>cup on table/placemat
>napkin on table/placemat
>fork on table/placemat
>knife on table/placemat
>spoon on table/placemat

The student performs the table-setting activity at Level 3, but makes one or two errors in the placement of objects. He can, however, perform Level 2 of the work activity correctly. His errors at Level 3 appear to be related to the movement involved. At Level 3 the learner must get each object (provided by the teacher) from a shelf a few feet from the table to be set. This particular learner's attention problems interfere with his performance when he is moving from the shelf to the table. Therefore, I have moved the table closer to the shelf and must provide one or two nonverbal cues (pointing to correct position on placemat) in order for him to perform correctly at Level 3. For this reason, we begin work on the language program at the mastered activity level (Level 2). I can then concentrate on the language, knowing that the learner can perform each step at that level correctly. (See Appendix A for a complete description of the language program within the table-setting curriculum unit.)

Receptive Level

The learner is seated at a table. I have put a placemat on the table and one of each object above the placemat, within the learner's reach. At the start of each lesson, I say and sign, "It's time to set the table." At Condition A, I say and sign, "Plate on table/placemat." The learner is unsure what is expected, so I put his hand on the plate and point to the correct position on the placemat. He puts the plate on the placemat. Next, I say and sign, "Bowl on table/placemat." I wait a second or two, and the learner does not respond. I repeat the phrase and move the learner's hand to the bowl. He picks up the bowl and puts it in the correct position on the placemat. I say and sign, "Cup on table/placemat."

This time the learner gets the cup and places it correctly on the placemat. Then I say and sign, "Napkin on table/placemat." The learner again gets the correct object and places it correctly. I say and sign, "Fork on table/placemat." The learner reaches for the knife, so I repeat the direction and point to the fork. He picks it up and places it correctly. I say and sign, "Knife on table/placemat." The learner gets the knife and places it correctly. I say and sign, "Spoon on table/placemat." He again responds correctly.

Looking at his performance, the learner actually needed only three interventions in order to perform the task correctly in response to the verbal directions. Of those three interventions, only the first two required physical manipulation of the learner through the appropriate step of the activity. If the learner had required physical manipulation through at least 50% of the task, whether because of difficulty with the task itself or because of resistive, uncooperative, inappropriate, or interfering behavior, we would have worked on Condition A until physical manipulation was no longer necessary.

Since the learner is nonverbal, I must decide whether to move to Condition B or repeat Condition A with only the signed directions. When we reach the expressive conditions, the learner will have to sign each phrase. Consequently, the receptive and imitative conditions (A–G) may be introduced, with both oral and signed directions being provided, or the learner may be taught to respond to the signed directions, without the accompanying oral words. I usually teach a learner to respond first to oral and signed directions at each condition, and then to respond to the signed directions. Therefore, in this case, I remain at Condition A, giving the directions in sign language. The procedure, as described, is repeated. After I sign each phrase and the learner responds correctly, I say the phrase. This reinforces the signed language and provides the learner with oral feedback. In testing the learner on Condition A, performing in response to signed directions, more physical manipulation through the appropriate step of the activity may be necessary. However, once a learner understands how he is expected to respond in this situation, he will probably perform correctly (unless behavior interferes). This is because he has already learned the correct responses through performing the activity. Now we are training the learner to perform these learned responses to a verbal direction. In fact, it may be necessary to prevent him from responding before I have given the verbal direction. He has been trained to set a place setting and may automatically take each object and want to put it on the placemat. If this happens, I tell him to "wait and listen," physically fold his hands, or otherwise prevent him from responding until I have given the appropriate verbal direction.

We work on Condition A, performing the correct step of the activity in response to signed directions, until physical manipulation through each appropriate step is no longer required for the seven directions. Then we move to Condition B. At this condition, I sit next to the learner, with my own placemat and set of objects. I give each verbal direction, perform the correct step of the activity, and indicate that he is to do the same. I might begin Condition B with only the signed directions, providing the oral feedback after he has responded in imitation of my correct response. If the learner has difficulty, I give oral and signed directions until he performs with 100% accuracy. Then I eliminate the oral directions (except for feedback), so that the learner responds to the signed directions. Keep in mind, however, that the teacher may skip any of the conditions, depending on the learner's performance. I am usually able to skip Condition B, when a learner eventually performs at Condition A with interventions other than physical manipulation. For example, when the learner understands what is expected in the task, he may need only a nonverbal cue (e.g., pointing to appropriate object) in order to perform correctly. In that case, we may go directly to Condition C, in modified form (e.g., providing a nonverbal cue). I am assuming that the learner is placing each object in the correct position, since he mastered that aspect of the task in performing Level 2 of the work activity. However, if he makes an error of placement during the language lesson, I point to the correct position on the placemat or otherwise correct him and do not record it as an error in following the verbal direction. I may note the error and work on it during the work activity lesson, but the specific objective of the language lesson is to follow the verbal directions, get the correct object, and put it on the placemat.

When the learner can perform the correct step of the activity in response to the signed direction, in imitation of the teacher (Condition B), we are ready for Condition C, in which the teacher presents verbal commands in sequence and the learner follows the commands and performs the steps of the activity. The teaching situation is the same as that for Condition A. With the nonverbal student, I begin by giving each direction in sign language. If the learner responds incorrectly 50% of the time or more, I may provide oral cues; that is, I say each command as I sign it. When the learner performs each step in response to the oral and signed command, I eliminate the oral commands and provide only the signed directions. If the learner is still responding incorrectly, it may be necessary to provide a nonverbal cue, such as pointing to the appropriate object to be placed on the placemat. I would systematically fade out the nonverbal cues, perhaps pointing only when the learner begins to pick up the incorrect object. I am recording his performance at the beginning (or end) of each session on each of the seven phrases. When he can perform each step of the activity in response to each of the signed directions without any verbal or nonverbal cues, we are ready for Condition D. A sample language lesson for Condition C is provided at the end of this chapter on page 92.

Note should be made that I am illustrating each condition by a relatively poor performance in this sample case. In other words, a learner most often does not perform with less than 50% accuracy on each subsequent condition. Whatever he has mastered in the previous condition carries over into the next, so that, although the teaching situation is more demanding, he has acquired the skill to perform at the next condition with few errors. From Condition B to Condition C the teacher's model for imitation is removed. However, the learner should have learned to respond to "Plate on table/placemat" by putting the plate on the table/placemat. We are gradually modifying the teaching situation and the cues each condition provides, so that the learner eventually responds to each verbal direction without those cues and intervention procedures.

Condition D tests a learner's understanding of the language involved, when the seven phrases are signed in any sequence. At Level 2 of the table-setting activity, the learner must listen (look) and respond to the specific signed object to be placed on the table/placemat. At higher levels of the table-setting activity, the language becomes more differentiated and specific. The learner must go to other rooms (e.g., kitchen, dining room) and open and close cupboards and drawers, as well as get objects and put them on the table, as directed. One of the problems that may arise at Condition D is the learner's initial confusion over performing the familiar steps of the activity out of sequence. I usually tell the learner to "do what I say," and, after several sessions at Condition D, he appears to understand what is expected in the task. A more difficult problem is the learner who is upset by the deviation from the routine. Condition D provides an appropriate means of getting the more rigid learner's responses under the teacher's control. The learner must perform the steps of the activity as directed, rather than in an established pattern.

When Condition D was first introduced to one of my students, he attempted to perform all of the activity steps preceding the verbal direction that I gave. For example, in the blackboard-cleaning activity (Level 5), I would say/sign, "Go to the bathroom." He would first go to the closet and get the tub and sponge. Or I would say/sign, "Go to the bathroom," "Turn on the cold water," "Turn off the cold water," "Go to the classroom." He wanted to first get the tub and sponge, go to the bathroom, turn on the cold and hot water, and fill the tub with water. He was understandably confused by the changes in the sequence of the activity, and engaged in tantrum behavior when I prevented him from performing the activity in the usual sequence. He screamed, stomped on the floor, and tried to grab and pinch me. We discontinued that lesson for the day, and instead did a reading lesson, which often calms him down. The next day, I began the lesson by telling him that we were going to play a game, and he must do just what I told him. I began giving directions that were unrelated to any work activity (e.g., "Get a pencil," "Put the pencil on the table"), and then slipped in several directions from the blackboard-cleaning activity. This approach seemed to be successful, and I therefore continued the lesson in this way each day, gradually eliminating the nonactivity-related directions and increasing the number of directions from the blackboard activity. This incident emphasizes that the teacher may, indeed, have to modify lessons and short term objectives in response to a variety of learning and behavior problems.

When a learner who has reached Condition D makes errors in performance, the errors are most likely caused by confusion about the task itself, resistance to performing the steps of the activity out of sequence, lack of attention, or interfering behavior. By the time the learner is at Condition D, he should understand that the verbal word "bowl" represents the object bowl. If the learner is not attending, getting his attention and repeating the word should improve performance. However, Condition D may reveal that he has been performing a learned set of responses (steps of the activity) in rote fashion without attending to or associating the verbal directions with the responses. In that event, more drills in selecting objects in response to the verbal words should be done in addition to work on the language unit. When problems occur at any condition, the teacher must decide whether to remain at that condition, add specific cues, design supplementary drills to reinforce a specific area of weakness, or go back to the previous condition. A sample lesson for Condition D is provided at the end of the chapter on page 93.

Imitative Level

When the learner performs each step of the activity in response to verbal directions, regardless of the sequence in which the directions are given (Condition D), he is ready for Condition E, in which the teacher provides verbal model and puts the learner through verbal behavior (at desk). This condition differs from Condition F in that the teacher may physically manipulate the learner to articulate clearly (orally or through sign) in imitation of the teacher's verbal model. However, at Condition F any physical manipulation must be recorded as an intervention and gradually eliminated. In both conditions E and F the learner is seated at his desk and removed from the activity situation. The learner must say (and/or sign) each phrase after the teacher has said/signed it. In Condition E, the teacher may manipulate the learner's mouth, hands, and fingers in order to improve speech articulation or to correct sign imitation. When the learner can imitate each word of the phrase without the need for physical intervention, he is then ready for Condition F.

At this level, the teacher should not need to put the learner through the verbal behavior. Of course, articulation should be worked on whenever the learner imitates or expresses language, but at Condition F the learner must also demonstrate the ability to say or sign a sequence of words (phrase) correctly, after the teacher provides the verbal model. With a nonverbal student, I usually present a simultaneous oral and signed model for imitation. As in the receptive conditions, I fade out the oral cues so that the learner is eventually signing the phrase without the oral cues. Each time he signs the phrase in imitation of my signed phrase, I provide the oral feedback. Any problems that the learner demonstrates in imitating a sequence of words/signs must be overcome at the imitative levels (Conditions E-G). He must be able to say or sign a complete phrase (even if that phrase is only two words) in imitation of a model, before he is expected to express a phrase without the verbal model (Conditions H[a]-K). A sample lesson for Condition F is provided at the end of the chapter on page 94.

For Condition G the learner is again in the activity situation. He is seated at a table with a placemat, with one of each appropriate object above the placemat. As in Condition F, I provide the verbal model; that is, I sign each step of the activity. The learner must imitate each phrase and then perform the appropriate step of the activity. A student who does not have difficulty imitating oral or signed language may go from Condition D directly to Condition G. However, I usually run through each of the phrases at the learner's desk, in order to determine whether it is necessary to work on articulation at Conditions E or F or if we can progress directly to Condition G. I would not move to Condition G unless the learner was able to imitate a complete phrase. It may become apparent at the imitative levels that the phrases are too lengthy for a particular learner. The teacher may then shorten the phrases, and lengthen them appropriately after the learner has mastered the modified phrases.

As with any variation of a given task, the learner may initially have problems in understanding how he is supposed to respond at each condition. In an attempt to communicate this, I first give a simple verbal direction, but demonstration, or putting the learner through the desired response, is most often necessary. It is especially important that the learner understands what he is expected to do at the various levels of the language program of the curriculum unit, because the same materials are used throughout the conditions and the teaching situations are so similar. If the learner has moved from Condition D directly to Condition G, I tell him to "say what I say." After he has imitated the verbal phrase, I tell him to "do it," and if necessary I point to the appropriate object or put him through the action. If the learner has moved from Condition F to Condition G, he will probably imitate the phrases automatically. Then I must indicate, either verbally or nonverbally, that he is to perform the appropriate step of the activity. At Condition G, the learner puts together the language that he is expressing with the appropriate step of the activity. Essentially, he is describing his actions before he performs them.

Expressive Level

When the learner consistently signs each phrase in imitation of the teacher's model and performs the appropriate step of the activity, he is ready for Condition H[a], in which the teacher presents a verbal cue in response to which the learner will produce the appropriate verbal behavior and perform the steps of the activity. This is the first condition at which the learner is expected to sign each phrase without the verbal model for imitation. Keeping in mind our case example at Level 2 of the table-setting activity and language program, for the expressive conditions the learner sits at the table where a placemat and the appropriate objects have been placed. I say/sign, "Tell me how you set the table." It is likely that the learner will not respond initially. I then provide a verbal (oral or signed) cue such as "What do you do?" or a more leading question such as "What do you put on the placemat/table?" At first, I may have to provide the verbal model as well; that is, I sign "Plate on placemat/table." The learner should imitate the verbal model and put the plate on the placemat/table. I then provide the oral feedback by saying, "Plate on table; good." I record this as an intervention because it was necessary for me to provide the model, as in Condition G.

Condition H[a] requires that a learner say or sign each step of the activity in response to a verbal cue, or leading question. Any time I must give the verbal model, whether the complete phrase or any of the words of the phrase, it is recorded as an intervention. These interventions should be eliminated before progressing to Condition H[b]. In some instances, it may be necessary to intervene in order for the learner to perform the appropriate step of the activity after he has expressed the phrase correctly. This is more likely to occur at higher levels (units) of the language program, where language may become more complex. It also may happen when the condition is first introduced or when working with a deaf student. The deaf student cannot benefit from the verbal (i.e., signed) cues unless he understands the language. Most often, these cues are questions like "What do you do?" "What do you get?" "Where do you go?" "Where do you put the plate?" etc. Although the deaf student (or any student with very limited receptive language) will not initially understand these questions, he may learn the correct responses through the repeated association of the signed phrases with the appropriate steps of the activity. I have also found that students recognize words within the complete cue (if not the whole question) and use these particular words as cues. For instance, when I ask, "What do you put on the table/placemat?" the student hears (or sees the sign for) "on table/placemat." He usually will then look at the objects and sign "(object) on table/placemat." Initially, he may need only the model for "on" in order to sign the complete phrase. This is recorded as an intervention, but it is usually easily and quickly faded out so that the learner is signing the complete phrase.

At the expressive conditions of the language program for the table-setting unit (Levels 1 and 2), the learner may sign the phrases in any sequence. At these levels of the table-setting activity, the order in which he performs the steps of the activity is unimportant. It does not matter whether he puts the plate or the spoon on the table/placemat first, unless performing the activity out of the sequence in which it was learned interferes with performance. If the student signs a phrase and performs the appropriate step of the activity, then he may perform the steps in any sequence. However, at higher levels of the table-setting activity (and in other activities) a specific sequence may be necessary in order to perform the activity. A sample lesson for Condition H[a] is provided at the end of the chapter on page 95.

When the learner can sign each phrase and perform the appropriate steps of the activity in response to verbal cues without verbal models or interventions to perform the appropriate actions, we move to Condition H[b]: (teacher provides a nonverbal cue in response to which the learner produces the verbal behavior and performs the steps of the activity). The teaching situation is the same as that for Conditions G and H[a]. In our case example, I say/sign, "Tell me how you set the table." In Condition H[b] I may cue the learner by pointing to an object, for example, a plate. He must sign the appropriate phrase, "Plate on table/placemat," and perform the action by putting the plate on the table/placemat. If I must provide a verbal cue or verbal model or intervene in order for him to perform the appropriate step, these interventions are recorded.

The interventions must be eliminated so that the learner signs each phrase before performing each step of the activity, with only a nonverbal cue for each verbal phrase. After the initial presentations at Condition H^b, interventions for performing the steps of the activity and verbal cues or models should not be necessary. The learner should have mastered the language and the actions in previous conditions. If he does make errors, I must determine if they are attributable to confusion about the task or to behavior; in order to have reached Condition H^b the learner must have demonstrated the ability to perform at Condition H^a several times consecutively (during different sessions or on consecutive days).

When he can sign each step of the activity before he performs it with only a nonverbal cue, he is ready for Condition I (teacher presents a situation in which the learner produces the verbal behavior and performs steps of the activity). It may not be convenient to conduct this table-setting lesson before a meal. If it is not, the verbal direction, "Tell me how you set the table," should be sufficient. Using no cues from the teacher, the learner must then sign each step of the activity as he performs it. Any interventions that are necessary must be recorded and gradually eliminated. Interventions given in response to inappropriate behaviors, lapses in attention, or other behavioral problems not directly related to the specific task may or may not be recorded. I usually record only instructional interventions necessary for the achievement of the condition's objectives. When the learner demonstrates consistently that he can produce the appropriate verbal behavior and perform the steps of the activity, I may decide to work specifically on the interfering behaviors. Then my objectives are work behavior objectives, rather than language objectives, and can be recorded separately. The teacher may use any of the tasks in a curriculum unit to work on behavior, but keep in mind the specific objectives so that the learner is evaluated on those particular goals.

Condition I is the first condition in which the learner has no cues other than those inherent in the teaching situation. At Level 2 of the table-setting curriculum unit and language program, those cues are the table-setting object themselves. Because the learner may have become dependent on external cues provided by the teacher, Condition I may require more time to achieve than some of the earlier conditions. However, the teacher's role in providing cues has been systematically reduced throughout the expressive conditions, so that the learner's dependence on them is also gradually decreased. A sample lesson for Condition I is provided at the end of the chapter on page 96.

In Condition J the learner uses his newly aquired language skills to instruct another person (teacher or student). I tell the student to "tell me how to set the table." At first, he will probably be confused by this reversal of roles. However, this condition provides a situation in which the learner uses the language to interact with another person. It is primarily a language exercise, but may be socially valuable in that the learner is using the language to communicate with another individual. For students who have learned the expanded language (e.g., "I put the plate on the table/placemat"), Condition J allows the teacher to teach him pronoun usage ("You put the plate on the table/placemat") or proper names ("Mary, put the bowl on the table/placemat").

In Condition K the learner must watch another person perform a step of the activity. He must then use the language he has learned to describe whatever step of that activity the person performs, in any sequence. I usually direct the student initially by saying and signing verbal cues, such as "What am I putting on the table/placemat?" When he is able to describe my actions in response to verbal cues, I make them less specific, such as "What am I doing?" This condition may also be used as a means of teaching pronouns, proper names, and grammar, if these are appropriate goals for a particular learner. For example, you might have another person (teacher, student, family member) perform the actions while you ask, "What is Mary doing?" The learner should learn to respond, "Mary put the bowl on the table/placemat." Or ask, "What is he doing?" The learner should respond, "He put the knife on the table/placemat." Once the learner can perform successfully at Condition I for any language unit, you may use your creativity to design different situations in which the structured language can be used, as appropriate to his needs and abilities.

Student Progress

How long does a learner remain at each condition? This, of course, depends on the learner's abilities. Most learners remain at Conditions G and H[a] longer than the other conditions, because these are the first conditions at which the learner expressively combines verbal behavior (phrases) with an action. Learners with very limited receptive skills may need to stay at Condition C for a relatively long period of time. The length of time the learner spends at each condition is relative only to his capabilities. I have students who begin at Condition C and progress to Condition I within several weeks. Others remain at a given condition for months. However, it is encouraging that many students learn the language for higher activity levels, or a second and third activity, much faster than the first language program taught to them. It appears that, as the students become familiar with the method (and the teacher becomes more familiar with it) and how they are expected to respond at the various conditions, they are better able to concentrate on learning the new language material that is presented.

RELATION OF RECEPTIVE AND EXPRESSIVE IDENTIFICATION TO THE LANGUAGE PROGRAM

The vocabulary words listed in objectives 1 and 2 of the language skills area of a curriculum unit are a breakdown of the language components of the work activity levels or of the units of the accompanying language program. The units (or levels) of the language program are comprised of phrases that describe the steps of an activity at each level, and the vocabulary words are those words that make up the descriptive phrases. Thus, a question may arise as to when and how to teach the vocabulary words in relation to introducing the language program. I do not usually begin the language program for a specific activity until the learner demonstrates reception of the nouns presented in Level 1 of that activity. For example, I would not begin the table-setting language program until the learner could consistently point to or otherwise select a placemat, plate, bowl, cup, napkin, fork, knife, spoon, and table in response to the verbal words for those objects. It is also essential that the learner perform the steps of a given level of a work activity before teaching the language unit for that level of performance. If the teacher begins teaching the language unit for Level 1 of the work activity (which the learner can perform) before the learner can correctly identify the task-related objects, then the learner will probably start at a lower condition than if he had mastered the objects receptively. The learner who can receptively identify plate, bowl, cup, napkin, fork, knife, spoon, and table will probably be able to follow verbal directions from the table-setting language program at Condition B. The learner who has not yet learned to identify these objects probably will have to begin at Condition A. He may also need to remain at the receptive conditions (A-D) longer than the learner who begins the language program after he has learned to identify the objects. Similarly, the learner who can identify the task-related objects expressively may require less time at the expressive Conditions (G-K) of the language program.

Another consideration is the learner's ability to follow simple verbal directions. At the lower activity levels of the table-setting curriculum, the basic language unit is very repetitive. Each object is placed on the table/placemat. However, other activities may involve more differentiated language and require better receptive skills. Consider, for example, language unit Level 1 of the blackboard-cleaning activity:

Basic	Expanded
tub down	Put (the) tub down.
wet sponge	Wet (the) sponge.
squeeze sponge	Squeeze (the) sponge.
clean/wash blackboard	Clean/wash (the) blackboard.
sponge in tub	Put (the) sponge in (the) tub.

The learner who has at least a receptive understanding of the objects and actions, and who can follow verbal directions, probably can begin the language unit at a higher condition than the learner who does not demonstrate these skills. Again, the purpose of the units and conditions in the language programs is to teach these skills by associating the verbal phrases with the appropriate actions. At Condition A, you may put the learner through the appropriate action after giving the verbal direction. It is basically the teacher's decision whether or not to teach a number of the vocabulary words separately before introducing the language program.

RELATION OF WORK ACTIVITY LEVEL TO UNITS OF LANGUAGE PROGRAM

Work on a level, or unit, of a language program generally should not commence until the learner can perform the task objective of the corresponding work activity level. This does not mean that you cannot work on language unit Level 3 of the table-setting activity if the learner makes errors in setting a table at activity Level 3. If he makes one or two errors in the placement of objects, but a language evaluation shows he may be ready to begin the language units, you may decide to work on Level 3 of the language program. However, if he needs interventions in order to proceed from one step of the activity to the next, the language program should not be introduced at that level of the activity. At a given level of any language program, the learner is learning the language through its association with a step of the activity. It would be confusing to both the learner and the teacher if interventions were necessary for both the language and the performance of a given step of the activity. By working on a language unit at a level of performance that the learner has already mastered, the learner does not have to learn two new things at once. He has demonstrated that he can perform the steps of the activity at a given level, so efforts can be directed toward associating the appropriate language with those steps. Learning the language should be less complicated if the learner can direct his attention to the language, rather than having to think about what he gets next, from where, and what he must do.

Obviously, teaching is simplified by working on only one objective at a time, and the objectives of the language program are to teach language through an activity, rather than to teach an activity through language. However, if it is necessary to provide verbal directions in teaching a level of the work activity, use the directions from the corresponding language unit so the learner becomes familiar with that language. Remember that the objective of the work activity area is for the learner to perform an activity adequately and independently, while the objective of the language skills area is to improve receptive and expressive skills.

VARIATIONS OF THE LANGUAGE PROGRAM

The fourth objective in the language skills area of a curriculum unit states: "Learner demonstrates reception of verbal phrases outside the context/structure of the activity situation and language units by following verbal directions consisting of functional combinations of the vocabulary in objective 1 and any previously learned vocabulary." The primary purpose of this objective is to improve receptive skills and to ensure that the learner understands the language from a curriculum unit even when it is not directly related to an activity situation. The teacher may implement this part of the language skills area at any time, while teaching reception and expression of vocabulary words and/or during the language program. How simple or complex the verbal directions are depends on the learner's needs and abilities. If he cannot select task-related objects from a group of objects in response to the verbal words (objective 1), I begin with very simple directions. For example, I might put 10 of the same object (e.g., forks) and a tub on the learner's desk. The learner must put a fork in the tub in response to the verbal direction "Fork in tub" or "Put the fork in the tub." The length of the phrase and number of nonessential words (e.g., the) should depend on the learner's ability to follow verbal directions. If he is nonverbal, I present the command orally and through sign. When he can respond consistently to the oral/signed commands, I present only the signed directions (with oral feedback after he responds). At this level of the task, I am teaching him primarily how he is expected to respond; that is, he learns to pick up an object (fork) and put it in a specific place (tub). Next, I teach him to discriminate two objects in a given number of trials (I present 10 test trials) by presenting two sets of objects (e.g., five forks, five cups). I give the verbal directions, "Fork/cup in tub" or "Put the fork/cup in the tub." When my data for the 10 test trials show that he responds correctly to the verbal directions given in random order, I can further complicate the task.

At these very basic levels of the task, it is important that the learner really attends to what the teacher is saying and/or signing. It is very easy at these simple levels for the learner to respond by rote rather than to the verbal directions. Make sure that he does not respond until you have given the complete verbal direction, as this will be especially necessary when the directions become more complex at higher levels of the task.

The teacher may begin training the learner to follow simple verbal directions by setting up the task situation for maximal success, that is, using all of the same object and putting each in one specific place as directed. Systematically require the learner to follow more complex directions by presenting two different sets of objects from which he must select the correct objects in response to the verbal directions. At this point, he may actually be responding only to the objects that you say/sign, since he is required to put each object in the same place. You may increase the difficulty of the task by the manner in which you present two sets of objects. Initially, place them on the desk in separate groups. When he consistently responds correctly, combine the two sets of objects so that he must really attend to the directions and the objects. It may be best to begin with objects that are different in appearance, sound, and function. Then, before adding more objects, places, or prepositions, you may present two sets of objects that are similar in appearance, sound, and/or function (e.g., two utensils).

When the learner performs correctly under these conditions, you may gradually add more variables to the task. I usually require the learner to select objects from a group of different objects (e.g., a fork, spoon, knife, napkin, plate, placemat, two cups, two bowls) that provides 10 trials before adding to the number of places he must put the objects. However, you could work from the other end and limit the number of different objects from which he must choose, while requiring him to put the objects in different places (e.g., in a tub, on a table). It is important, though, that he select from at least two groups of objects and put the objects in two different places as soon as he demonstrates that he is ready (for example, by correctly selecting from two or more groups of different objects and putting them in one place, or by putting each of 10 of the same object in two or more different places). If you only increase the variety of objects or the number of places in which he must put the objects, rather than increasing both as soon as possible, the learner may begin to attend to only the beginning or the end of the verbal direction.

The teacher may then increase the number of different objects from which the learner selects, the places he must put them and the amount of movement through the environment, the prepositions used in the verbal directions, and the length of the direction. You may use the objects and places related to a work activity that the student is currently performing and objects and places that he has learned in other work activities or areas of his program. Within the table-setting curriculum unit, verbal directions to which the learner might learn to respond could include:

        Put (the) (object) in/on/under (the) tub
                                                   chair
                                                   table
                                                   closet
                                                   drawer
                                                   shelf
                                                   kitchen
                                                   cupboard, etc.

and, when and if he demonstrates the ability to follow those directions,

Put (the) (object) and (the) (object) in/on/under (the) (place).

Remember to carefully evaluate the learner's performance with each variation of the task, so that you may systematically and appropriately increase the complexity of the verbal directions.

Although it is not listed in the curriculum units as an objective, you may also use this task to work on improving expressive language skills. You might put an object or objects in a specific place while the learner watches, and ask, "Where is/are the (object/and object)?" The learner should respond, "(The) (object/and object) is/are in/on/under (the) (place)." You should not work in the expressive level of the task until the learner can consistently perform correctly at the receptive level. You may initially have to provide verbal models for imitation, but these interventions should be faded out so that the learner is eventually responding to the verbal cue (e.g., the questions, "Where is the _____?" or "What is in/on/under (the) (place)?"). With some learners, you may eventually eliminate the verbal cues, so that the learner responds to your nonverbal cues with an appropriate verbal phrase, such as pointing to the object or objects, after you put them in a specific place.

With this task, or any objective in the curriculum unit, the teacher should feel free to develop new objectives that are appropriate to the learner's level of functioning. The curriculum unit is presented as a model, and objectives may be modified and expanded to suit individual needs and abilities. A sample language program variation lesson is provided at the end of the chapter on page 97.

EXAMPLES OF LANGUAGE OBJECTIVES FOR INDIVIDUAL STUDENTS

Two examples of students' work activity and language objectives are presented below to illustrate how the objectives fit together to teach new skills and reinforce each other in the students' programs.

Student A

Table-Setting Work Activity Level 2:
　　Learner places table-setting objects provided by teacher in correct positions *on a placemat.*
Receptive Language Objective 1:
　　Learner demonstrates reception of the following task-related objects by selecting objects in response to verbal directions: placemat, plate, bowl, cup, napkin, fork, knife, spoon.

Language Unit Level 1, Condition A:
  Learner performs steps of the table-setting activity in response to verbal commands given in activity sequence, with physical prompts provided as necessary.
Variations of Language Program:
  Learner demonstrates ability to follow simple verbal directions by selecting the appropriate objects from two sets of objects (forks, cups) and putting them in specific places (in a tub, on the table), in response to verbal directions ("Put (the) fork/cup in/on (the) tub/table").

Student B

Bed-Making Activity Level 8:
  Learner goes to appropriate place (e.g., linen closet) and gets bottom sheet, top sheet, pillowcase, pillow, blanket, and bedspread and makes the bed properly.
Language Unit Level 8, Condition G:
  Learner expresses orally each step of the bed-making activity in imitation of the teacher's verbal model, before performing each step of the activity.
Variations of Language Program:
  Learner demonstrates ability to follow simple verbal directions comprised of functional combinations of vocabulary from the bed-making activity and previously learned vocabulary (from the table-setting activity) by getting objects and putting them in specific places within and outside of the classroom (e.g., "Put a blanket on the table," "Put a pillow on the chair," "Put a pillowcase in the tub," "Bring the tub to the kitchen").

Student A is at a low level of the table-setting activity (Level 2). His receptive skills are poor, and he is not able to correctly select the objects listed in response to the verbal words. Therefore, one part of his program is a lesson designed specifically to teach reception of those objects. Another part of his language program is the selection of the appropriate language unit. He works on the language unit corresponding to the work activity level that he has mastered, so we may concentrate on the primary objective: learning to associate each of the verbal directions with each step of the activity. Because Student A cannot consistently select each object in response to the verbal word, he is at Condition A. At this condition, I present a verbal direction (e.g., "Plate on table") and physically put him through the appropriate steps of the activity if necessary. In the lesson involving variations of the language program his ability to listen and respond to a very simple verbal direction involving task-related objects is again reinforced.

Student B has mastered the table-setting activity and accompanying language skills. He is now working on the bed-making activity at a high level of the task (Level 8). His errors in performance at this level are related to the quality of his performance, rather than errors in the step-by-step procedure. Therefore, he is working at a matching language unit and work activity level. He has demonstrated the ability to follow the verbal directions from the language unit out of the activity sequence (Condition D), and is able to clearly articulate the verbal phrases in imitation of the verbal model (Condition F). Therefore, we are working on Condition G, where he must imitate a verbal phrase and perform the appropriate steps of the activity. In addition, his receptive skills have developed enough so that he can follow simple verbal directions involving a wider variety of vocabulary words (from both the table-setting and bed-making units) and movement through the environment.

In scheduling these work activity and language lessons, I usually do not conduct the work activity and language unit lessons during the same lesson period. I also preface the language lesson by telling the student that he is going to "tell me how (he) makes the bed." In this way, the objectives remain separate, and the student soon learns what he is expected to do in each lesson situation. Sometimes, however, a student will spontaneously express each step of the activity as he performs it during the work activity lesson. This, of course, is one of the objectives of the language skills area, and should not be discouraged. However, keep in mind the particular objectives of each area (work activity and language), and direct teaching efforts to the achievement of those area-specific goals.

DEVELOPING SUPPORTIVE AND ADDITIONAL SKILLS

Task-related materials and the activity situation may be used as a basis for supportive language work and to teach additional language-related skills. The teacher may develop a variety of objectives and tasks according to the needs and abilities of each learner. In this section, some suggestions are provided for skills that may be taught or reinforced using the curriculum unit activity and materials. The teacher must determine what specific types of language skills may require supportive or remedial work. Speech articulation, auditory memory, or sequencing skills may all benefit from supplemental work, and other skills such as question answering, color identification, the use of pronouns, size concepts, and verbal or written descriptions of activity-related pictures, can be developed through the curriculum unit. The teacher should consider both the learner's areas of weakness and his demonstrated abilities, in order to identify appropriate objectives and create new activities to supplement those provided by the curriculum unit. By using task-related materials and the activity as a base, the student learns new skills through a familiar situation. This approach simplifies learning and heightens efficiency by limiting the amount of new material presented to the learner at a given time. For example, an auditory sequencing task might require the learner to pick up two or more objects in the order in which the teacher says/signs them. By using objects that the learner can consistently identify correctly, the learner can attend to the sequence itself, without first having to learn to identify new objects.

This section was added to the original curriculum model to illustrate the potential for developing new learning situations from those presented within the curriculum units. The suggestions are based on activities that were developed in response to Benhaven students' needs and capabilities. The teacher should feel free to expand the scope of the curriculum as far as students' abilities allow, using work activities and structured language as a springboard for a wide range of language-oriented activities.

At the end of the chapter several sample lesson plans, based on some of the suggested activities, are provided for the reader's reference (pages 98-104). Note that the materials used are always those with which the learner is familiar.

CONCLUSION

The language program presented in the curriculum is highly structured and systematic and is based primarily on the work activity of each curriculum unit. The rationale behind this approach is that language related to an activity with which the learner is familiar can be concretely demonstrated, will be meaningful, and thus will be learned more readily. The general, long term objectives of the language skills area are to improve receptive skills and to develop expressive language skills. The specific objectives and tasks may be used to teach individuals who demonstrate a broad range of language and communication difficulties — from individuals with severely limited receptive and expressive language to persons who do not use language appropriately or spontaneously. Through the highly structured language components of the curriculum units, as well as supportive and supplementary skills, progress toward increasing the learner's ability to communicate can be made. This training should enable the learner to use language, not only in the structured situations within which it is taught, but in other situations where the language is appropriate. The more language the learner acquires and the more opportunities with which he is presented to use that language, the greater the chances for the learner to use the language spontaneously and to generalize it to a variety of situations.

In the language skills area and other areas of the curriculum units, the teacher may use the performance objectives and tasks in a variety of ways. The curriculum provides a model rather than a strict "recipe" for teaching individuals with severe learning and behavior disorders. The principles and methods presented should be adapted and used to develop appropriate, prescriptive educational programs that effectively meet the needs of individual students.

Language Program Lesson — Condition C

Objective: Learner will perform appropriate step of an activity in response to verbal phrases/directions given in sequence.
Materials: objects necessary for performance of the activity
Procedure:
1. Structure environment as needed for performance of the activity.
2. Tell learner it is "Time to (activity)."
3. Say/sign each phrase from the appropriate language unit in the activity sequence.
4. Help learner to perform the appropriate steps of the activity in response to the verbal phrases/directions, by demonstration or physical manipulation through task, as needed.

All the above verbal and nonverbal interventions (4) other than the verbal phrases/directions from the language unit are to be faded out.

Evaluation procedure: Count and record the number of teacher interventions needed, both verbal and nonverbal, for learner to perform appropriate step of the activity in response to the verbal phrases/directions from the language program.

Language Program Lesson — Condition D

Objective: Learner will perform appropriate step of an activity in response to verbal phrases/directions given out of the activity sequence.

Materials: objects necessary for performance of the activity

Procedure:
1. Structure environment as needed for performance of the activity.
2. Tell learner, "Listen, and do what I tell you."
3. Say/sign phrases from the appropriate language unit out of the visual activity sequence.
4. Help the learner to perform the appropriate steps of the activity in response to the verbal phrases/directions, by demonstration or physical manipulation through the task, as needed.

All the above verbal and nonverbal interventions (4) other than the verbal phrases/directions from the language unit are to be faded out.

Evaluation procedure: Count and record the number of teacher interventions needed, both verbal and nonverbal, for learner to perform appropriate step of the activity in response to the verbal phrases/directions from the language unit.

Language Program Lesson — Condition F

Objective: Learner will produce verbal behavior (phrases from the appropriate language unit) in imitation of the teacher's verbal model.

Materials: none (sit across from or next to student)

Procedure:
1. Tell student, "Listen/look, and say/sign what I say/sign."
*2. Say/sign each phrase.
3. Learner imitates complete phrase correctly.
3. Learner imitates complete phrases correctly.
4. Repeat and work on any phrases, or parts of phrases, with which learner has difficulty.

*If presenting only signed phrases for imitation, say each phrase after learner signs it.

Evaluation procedure: Count and record the number of complete verbal phrases/directions learner imitates correctly, and the number of verbal phrases/directions requiring interventions (e.g., incomplete or incorrect imitation).

Language Program Lesson — Condition H[a]

Objective: Learner will express an appropriate phrase, orally or through sign, before performing each step of the activity (with verbal and nonverbal cues provided as needed).

Materials: objects necessary for performance of the activity

Procedure:
1. Structure environment as needed for performance of the activity.
2. Direct learner, "Tell me how you (activity)."
3. Teacher may point to appropriate place or object (nonverbal cue) and/or ask a leading question (verbal cue) such as, "Where do you go?," "What do you get?," "Where do you put the _____?" etc.
4. Learner says/signs an appropriate phrase before performing each step of the activity.

Evaluation procedure: Count and record the number of times learner says/signs phrase correctly and performs appropriate step of activity, and the number of verbal phrases that require intervention (e.g., verbal modeling of correct word or phrase, or demonstration/physical manipulation through step of activity).

Language Program Lesson — Condition I

Objective: Learner will express verbally each step of an activity before performing each step, in response to the direction, "Tell me how you (activity)."

Materials: objects necessary for performance of the activity

Procedure:
1. Structure environment as needed for performance of the activity.
2. Direct learner, "Tell me how you (activity)."
3. Learner says/signs the appropriate phrase before performing each step of the activity.

Evaluation procedure: Count and record the number of teacher interventions needed, both verbal and nonverbal, for learner to express verbally the appropriate phrase for each step of the activity as he performs it.

Language Program Variation
Lesson — Following Verbal Directions

Objective: Learner selects correct object(s) and puts it in appropriate place in response to verbal directions.

Materials: task-related materials: table, tub, shelf, closet, etc. (various places to put objects)*
*Check data chart for specific number of objects and specific places to put them for particular learner.

Procedure:
1. Place objects where indicated on chart (on a desk near the learner, a few feet away, or in another room).
2. Stand next to learner and give direction
(Object) in/on/under (place)
or
Put (the) (object) in/on/under (the) (place).
3. Learner gets correct object(s) and puts it in appropriate place.
4. Continue, varying the verbal directions.

If learner selects incorrect object and/or puts it in incorrect place, try the following:
— Break down direction, for example,
   "(Object)" learner gets correct object
   "in/on/under (place)."
If necessary, put learner through the actions physically. — Repeat same direction several times, for example,
   (Object) on table.
   (Object) on table.
   (Object) on table.
or vary just one element of the direction, either the objects or the places.

Evaluation procedure: Count and record the number of times the learner performs correctly/incorrectly (gets correct object and puts in appropriate place) in response to verbal directions on first 10 trials.

Additional Language Skills Lesson — Auditory Sequencing

Objective: Learner will place two objects in a tub, in the sequence in which the teacher says/signs the objects.

Materials: task-related objects that the learner consistently identifies correctly (orally or through sign)

Procedure:
1. Put a tub on the learner's desk or on a chair next to the desk (within the learner's reach).
2. Begin with two different objects placed on the learner's desk.
3. Demonstrate by saying/signing object, and placing each object in the tub in the order you said/signed each object.
4. Put the objects back on the desk.
5. Say/sign each object.
6. Learner places each object in the tub in the order in which you said/signed each object.

If the learner responds incorrectly, try breaking up the direction, for example,

Say/sign "(object)" — Learner places object in tub.
Say/sign second object — Learner places object in tub.

Continue in this way, gradually shortening the length of the pause between objects, until the learner performs as in steps 5-6.

Evaluation procedure: Count and record the number of times learner responds correctly/incorrectly on a given number of trials. When the learner performs steps 5-6 with 100% accuracy on a given number of trials, go on to step 7.

Procedure:
7. Put three objects on the learner's desk.
8. Say/sign two of the objects.
9. Learner places each of the two objects in the tub in the order you said/signed each object.

Evaluation procedure: Count and record the number of times learner responds correctly/incorrectly on a given number of trials.

Additional Language Skills Lesson — Introducing Big/Little

Objective: Learner will identify objects, orally or through sign, as big or little.

Materials: task-related objects that the learner consistently identifies correctly (orally or through sign); two sets of each object, big and little, with each set of objects the same except for size; two shallow containers, such as shoe box covers

Prerequisite: (Steps a-e are designed to determine whether the learner can visually discriminate big/little).
  a. Place two shallow containers on the learner's desk.
  b. Put a big object in one container and a little object (same object as big object) in the other container.
  c. Hand the learner big and little objects (the same objects as in the containers).
  d. Learner places the big/little objects in appropriate containers.
  e. Repeat steps 1-4 below several times, with different sets (big/little) of objects.

Procedure:
When learner can sort different sets of objects according to size (big/little), begin step 1:
1. Put an empty shallow container on learner's desk.
2. Place two of the same object on learner's desk — one big, one little, for example, a big fork and a little fork.
3. Say/sign "big," and point to the big object and the container, demonstrate, or physically manipulate learner to pick up big object and put it in container.
4. Place two other same objects, big and little, on learner's desk (e.g., big plate, little plate).
5. Say/sign "big."
6. Learner selects big object and puts it in container. (If learner does not respond, or responds incorrectly, say/sign "big" and direct him to respond correctly as in step 3.)
*7. Repeat steps 4-6 with a variety of objects, presenting two of the same at a time (big and little) until learner consistently selects the big object independently (10 times consecutively).
   *Make sure that big and little objects are presented in different positions on the desk; for example, do not put the big object to right of the little object each time, present objects in horizontal and vertical rows, place objects upside down as well as right side up, etc.
8. Take big objects out of container.
9. Follow steps 1-6, saying/signing "little" and requiring learner to select the little object each time.
10. Repeat with a variety of objects, presenting two of the same at a time (big and little) until learner consistently selects the little object independently.
11. Take little objects out of container.
12. Present two of the same objects, big and little, at a time.

13. Say/sign "big" or "little."
14. Learner selects correct size object and puts it in container.
    (If learner does not respond, or responds incorrectly, say/sign "big" or "little" again, and direct him by pointing, demonstrating, or physically manipulating him to respond correctly.)
15. Continue presenting two objects at a time, big and little, and saying/signing "big" or "little."
16. Learner selects correct-size object and puts in container.

Evaluation procedure: Count and record the number of times learner selects correct/incorrect-size object in response to verbal words ("big," "little") on 10 test trials (steps 15-16).

Additional Language Skills Lesson — Introducing "Yes/No"

Objective: Learner will answer questions correctly, "Yes" or "No," when the teacher presents an object and asks, "Is this a _____?"

Materials: task-related objects that the learner consistently identifies correctly (orally or through sign)

Procedure:
1. Hold up an object, for example, a cup.
2. Say/sign, "Is this a cup?"
3. Provide the verbal model "Yes."
4. Learner imitates: "Yes."
5. Repeat steps 1 and 2 until learner responds "Yes" several times consecutively, without needing a verbal model.
6. Hold up another object, for example, a plate.
7. Say/sign, "Is this a plate?"
8. Follow steps 3-5.
9. Hold up another object, for example, a spoon.
10. Say/sign, "Is this a spoon?"
11. Follow steps 3-5.
12. Hold up, one at a time, each of the objects (cup, plate, spoon), and ask, "Is this a cup/plate/spoon?"
13. Learner should respond correctly ("Yes") to each object and question.
    When learner responds "Yes" with 100% accuracy to each object presented (you may present any number of different objects), go on to step 14.
14. Hold up an object, for example, a cup.
15. Say/sign, "Is this a (chair)*?"
    *(Use an object word the learner knows, but which you have not presented in steps 1-13).
16. Provide the verbal model "No."
17. Learner imitates: "No."
18. Repeat steps 14-15 until learner responds "No" several times consecutively, without needing a verbal model.
19. Hold up another object, for example, a plate.
20. Say/sign, "Is this a (chair)?"
21. Follow steps 16-18.
22. Hold up another object, for example, a spoon.
23. Say/sign, "Is this a (chair)?"
24. Follow steps 16-18.
25. Hold up, one at a time, each of the objects (cup, plate, spoon) and ask, "Is this a (chair)?"
26. Learner should respond correctly ("No") to each object and question.
    When learner responds "No" with 100% accuracy to each object presented (you may present any number of different objects), go on to step 27.
27. Hold up an object, for example, a cup.
28. Say/sign, "Is this a cup?"
29. Learner should respond, "Yes."

30. Hold up the same object used in step 27.
31. Say/sign, "Is this a (chair)?"
32. Learner should respond, "No."
33. Hold up another object, for example, a plate.
34. Say/sign, "Is this a plate?"
35. Learner should respond, "Yes."
36. Hold up the same object used in step 33.
37. Say/sign, "Is this a (chair)?"
38. Learner should respond, "No."
39. Hold up another object, for example, a spoon.
40. Say/sign, "Is this a spoon?"
41. Learner should respond, "Yes."
42. Hold up the same object used in step 40.
43. Say/sign, "Is this a (chair)?"
44. Learner should respond, "No."
   When the learner responds with 100% accuracy to each object and question, go on to step 45.
45. Hold up an object, for example, a cup.
46. Say/sign, "Is this a cup?" or "Is this a (chair)?"
47. Learner should respond correctly, "Yes" or "No."
48. Continue with each of the other objects, asking a question that requires a "Yes" or "No" response.

Evaluation procedure: When evaluating performance, present a given number of trials, using a set number of different objects, and ask questions requiring an equal number of "Yes" and "No" responses (in any sequence). For example, present each of the following objects twice: cup, plate, bowl, spoon, knife. On these 10 trials require five "Yes" and five "No" responses. Count and record the number of correct responses within a given number of trials (steps 45–48), and count and record responses requiring interventions (incorrect responses or any response requiring the verbal model for imitation).

Additional Language Skills Lesson — Verbal Expression

The following lesson sample is for students who demonstrate the ability to answer simple, concrete questions and who can speak/sign in complete sentences. They must demonstrate good receptive and expressive language and should have completed the language units for one or more work activity (curriculum unit) at Condition K (learner describes steps of an activity as another person/teacher performs them out of sequence). The purpose of this lesson is to expand the learner's understanding and use of activity-related vocabulary to situations other than the activities within which the vocabulary was learned. The teacher should provide the person conducting the lesson with a variety of appropriate questions (verbal cues) for each vocabulary word, so that the learner's responses do not become simply rote answers.

Objective: Learner will use activity-related vocabulary words appropriately in nonactivity-related sentences, in response to verbal cues (questions, descriptions, etc.).

Materials: list of activity-related vocabulary words that learner has mastered expressively

Procedure:
(Begin with nouns from any curriculum units that learner has mastered).
 1. Ask questions to which the response is an activity-related vocabulary word. For example,
    "What do you drink from?" (cup, glass)
    "What are you sitting on?" (chair)
    "What room do you eat in?" or "Where do you eat breakfast, lunch, dinner?" (kitchen, dining room)
    "Where do you brush your teeth?" (bathroom, sink)
    "Where is your toothbrush?" (cabinet)
    "What do you cut your sandwich with?" (knife)
 2. Learner responds with an appropriate word or phrase.
 3. Tell learner to "say the whole thing."
 4. Learner says/signs an appropriate sentence.
    (If learner does not respond or responds incorrectly, repeat the question, provide more cues if necessary, and/or present a verbal model, e.g., "I drink from a cup.")

Evaluation procedure: Count and record the number of appropriate responses and the number of responses requiring a verbal model.

Additional Language Skills Lesson — Eliciting Spontaneous Language

Condition: J^b (an additional condition)
Objective: Learner will instruct another person (i.e., the teacher) to perform an activity by giving verbal directions for each step of the activity and will correct the teacher when he purposely performs steps of the activity incorrectly.
Materials: materials necessary to perform activity
Procedure:
1. Structure environment so materials are readily available.
2. Tell learner to "tell me (name) how to activity."
3. Learner says/signs directions for each step of the activity.
4. Teacher purposely performs steps of activity incorrectly.
5. Learner verbally corrects teacher. (If necessary, provide verbal model, e.g., "No. Get the _____," or "Pick up the _____."

Some suggestions for eliciting spontaneous language:
Get wrong materials.
Go to wrong room or different area.
Do the wrong thing (e.g., write on blackboard instead of washing it).
Drop things.

Evaluation procedure: Count and record the number of spontaneous phrases/directions learner expresses as teacher performs activity.

8
IMPLEMENTING THE READING SKILLS AREA OF A CURRICULUM UNIT

The reading skills area of the curriculum is designed to develop word recognition and reading comprehension skills. The long term objective is for the learner to function with a greater degree of independence as a result of acquired reading skills; the specific goals are geared toward the development of the ability to read, understand, and follow directions. The program is highly structured, and based on the work activity of a curriculum unit. The reading vocabulary is the same as that in the language skills area, and the written phrases closely correspond to the language units in the language skills area of a curriculum unit.

The methods used to develop reading skills are based primarily on a whole word recognition approach. Because many of the students at Benhaven have not demonstrated the ability to learn to read through a phonetic approach, lesson procedures are designed to develop sight-reading skills. If a student can read phonetically, or if evaluations indicate the potential for developing decoding skills, a program designed for that purpose should be used in conjunction with the reading program of the curriculum. The performance objectives may be as appropriate to a phonetic reader as to a sight-reader, although the method of achieving them will be different. For instance, in a given curriculum unit, the phonetic reader (like the sight-reader) may be taught to read the listed vocabulary words (using methods designed for that purpose) and then to read phrases and sequences of phrases composed of those vocabulary words. The order in which you teach specific vocabulary words will depend on the reading method used. For example, a sight-reader might first learn to recognize familiar nouns (e.g., *table, fork*), because they are more concrete and meaningful than verbs or other parts of speech. However, the phonetic reader is taught to read words based on their phonetic components; thus, the first words introduced may be closed syllables (e.g., *in, on*) and consonant-vowel-consonant words (e.g., *get, set*). The reading objectives may be the same, regardless of the approach used, but the method will determine the sequence in which specific vocabulary is presented and how it is taught.

WORD RECOGNITION SKILLS

Most of the students in my classroom initially demonstrated no word recognition skills or very limited sight-reading vocabularies. The vocabulary words of the reading program are based on the specific work activity of a curriculum unit. In this way, reading words correspond to language vocabulary, which, in turn, corresponds to a work activity with which the learner is familiar. Each skill area, then, reinforces the other areas. A learner should not be taught to read a word until he has demonstrated an understanding of that word in his language program. For example, I do not teach a student to read the word "cup" until he can at least receptively identify the object cup. I am not trying to teach the learner to recognize a meaningless configuration of symbols, but rather to associate that configuration with a specific object, place, quality, or action. He does not learn to read "in" or "on" until he has performed the actions of putting something in or on an object in a task situation. Therefore, the reading program of the curriculum should closely follow a learner's language program. There may, of course, be exceptions, but the learner's understanding of spoken/signed words should always be a prime consideration in determining the sequence in which reading vocabulary is introduced. The learner is more likely to learn to recognize a word that is somehow meaningful or concretely demonstrable to him than one that is not.

Developing Readiness Skills: Visual Matching

A learner must demonstrate visual discrimination of words before he can learn to recognize and identify them. Simple word-matching tasks will reveal whether or not the learner can match words, his present level of performance on a visual discrimination task, and specific problems that may be interfering with performance. When you make up your materials, remember that the learner is going to memorize a visual configuration, so printing should not reflect your own personal way of printing. Letters should be uniform, regularly spaced, lowercase, and probably no larger than one-half to one inch tall. As the learner acquires more sight-word skills, you may make the letters even smaller, to approximate normal printed material. (For further discussion of reading materials refer to Chapter 12, "Introducing the Curriculum: Teacher and Materials Preparation.")

The learner also should learn to recognize words printed on a variety of media, such as word cards, lined paper, and the blackboard. Initially, print words in black on cards, such as blank three-by-five index cards. I usually begin with a task that requires discrimination of two very dissimilar-looking words printed on cards. I place one of each word card on the learner's desk side by side and several inches apart. I have at least five or as many as ten matching word cards for each of the two words on the desk, and I hold up each of one of the words for the learner to take and match appropriately. When the learner has correctly matched each of the word cards for one word, I do the same with the other word cards. For example, I might begin with "cup" and "table." They differ in length, are comprised of different letters, and "table" includes three tall letters. I first hold up each of the ten "cup" cards to be matched, one at a time. This is a visual discrimination task, so I may either not say the word "cup" or say it only after the learner has correctly matched the word card. I then do the same with each of the "table" cards. If the learner is able to correctly match the words presented this way, I then repeat the task, presenting the words in random order. That is, I hold up "cup" to be matched, then "table," "table" again, then "cup," and so on, until each word card has been matched. If the learner demonstrates problems at this simple level of visual discrimination, he may need more readiness work, such as matching objects, pictures, colors, shapes, and forms.

The teacher must observe the kinds of errors that the learner makes to determine whether problems are attributable to poor visual discrimination, off-task behaviors, or lack of attention to the task. When holding up each word card, observe whether the learner makes sufficient eye contact with the word card. If he merely glances at it, do not release the card until he has looked at it for several seconds. This may help you to determine whether the learner's difficulties are primarily attentional. You might also hold the card in different positions or even move it slowly in the air (not too far above or below eye level). This enables you to see whether or not the learner is actually looking at the word card. The word cards on the desk may also be placed in various positions for each trial: in a horizontal, vertical, or diagonal configuration; or close together or far apart.

If the learner looks at the card to be matched, and then engages in off-task behaviors or looks away from the task, try speeding up the pace of presentation. A verbal direction, such as "Look," may be needed to get the learner's wandering attention. If so, try pairing the verbalization with a nonverbal cue, such as tapping on the desk, and gradually fade out the verbal direction.

Another way to modify the task in order to improve attention might be to use high interest pictures, such as illustrations of food, with the appropriate words printed above or below the pictures. Gradually present cards with smaller pictures and larger words, until the learner is looking at cards with just the printed words.

Color coding the printed words may also improve performance. However, the learner may then only attend to the color. Therefore, if color coding is used, gradually switch from easily discriminated colors, such as red words and black words, to blue and black, purple and black, and, finally, all black printed words.

When the learner is able to correctly match two sets of dissimilar-looking words, try three sets, and then four sets of different word cards. When he consistently matches four sets of word cards correctly, you may use similar-looking word cards. Do not introduce very similar words (e.g., in, on; plate, table; cup, tub) until the learner has demonstrated the ability to correctly match four different sets of less similar words (e.g., bowl, spoon, cup, knife). Observe any difficulties in recognizing letters, such as confusing f and t, b, d, p, or n and u. These types of errors should have been apparent in pre-word-matching readiness tasks (such as matching letters) and overcome at that level. If the errors recur during word-matching tasks, you may have to do extra drills with the isolated problem words. Gradually increase the number of different sets of words to be matched, and incorporate similar-looking words (refer to Reading Readiness — Visual Matching, page 135).

Developing Readiness Skills: Reception

When the learner successfully matches eight different words on the desk at one time, work can be begun on the first reading objective under word recognition skills in the curriculum units, which states: "Learner demonstrates reception of the following task-related words by selecting/circling written words in response to verbal words...." Two or three different lessons may be used for beginning work on receptive reading skills. Depending on the learner's abilities, one method may be more successful than another. After trying one lesson plan for several days and evaluating progress or noting lack of progress, it should become apparent whether one method of presentation is more effective than another. You may find it necessary to either modify the lesson plans or design your own, using the principles involved.

The sample lesson plans provided at the end of the chapter are based on the learner's ability to match word cards. It is not usually necessary to demonstrate the association between the written word and the object or action it represents, because a reading (written) word is introduced only when the learner can consistently select an object or perform an action in response to the verbal (oral or signed) word. When the teacher presents a written word and says/signs it (during a reading lesson), the learner should associate the written word with the verbal word and its meaning. The object or action is reintroduced during reading comprehension tasks, but is usually not a part of word recognition training. Because the words the learner reads are vocabulary words from a given curriculum unit, they are used and reinforced repeatedly during other lessons (e.g., work activity, language). I prefer to begin receptive reading lessons with word cards rather than writing words on a blackboard because this allows more control over the lesson presentation. You may change the position of word cards on the desk quickly, and the pace of the lesson is smoother. The learner demonstrates reception by selecting a word card in response to a verbal word, which does not require the fine motor skill of circling a word on the blackboard, and is a more definitive and active response than pointing to a word.

Several lessons are included at the end of this chapter in which the learner must associate a verbal word with a written word, selecting words in response to the spoken/signed words. The issues that must be considered in the preparation and presentation of these lessons are discussed below.

Reading Readiness — Reception (1) (page 136) In this particular lesson, the learner initially uses the concept of *sameness* to select the correct word card; the word that is different is never selected. If the learner does select the different card, the teacher says "No" and redirects him (if he does not self-correct) to the correct word card after saying/signing the word. The teacher virtually ignores the one card, directing the learner's attention repeatedly to the word to be learned.

In steps 1-5 on page 136, the learner is learning the correct way of responding. These steps may need to be followed before each session, or only for the first few sessions. They are designed to teach the learner that he will hear a word (or see a sign), and he must pick up a word card and turn it facedown. Step 5 identifies a criterion for progressing to step 6. However, the learner may require a cue, such as tapping the desk or hearing "Look" in order to bring his attention to the task. The teacher must decide whether to remain at this level of the task or to work on improving on-task behaviors at higher levels of the task.

The issue of inappropriate work behavior will demand the teacher's judgment in any lesson activity. If the behaviors do not significantly interfere with performance, and I am still able to clearly evaluate task performance in spite of the off-task behaviors, I usually move to the next level of an activity. Behaviors must be dealt with during any lesson, even if that means ignoring the behavior and redirecting the learner to the lesson. However, in evaluating performance, I am evaluating the learner on what he has or has not learned as defined in the lesson objective. I may, at any point, decide that a learner has achieved an objective and then use that task to work specifically on behavior. For example, a learner may consistently select the correct word card in response to the verbal word but require many nonverbal cues (e.g., tapping the desk) in order to stay on-task. I might then design a specific behavioral intervention procedure and record, not his academic performance (which he has demonstrated that he has achieved), but his behavior. Sometimes it may be necessary to record data on performance and behavior at the same time. For instance, if a persistent behavior is throwing task materials off the desk, you may be recording the number of incidents as you conduct a lesson and record this on the lesson objective. However, it is important to keep the two records separate, in order to know what has or has not been achieved. You may, of course, compare both sets of data to observe the effect of behavior and of a behavioral procedure on lesson performance.

Timing is another issue to consider when presenting this lesson or any lesson in which the learner responds to a verbal cue. This lesson is designed to minimize errors; that is, there is only one word card that the learner must not select. Nevertheless, you must teach the learner to wait and listen to (or watch for) the oral/signed word before he responds. It is very easy for the learner to get into a pattern of selecting and turning over word cards before you say/sign the word. It may be necessary for you to 1) hold the learner's hands, 2) direct him to keep them folded, in his lap or on the desk, and/or 3) look at you, before he responds to the verbal word.

Whether or not the learner self-corrects is another factor that enters into the way in which a lesson is conducted. It will become apparent whether he can self-correct if the word is repeated or if he responds incorrectly again. In this particular lesson, most learners will select a correct word card when the teacher says "No" to the one possible incorrect response. However, I have observed students perseverate, that is, continue to select the incorrect word card, even when the chances of responding incorrectly are one in six. If the learner does not correct himself, it is better to show him the correct response, rather than allow him to make several errors and perhaps frustrate both of you.

With a nonverbal learner, you may present this lesson by saying and signing the word to be selected. When he consistently performs correctly, eliminate the oral command to ensure that he can respond to the sign alone. This becomes crucial when the learner is required to read expressively through sign. He must learn not to rely on external cues, such as the oral word, so that he will be able to sign in response to a written word at the expressive levels of reading. However, you should provide the oral feedback after the learner responds to the signed word.

Reading Readiness — Reception (2) (page 137) This lesson plan is based on the previous one and should not be presented until the learner achieves the first lesson objective. In this lesson the learner must consistently select a specific word card, in response to the verbal word, from a group of several other word cards.

If a performance evaluation consistently shows that the learner performs with 50% accuracy or less, you may need to modify the lesson presentation. One way is to hold up another word card of the word to be learned as a visual cue. The learner may then use his matching ability to select the correct (matching) word card. When the learner consistently performs correctly with the matching word as a cue, eliminate it. At this point his performance should have improved from that noted in the initial evaluation.

With a nonverbal learner who will have to read expressively through sign, conduct the lesson with both the oral and signed word and then with the signed word only. Remember to provide the oral feedback, by saying the word after the learner has responded to the signed word. This reinforces the association between the verbal and written word and also provides an affirmation of the correct response. The oral word may also be used as an extra cue if the learner occasionally responds incorrectly to the signed word. When the nonverbal learner's objective is to respond to the signed word alone, any time that you must provide the oral word should be recorded as an incorrect response.

If the learner does not seem to be looking at each word, place the word cards far apart. Sometimes placing the three or four word cards in the corners of the desk helps make the learner look at each word. You may even direct him to look in a specific pattern, if necessary, by pointing to each word in a left to right, top to bottom (reading) sequence.

Use nonverbal cues when necessary, but try to minimize verbalizations other than the word(s) to be selected. Verbal input beyond that which is necessary to the task may confuse the learner. It is especially important not to precede each word with a phrase like "Robert, find (word)." Presentation is much clearer and smoother if you just say/sign the word itself. The learner can focus his attention upon the association of that particular verbal word with the written word. Occasionally learners respond expressively to a written word with "Find (word)" or "Show me (word)." Each lesson is designed so that the learner's responses are consistent, and he will learn how he is expected to respond (e.g., by turning over word card) through repetition.

Note that in each lesson plan there is an established and consistent way to respond; the learner's manner of responding does not change throughout the lesson. The demand is always the same: look, listen, pick up a card, and turn it over. This consistency of format also simplifies the task of conducting the lesson for the teacher. Presentation may vary from step to step, but the format remains constant.

The Reading Readiness — Reception lesson plans 1 and 2 are designed to introduce only one word at a time. When a learner performs correctly with a given word, teach a new word. Continue to review the learned word, but each new word should be presented and drilled separately. For example, if the learner consistently selects "cup" from a group of four different word cards, continue this lesson as a review. In a separate lesson, a new word, e.g., "spoon," can be presented. First, the learner must select "spoon" when presented with four other "spoon" cards and one other word card. When he achieves this objective, he must select "spoon" from a group of four different word cards. If I am teaching "spoon" and reviewing "cup," I do not yet put the two words together in the same lesson. That is, "cup" and "spoon" should not yet appear on the learner's desk at the same time. This may lead to confusion, and should not happen until the learner has "overlearned" each word separately.

Reading Readiness — Reception (3) (page 138) The third lesson provided at the end of the chapter presents two learned words at the same time. I usually use it after the learner has learned to select two (or three) word cards in response to the verbal words, in separate lessons. That is, he consistently selects "cup" when presented with two or three other word cards (e.g., "bowl," "knife," "plate"); and consistently selects "spoon" when presented with two or three other word cards (e.g., "bowl," "knife," "plate"). The learner is required to select each of the word cards ("cup," "spoon") in response to the verbal words.

In this lesson, as in the other two lessons presented, the first steps (which are not part of the evaluation procedure) may be necessary for many sessions, or at least the first few sessions. With some learners, I conduct the lesson by first evaluating performance on steps 13-15 and then spending the remainder of the session drilling the words as in steps 1-11, or drilling a specific problem word or words.

If a learner cannot perform steps 13-15 with more than 50% accuracy, but has achieved the prerequisite objectives (e.g., matching and the first two lesson plan objectives), you may need to provide an extra visual cue by holding up a matching word card as you say/sign a word. For example, as you say/sign "cup," hold up the word card "cup." The learner then selects the "cup" card from his stacks of word cards. When you say/sign "spoon," hold up a "spoon" word card. The learner looks at his stacks of word cards and selects the "spoon" card. When the learner consistently performs correctly with the visual cue of a matching word, eliminate it.

In any matching tasks where the learner merely glances at a word or does not appear to be looking, hold the word card in different positions at, or slightly above or below, eye level each time. Do not release the card until the learner appears to have made sufficient eye contact.

In the third presented lesson, it is especially important to time the verbal word so that the learner selects a word card after you say/sign it. Do not let the learner begin to respond until you have said/signed the word. In the matching part of this lesson (steps 1-4), be sure to say/sign the word as or immediately after the learner matches it. If your timing is off, you may appear (to the learner) to be saying/signing "cup" as you are getting ready for the next word and holding up the "spoon" word card.

Developing Readiness Skills: Expression

When the learner consistently selects two or three different word cards in response to the verbal words, separately (as in the first two provided lessons) and/or together (as in the third lesson), he may be ready to begin work on the expressive level of reading. I usually teach the learner to read expressively two or three words that he already can select before adding more vocabulary words.

As discussed earlier, the reading program should correspond closely to the language program for a particular student. He should not learn to recognize words that are meaningless to him. In addition, you should initially introduce reading words that the learner can say or sign relatively clearly. When you begin expression, which requires the learner to say or sign a word in response to a written word, you are likely to have more problems with a word that presents articulation difficulties. For example, I have a student who has a terrible time saying "spoon." Unless I set up a language lesson (e.g., orally identifying objects) in a specific way, it is unclear whether or not he has correctly identified a spoon. Not realizing problems to come, I taught him to select "cup" and "spoon" in response to the verbal words. When we began work on expression of these words, it was evident that I would have a difficult time knowing whether or not he was saying "spoon" when I held up the word card "spoon." I worked on selecting a different word ("plate") in response to the verbal word, until he could consistently select "cup" and "plate" as directed. This simplified expressive reading lessons, since it was clear when he identified a word correctly or incorrectly. Furthermore, I did not need to correct articulation during the reading lesson, which could confuse the learner as to whether he had read a word wrong or said it incorrectly. "Spoon" could be added at a later time when the reader had demonstrated that he could, in fact, identify written words orally.

For maximal effectiveness, the lessons for teaching and testing expressive reading skills should initially be conducted immediately after a receptive reading lesson. For example, follow the lesson procedure described in the third Reading Readiness — Reception lesson (page 138), steps 13-15, before going on to expression of those words. Keep in mind that each of these lessons is designed primarily for the first stages of word acquisition.

Once the learner can read two or three words consistently, a more simple format with less repetitive drill may be used.

Reading — Expression (1) (page 139) In this lesson, any word for which you must provide the verbal model (step 4) is recorded as incorrect. Because the reading words are words with which the learner is familiar through the work activity and language lessons, a nonverbal learner may need only the oral word in order to sign correctly in response to the written word. This, too, should be counted as incorrect, because the nonverbal learner must eventually learn to express the sign in response to the written word itself. You should, however, provide oral feedback for every signed response; that is, after the learner looks at the written word and signs it, you should say the word. This reinforces the association among the written word, the verbal word, and its meaning, and serves as positive feedback for a correct response.

In presenting each word card, you may place the stack on the desk and turn over each card as the learner responds. If he responds incorrectly, you may simply not turn the card over; the learner will learn that this indicates he must try again. If you turn over a word card each time the learner responds correctly, this can serve as positive feedback and eliminate the need for a verbal response (e.g., "good") for every word. When a learner performs with almost 100% accuracy, and when behavior allows, you may have him turn over each card as he reads. If the learner appears to not be making sufficient eye contact with the word card, hold up each card in different positions (e.g., to the right, to the left, slightly above or below eye level). This allows observation of the learner's eyes in relation to each word card presented.

When the learner demonstrates the ability to read (expressively) two or three different vocabulary words, you may begin to add new words from the curriculum unit. It should not be necessary to introduce each new word through the previous lesson plans for receptive reading (pages 136-138). Instead, the teacher can present one new word at a time, grouping it with previously learned reading words. The learner should be able to select the new word in response to the verbal word by a process of elimination. In other words, if he has learned to select "cup" and "spoon" from a group of three or four words, and can read "cup" and "spoon" orally or through sign when the written words are presented, a new word, e.g., "bowl" can be introduced (see Reading — Reception, page 140).

Reading — Reception (page 140) Using this procedure, I have never had a student who did not learn the new word. It is, of course, possible that the learner may respond incorrectly to the learned words. This is especially true if words that are similar (e.g., cup, tub; table, plate) are presented.

When this happens, or with any problem words, I use any of the receptive lessons or variations (page 140) to drill those words.

Reading — Expression (2) (page 141) As you add more vocabulary to the initial three or four mastered words, steps 1-6 of the Reading — Reception lesson may be omitted and used as a drill for problem words. An expressive lesson plan that can be used once the learner has mastered three or four words expressively is provided at the end of the chapter (page 141).

When a learner begins to acquire more vocabulary words, for example, eight to ten, you may evaluate his performance by presenting each word once. Until he has acquired eight to ten words, I usually present each word several times, so that my evaluation is based on at least ten presentations. For example, if he is working on five different words, I would present each twice, for a total of ten trials. Some curriculum units have as many as 30 or more vocabulary words; the evaluation procedure should be done on the basis of the total number of words presented (receptive and expressive lessons).

New words may be introduced in any sequence, provided the learner has demonstrated an understanding of the verbal word. For example, although "kitchen" (table-setting curriculum unit) does not appear in the language program until Level 11, you may decide to teach it if the learner can read most of the vocabulary corresponding to his present language level. If he is at Level 3 of the language units, you might bring him to the kitchen and say/sign "kitchen." After several times, you might stand outside the kitchen door and say/sign "kitchen." When the learner consistently goes to the kitchen in response to the verbal word and/or says/signs "kitchen" when he is in the kitchen, you may introduce the reading word. It is not necessary to teach him to read only those words corresponding to his present level in the language units. If he has acquired those reading words, but his language performance is not such that he is ready to move to the next language unit, you may introduce language vocabulary in isolation so that progress in the reading area is not delayed.

The learner must be able to read the words presented on a variety of media and printed in different sizes. Therefore, at any time you may follow the lesson plan formats by printing words on a blackboard for the learner to circle or point to (reception) or for him to read as you point to them or write each word. I also make up a second set of word cards, with words printed smaller than in the original set, to ensure that the learner can read the words. This might not be necessary if the learner can work with the blackboard, which allows you to print the words in any size. When beginning work on the blackboard, it is sometimes easier for a student to circle words on a flat surface rather than an upright surface like the classroom blackboard. A small portable board that can be placed flat on the learner's desk can be used. This is also convenient for students whose behavior is more easily controlled when they are seated behind a desk.

If the learner has difficulty transferring learning from reading word cards to reading words on the blackboard, try an intermediate step. Using a portable board on the learner's desk, place the word cards on the blackboard. Gradually start printing some of the words directly on the blackboard, with the remaining words on word cards. Increase the number of written words and decrease the number of words presented on cards. This procedure may aid the learner in working through the new medium of the blackboard.

When a student can read all of the words from more than one curriculum unit (or all the vocabulary from one unit and several words from another), try presenting vocabulary from both units together. This will help determine if the student can read learned words when presented out of the context of the given activity vocabulary. The learner may initially demonstrate some confusion, but this is usually overcome after several presentations of the learned vocabulary in this manner.

READING COMPREHENSION SKILLS

Comprehension of reading words is ongoing, since the learner sees the objects and performs the actions in the work activity. The vocabulary words also comprise the learner's language program. I begin formal reading comprehension work when the learner can read between five and ten object vocabulary words, even though the reading comprehension objective is listed in the curriculum units after reception and expression of all the vocabulary words. In this way, the learner becomes familiar with the task of reading a word or words and performing an action — the objective of reading and following directions.

A lesson plan that can be used to teach and test reading comprehension of activity-related noun object vocabulary words is presented on page 142 (Reading Comprehension — Words). In order for the learner's response to be counted as correct in this lesson, he must read the word correctly and get the correct object/picture. If he either reads the word incorrectly, or selects the incorrect object/picture, the response is recorded as incorrect.

Theoretically, the learner should never read a word incorrectly in this lesson. The words used in the reading comprehension task should be those that the learner consistently reads correctly. This will minimize the need for interventions other than those necessary for the learner to achieve the comprehension objective.

In preparing for this lesson, the teacher may place one of each object/picture on the desk and return each to the desk after the learner puts it in the tub. Or you may put out several "extra" objects/pictures so that once the learner places an object/picture in the tub it can remain there. Always make sure that the learner must select the object/picture from several, so that his performance does not reflect some lucky guesses, as might happen when only two or three objects/pictures remain.

When the learner performs with at least 80% to 85% accuracy, and when behavior allows, begin letting him turn over each word card after he selects the correct object. In this way he will learn to go through a stack of cards, reading each, performing an action, and going on to the next card. This prepares him for higher level reading comprehension tasks, in which he must read and follow directions printed on several cards. The primary objective of the reading comprehension program is to enable the learner to carry out a task independently, by reading and following directions. An important aspect of this goal is that the learner goes from one card to the next; thus it is beneficial to teach him this response pattern as early as possible.

RELATION OF THE LANGUAGE UNITS TO READING SKILLS

As the learner's reading program expands to include simple comprehension tasks, such as selecting objects/pictures in response to a written word, lessons to increase his reading vocabulary should continue. Simple verbs and prepositions can probably be introduced, because the learner responds to and uses these words in his language lessons. Whether he is at Condition C of a language unit (performing steps of an activity in response to verbal phrases), or Condition I (expressing each step of the activity before he performs it), he is becoming familiar with the concept and meaning of the vocabulary words within a functional context (i.e., the work activity). In language lessons designed to teach the learner to follow simple directions (see Chapter 7), the vocabulary is again used functionally, but without the context of the specific activity. In this way, the language units and language skills area, in general, reinforce the material presented in the reading area of the curriculum. For example, I have had several students respond to a reading word (e.g., "fill") with a phrase from the corresponding language unit (e.g., "Fill the tub with water"). Or they may initially read "plate" as "Plate on the table." When the learner reads phrases based on the language units, his ability to say/sign those phrases during his language lessons improves significantly. This illustrates both the extent to which the learner may associate the content of the various skill areas (e.g., work activity, language, reading) and how they reinforce each other.

Reception and Expression of Simple Phrases

The third objective under word recognition skills in the reading skills area states: "Learner demonstrates reception of the following written phrases from the (activity) language units by selecting/circling each written phrase in response to a verbal phrase." These phrases correspond directly to the various language units of the specific curriculum unit. However, a learner may acquire reading vocabulary from a given level of a language unit faster than he progresses from one language unit level to the next in his language lessons. Therefore, the written phrases do not appear in the curriculum in the same sequence as the language unit levels. They are grouped, rather, by similarity in structure (e.g., all "get" phrases, all "on table" phrases, all "go to" phrases together, etc.). This sequence of presentation may simplify the learner's task by limiting the amount of new material presented at one time.

There are two criteria for introducing a given phrase: 1) the learner demonstrates an understanding of the verbal phrase, and 2) he reads (expressively) each word in the phrase. You may begin work on reading phrases as soon as the learner has acquired several noun object reading words and one or two verbs. For example, "get" appears in every curriculum unit presented in the model. Once the learner can read several nouns and the word "get" correctly, phrases like "get (object)" can be presented. The lessons for teaching reception of phrases follow the same format as lessons for teaching simple words. You may present two to four phrases printed on cards or on the blackboard, which the learner must then select and turn over or circle. He should be familiar with this format from his reading word acquisition lessons. When presenting several phrases that differ in only one word (e.g., "get fork," "get plate," "get bowl"), the learner is likely to look only at the second word. You may either present phrases in which both words of each phrase differ (e.g., "put bowl," "get plate," "put spoon," "get fork") or work on looking at and responding to the complete phrase at the expressive level. In fact, I am usually able to skip reception of phrases and move directly from word acquisition to expression (reading) of simple phrases. Selecting or circling a phrase in response to a verbal phrase may then be used as a drill for phrases presenting problems at the expressive level.

One of the most frequent problems learners encounter when reading a phrase is reading in a left to right sequence. It may therefore be necessary to point to each word in the phrase. Because the learner should be able to read each word in the phrase, it is fairly easy to identify problems at this level. If you cover all but one of the words, can the learner read it correctly? If so, the problem is probably in reading a sequence of words. It may be helpful to initially point to each word in a left to right sequence or to print the words of the phrase far enough apart so that they may easily be viewed separately. It may take much drilling at this level, with instructional interventions (e.g., pointing to each word) from the teacher, for the learner to correctly read a phrase. However, once this is achieved, it does not usually need to be taught again, provided the phrases contain simple words with which the learner is familiar. Remember that with nonverbal students you should say each phrase after the learner signs it to reinforce the association between the signs, oral words, and meaning, as well as to provide positive feedback.

Begin with simple two-word phrases, composed of a verb and a noun. Once the learner can read these phrases, move immediately into reading comprehension, even though reading comprehension objectives appear in the curriculum after reception and expression of a sequence of phrases. As in the language skills area, the learner probably will be working on several reading objectives at one time. For example, he may have a word acquisition lesson to build and expand vocabulary. He may also be working on expression (reading) of single phrases (as opposed to a sequence of phrases).

Comprehension of Phrases

As soon as a learner is able to read a phrase, it seems logical and efficient to teach him the meaning of the phrase through a reading comprehension task. Therefore, as soon as the learner can read a set of phrases, whether from a language unit or based on "Variations of the Language Program," he should learn to respond to the phrases with an action to demonstrate reading comprehension. In the curriculum units (see Part IV, Appendices A-E) word recognition skills (A) and reading comprehension Skills (B) are presented as separate sections of the reading skills area because they are essentially different skills. However, it is more practical and efficient to teach comprehension of a set of *single,* simple phrases before teaching the learner to read and then comprehend a *sequence* of phrases (A — objectives 5 and 6). The actual phrases the learner reads are determined only by his language skills (demonstrated understanding of specific words, phrases) and his single-word reading vocabulary.

Lessons for reading comprehension of single, simple phrases follow the same basic format as reading comprehension of single words. The teacher may present phrases with the verb "get" and an object, e.g., "get fork." The learner must read each phrase and actually get the appropriate object or picture. He may, of course, be attending only to the object word, but as phrases become more varied the task will demand attention to the complete phrase. A lesson plan designed to teach and test comprehension of simple, repetitive, two- to three-word phrases composed of "get" and a noun object is presented on page 143 (Reading Comprehension — Simple Phrases). In order for the learner's response to be counted as correct in this lesson, he must read the phrase correctly and get the correct object/picture. If he reads any part of the phrase incorrectly, requiring teacher intervention, or gets the incorrect object/picture, the response is recorded as incorrect. Theoretically, the learner should be able to read each word of the phrase correctly and get the correct object/picture in response to the written words.

Any problems that arise are most likely attributable to the fact that this task combines several prerequisite skills: reading a word, responding to a written word with an action, and reading a sequence of words. Observe the learner's errors and identify which aspect of the task presents particular difficulty. It may be necessary to modify the lesson presentation, or to do additional work on some aspect of the task. If errors are primarily the consequence of incorrect reading of the object word when it is part of a phrase, work on selecting the phrases in response to the verbal phrases and/or reading the phrases immediately before testing comprehension. If errors occur in selecting the correct object/picture (after reading the phrase correctly), perhaps a review in verbally identifying the objects is necessary. Or you might limit the number of objects from which the learner selects. For example, present only two different sets of objects/pictures and two different sets of phrases (e.g., five bowls and five "get bowl" cards; five cups and five "get cup" cards). Follow the same basic format, gradually increasing the variety of objects/pictures and phrases as the learner's performance improves.

When the learner can read the phrases and get the correct objects, the manner of presentation may be changed to increase the learner's level of independence. The teacher can gradually move the objects/pictures further from the learner's desk, requiring him to take each phrase card over to the objects/pictures and bring the correct object/picture back to his desk. For example, you might begin by simply moving the table or chair, on which the objects/pictures are placed, a few feet from the learner's desk. Depending on his performance and his work behavior, gradually move the objects across the room to a specific place in view or out of view (e.g., shelf, cupboard, drawer, closet) or even outside of the classroom. These gradual changes require the learner to follow the direction with a higher degree of independence and to move through the environment appropriately. These skills are especially important in order for the learner to eventually read and follow directions in carrying out various activities. The sooner he can follow even a simple two-word direction that requires an awareness of, and the ability to move through, the environment, the easier it will be when directions are more varied and complex. However, you may decide, for a variety of reasons, including the learner's behavior, to introduce these types of task modifications later (for instance, when the learner can read and follow a sequence of several directions on a card when objects are provided).

Reception and Expression of Longer Phrases

Reading phrases may correspond to the "Variations of the Language Program" as well as to the language units themselves. For example, if the learner can follow simple verbal directions composed of vocabulary from the curriculum unit and can read each word used in those verbal directions, he can learn to read and follow the corresponding phrases. The objective of "Variations in Reading," which is included as the fourth reading comprehension objective, states: "Learner demonstrates understanding of written phrases outside the context/structure of the activity situation by following written directions consisting of functional combinations of the vocabulary in objective A1 and any previously learned vocabulary."

Obviously, you must first teach the learner to read the phrases. If, in his language lesson, he can follow verbal directions like "Put (the) object in/on/under (the) (place)," and can read each of the words, then he is ready to read the corresponding phrases. You would not, or course, introduce a phrase that is longer than two words until the learner can consistently read and follow a two-word phrase correctly. Increase the length of phrases gradually, depending on the learner's performance. If a learner has mastered expression of two-word phrases, three-word phrases can be presented. Many students are able to progress from reading simple two-word phrases to reading four- and five-word directions (e.g., "Put (object) in/on/under (place)," "Go to the bathroom"), once they have learned to consistently read each word in a left to right sequence. The teacher may initially need to provide an external cue, such as pointing to each word in the phrase, but these cues can usually be faded out quickly.

Once the learner can read a variety of phrases beyond the simple two-word "get (object)" phrases (e.g., "Open the drawer," "Go to the closet"), reading comprehension work on these phrases can begin. The basic format of such a lesson is provided in Reading Comprehension — Longer Phrases on page 145. In this lesson, the learner must read the phrase correctly and perform the appropriate action in order for a response to be counted as correct. However, the teacher should note what kinds of errors the learner makes. Are the errors in the reading, which, in turn, affects the response? Or does the learner read the direction correctly but perform the action incorrectly? If the errors are in reading the direction, the learner may need some supportive work in reading a phrase. Sometimes simply reading through each phrase before beginning the lesson improves performance.

If the learner consistently misreads specific words when they appear in a phrase, it may be necessary to review these words in a separate lesson. For instance, one of my students consistently confused "tub" and "table" when they appeared within a phrase. I made up a set of ten phrase cards with five "(object) in tub" cards, and five "(object) on table" cards. Using the same lesson format, we had a practice session with just these two sets of phrases before the regular lesson. This improved the learner's performance within a few weeks and could then be eliminated.

If the learner's problem is in carrying out the direction after reading it correctly, perhaps rearranging his lesson schedule will help. For example, go through the language lesson that most closely corresponds to the reading lesson before conducting the reading comprehension task. If he is reading phrases like "Put the plate on the table" and "Put the cup on the shelf," having the learner perform these actions in response to the verbal directions before presenting the reading comprehension lesson may improve performance.

When the learner performs correctly (reads and follows) a set of phrases of the same format or structure, try varying the directions presented. For example, a set of ten direction cards might be made up of two "Go to_____" phrases, two "Put the _____" phrases, two "Get the _____" phrases, two "Open the _____," and two "Close the _____" phrases. As long as the phrases are composed of vocabulary words and phrases that the learner has demonstrated he understands and can read, he should be able to read and follow these directions.

Remember that the blackboard may be used in addition to cards or paper for each of the reading lessons presented at the end of the chapter. However, the learner should master a task presented on one medium before another medium is introduced or before words are printed in different sizes.

In any of the reading comprehension tasks, you may also systematically require the learner to perform with a higher degree of independence. As described earlier, the teacher can arrange the environment so that the learner has fewer external situational cues upon which to depend. Objects necessary to perform an action may be gradually moved further from the learner and even removed from view. The individual who can read and follow directions or perform an activity in a situation not arranged specifically to suit his needs and abilities can function in a wider variety of situations with a greater degree of independence. For instance, the learner who can read and follow a recipe and get all the necessary materials from the appropriate places in the kitchen is functioning at a higher level than the learner for whom you must provide the necessary materials. Of course, you must work toward this goal gradually. When the learner can perform an activity or read and follow directions under one set of conditions, the conditions can be altered to more closely approximate the "natural" situation. With these and any changes in a lesson presentation, remember to vary only one aspect of the task at a time. For example, do not introduce a new set of phrases at the same time that you move objects from the learner's desk to a shelf several feet away. Changing only one variable at a time allows the teacher to determine what aspect of a given task presents difficulties to the learner and increases the learner's chances of mastering the new aspect of the task.

Reception and Expression of a Sequence of Phrases

When the learner can consistently read and follow a written direction, whether simple "get (object)" phrases or a set of more varied phrases, he is ready to read (and then follow) a sequence of phrases. The fifth objective of the word recognition skills in the reading skills area states: "Learner demonstrates reception of a sequence of written phrases from the (activity) language units by selecting/circling a sequence of written phrases in response to verbal phrases." Although stated as an objective, receptive work on reading a sequence of phrases is usually not necessary. By the time a learner can read and follow a phrase or direction, he should be able to learn to read a sequence of phrases expressively.

If you decide to test the learner's receptive ability to select/circle a sequence of phrases in response to the verbal phrases, make sure that the phrases require attention to the sequence. For example, present

        get the fork   and   get the plate
        get the plate   get the fork

Say/sign one of the sets of phrases, which the learner must select.

However, it may be best to skip this task, because it may confuse the learner, especially if he has an auditory sequencing problem. If he performs incorrectly, it may not reflect an inability to read a sequence of directions but, rather, an inability to attend to or remember a verbal sequence. Therefore, progressing directly to expressive reading of a sequence of phrases, at which point any problems that may be encountered can be directly confronted, may be advisable.

The new aspect of the reading task will be, not the vocabulary used, the length of the phrase, or the lesson arrangement, but the number of phrases presented at one time on cards, paper, or blackboard. The learner must now read from left to right and top to bottom. The teacher should begin by presenting two phrases at a time, each of which the learner can correctly read when presented individually. Initially, I present sets of two very simple phrases, such as, "get the plate" and "get the fork" (from the table-setting curriculum unit). Test the learner by directing him to "read."

If he reads both phrases correctly, top to bottom, you may begin with the expressive objective of word recognition skills (A6), which states: "Learner verbally expresses (reads) each phrase from the (activity) language units when a sequence of written phrases is presented (on cards, blackboard, paper)." If he reads either the top or bottom phrase or both, but in the incorrect order, you will need to design an instructional intervention procedure to teach him the correct sequence for reading both the phrases. Many students who can read and follow directions from the language units and variations of the language program, demonstrate difficulty when more than one phrase is presented at one time.

A variety of task modifications can be effective in overcoming most of the difficulties in reading a sequence of phrases. With some students, pointing to each direction is necessary during the first few sessions. Then point to the top direction, and either provide a verbal cue (e.g., "finish") or merely do not turn the card over, and the learner should be able to read the next phrase. With some students, even this step is unnecessary; after several sessions during which the teacher points to each phrase, the students are then able to read each phrase in the correct sequence without the nonverbal cue. This same simple intervention (pointing) may be used when presenting any number of phrases at one time. For some students, pointing to each phrase in sequence and gradually fading out this cue are not enough. It may be necessary to provide additional cues, such as printing the top direction larger than the second. This may be particularly helpful if the learner consistently reads the second phrase first. Or you might print the top direction in a color other than black to draw the learner's attention to it.

As in all lessons, observe where the learner's performance breaks down, and try to modify the task or provide instructional cues that direct attention to the specific problem. With higher functioning students who demonstrate an understanding of numerical sequence, you might number each direction, or, for some students, consider providing a "marker." I sometimes take a piece of cardboard or oak tag, color it, cut out a window the size of each phrase and move the cardboard over the phrases so that only one phrase is exposed at a time. When the learner can read each phrase correctly as I move the marker down the card, blackboard, or paper, I teach him to move the marker himself, so that only one phrase appears at a time. Some learners will always need to use a marker; for others, you may be able to eliminate this aid. Remember that with whatever method(s) you try, you must allow enough time and keep accurate data to determine its effectiveness or ineffectiveness. Do not try a new method if the learner's performance has not improved after one or two sessions, unless other factors indicate that the method is inappropriate.

A verbal cue provided by the teacher may also help the learner move from one phrase to the next. Simply saying/signing each phrase after the learner reads it may cue him to read the next phrase. It is important that these external cues be faded out, especially with nonverbal learners, whose dependency upon the oral feedback may interfere with eventually reading and following a sequence of directions independently.

When a learner can read a sequence of two directions correctly, without external cues, such as pointing or verbal directions, the teacher may either move directly to a reading comprehension task, or increase the number of phrases presented at one time. A comprehension task may follow the same format as the lessons for reading and following one direction at a time. The learner must read the first phrase, perform the appropriate action, read the next phrase and perform the appropriate action, and so on. Depending on the learner's abilities, you may present a sequence of phrases following the same pattern, such as:

>get fork
>get knife
>get plate
>*or*
>Put a plate on the table.
>Put a knife in the tub.
>Put a cup in the cupboard.

Or present a variety of phrases at one time, such as:

>Go to the closet.
>Get a tub.
>Put the tub on the table.

Before presenting this task, the learner must be able to: 1) perform each action in response to the verbal directions, 2) read each word in the phrases, 3) read each of the phrases presented one at time, 4) perform each action in response to the written directions presented one at a time, and, 5) read a sequence of phrases presented together. The teacher may expand the variety of vocabulary used in the phrases, increase the length of the phrases and the number of phrases presented in sequence, and arrange the task so that it requires movement within and outside of the classroom. However, any of these changes should be incorporated gradually and introduced one at a time. If you add new reading vocabulary to the phrases, do not increase the number of phrases presented in sequence until the learner consistently performs correctly with the new vocabulary additions. Do not present a sequence of four phrases until the learner consistently reads, or reads and follows, a sequence of three phrases. If the learner has difficulty reading, or reading and following a sequence of two phrases, do not require him to turn over each card. Even this seemingly simple response may present difficulties to the learner, especially if he has problems performing the task itself.

Length of Time Needed for Instruction

Once the learner can read and follow a variety of phrases presented at one time (e.g., a set of five cards with five directions on each card), it should not be necessary to re-teach these skills when a new curriculum unit is introduced. The learner who can read and follow a sequence of directions that relate to a specific curriculum unit will demonstrate these skills in the reading activities of any curriculum unit. The only prerequisites are that he first learn to follow the corresponding verbal directions and to read the new vocabulary from the curriculum unit. Thus, the first curriculum unit that the teacher uses will generally present the most difficulties and may require the most energy, effort, and time. For instance, it took almost 1 year for one of my students (a "non-reader") to learn to read 30 vocabulary words from the table-setting unit. It took several months for him to learn to read and follow a phrase and then to read and follow a sequence of four phrases presented at one time. Then, within 8 months, he learned to read 20 words from the blackboard-cleaning unit. As soon as he was able to perform a variety of actions in response to verbal directions from the blackboard-cleaning unit, I introduced the corresponding written phrases. Within several sessions, he demonstrated the ability to read and follow a sequence of four directions from the blackboard-cleaning unit. He has learned a skill and can use that skill with any new material that is presented.

Other students (non-readers) may require even more time to learn to read even the single vocabulary words from a unit. When, then, does the teacher "give up"? Although there may be no definitive answer to this question, several issues should be considered in making such a decision. Is slow progress caused by a persistent behavior problem? For example, a student at Benhaven engaged in frequent tantrum behavior during his first several months in my classroom. Of the 5 hours he spent in the classroom each week (1 hour per day, 5 days a week), he engaged in tantrum behavior an average of 90 minutes a week during the first several months. Tasks either were interrupted frequently or required modification in order for work to continue. Therefore, progress in all areas was painfully slow. As behavior improved, there was more time to teach, the learner functioned better, and the teacher was more relaxed and able to "push" the learner. The learner still exhibits this behavior, but episodes are much less frequent, less intense, and, usually, brief. His rate of learning has improved significantly.

Rate of acquisition of initial words should also be considered. I have several students who learned to read only two or three words during the first 3 months of training. This was discouraging, but after those first two or three words new words were mastered at a more encouraging rate of two or more per month.

How long one spends on any objective also may depend on the judgment of other staff members and supervisors. If a learner has a reading vocabulary of ten words after 2 years of work plus ongoing reevaluation and modification of lessons, perhaps his general program should be scrutinized.

If the teacher and others involved in planning and implementing his program determine that each available method has been tried fairly, perhaps he cannot learn to read. The teacher must keep in mind that some students will fail repeatedly, progress painfully slowly, and then, almost suddenly, "catch on" and begin to demonstrate that they can, in fact, learn. There is, unfortunately, no formula for assessing the instructional time required other than appropriate programming, careful observation and evaluation, ongoing modification of objectives and tasks, and perseverance.

RELATION OF READING COMPREHENSION TO WORK ACTIVITY

The primary objective of the curriculum's reading program is to teach the learner a skill that will enable him to function more independently. Therefore, the final reading objective is for the learner to read and follow directions to perform an activity. Note that each work activity also states, in its highest level of performance, that the learner will perform the activity in response to written directions.

When the learner can read and follow a sequence of directions composed of phrases from the language units presented in any order or from variations of the language program, the teacher may present a list of directions from any level of the work activity. The learner should first be able to perform the specific level of the activity correctly. However, some learners may be able to perform the steps of a given activity, but have difficulty in moving from one step to the next without some external cues from the teacher. The written directions should provide these cues, enabling the learner to perform the activity independently. Reading each step of the activity may allow the learner to perform each step of the activity, without these verbal cues.

The teacher may, of course, modify the written directions. As discussed in Chapter 7, the language units may be designed to suit individual needs. Vocabulary words may be added or omitted, or other words substituted for those presented in the model. The written directions should, however, correspond closely to the language units or to any variations that the teacher develops. For example, with some of my students, I have modified the language and written directions for the blackboard-cleaning unit. The model for the language unit and written directions for activity level 6 are changed to:

> Go to the closet.
> Get the tub and sponge.
> Go to the bathroom.
> Turn on the water.
> Fill the tub with water.

> Turn off the water.
> Pick up the tub.
> Go to the classroom.
> Put the tub down.
> Squeeze the sponge.
> Wash the blackboard.
> Go to the bathroom.
> Empty the tub.
> Squeeze the sponge.
> Pick up the tub.
> Go to the classroom.
> Put the tub in the closet.

These changes, including omission of steps and substitution of vocabulary, were implemented to follow the way in which the student performed the task. For example, some learners get the tub and sponge in one movement, turn on the hot and cold water simultaneously, and squeeze the sponge after emptying the tub. If the learner has previously demonstrated that he can identify the sponge and tub, and can verbalize and read the five-word sentence, you may combine the two phrases. If you decide that you want to specifically teach the difference between hot and cold water, you can include both of those phrases. If the learner has not demonstrated that he knows what a sink is, then include "Go to the sink" as a step. When presenting the learner with a list of written directions to follow, it may not be necessary to include all the elements of vocabulary that were necessary in order to teach the specific language for each action.

When presenting a list of written directions for the learner to follow in performing an activity, it should not be necessary to do much *teaching*. The learner has demonstrated the necessary skills for performing the steps of the activity in response to written directions. He can read and follow a sequence of directions and he can perform the actions dictated by each direction. The only new aspects of this activity are the length of the list of directions and, perhaps, the order in which they are presented. Depending on the performance of the learner on previous reading comprehension (of a sequence of directions) tasks, you may present written directions from any of the levels of an activity or from the highest level of the activity that requires performing the complete activity. Depending on the kinds of errors the learner makes, you would probably not present written directions for a level of the activity that he could not perform correctly.

If interventions are required for him to perform each step in the logical activity sequence, but he can perform each step correctly, you might present written directions for that level of the activity. For example, do not present written directions for table-setting activity Level 4 if the learner cannot set two place-settings correctly. However, if he can place all of the objects in the correct positions on the placemats, but requires a verbal or nonverbal cue in order to get each set of appropriate objects from the shelf, written directions might help him to perform the activity independently at Level 4. There may be exceptions, depending on the language and reading skills of the learner. For instance, I have a student who understood the concepts of "left," "right," and "above." He could not consistently set a place setting correctly without the verbal directions to put the napkin to the left of the plate, the knife to the right of the plate, and the cup above the knife. I taught him to read the words "left," "right," and "above" and wrote out written directions for him to follow. After several weeks of preparing a place setting correctly in response to written directions, the written directions were removed. He could then set the place setting correctly and was able to progress to subsequent levels of the activity. In this particular case, the written directions provided a means of achieving the work activity objective.

For the student who has attentional or other cognitive problems that make it difficult to remember a sequence of steps, written directions may either serve to remediate the problem (as in the above case) or provide him with a means of performing activities independently.

Reading Comprehension and Work Behaviors

What about the student who has learned to read and follow directions but whose inappropriate off-task behaviors or inadequate rate of performance interfere with the achievement of independence in an activity? As with any of the work activity tasks, these behaviors may be worked on directly through the reading comprehension activities. Once a learner has consistently demonstrated the ability to perform an activity, or to read and follow directions, the teacher may use these tasks to concentrate efforts on improving work behaviors. Instead of evaluating performance on the basis of interventions needed for him to perform the activity correctly (e.g., recording the number of directions the learner follows correctly or incorrectly), you may institute procedures designed to improve a particular work behavior and evaluate the learner on that specific behavior. For example, if the learner performs the activity correctly but twiddles the objects involved, design a procedure to eliminate this behavior and record the number of times it then occurs. In this way it should not be necessary to intervene for instructional purposes at the same time you intervene for behavior. Or, if a learner stops and stares into space frequently during the task or otherwise moves too slowly, you might prod him with a word, a touch, or a stamp of the foot. You can then record the number of prods needed for him to perform the task within a given amount of time. The main point is that by using a task that the learner has demonstrated he can perform, whether reading and following directions or performing the work activity without written directions, the focus can switch from instruction and correction to behavioral intervention.

DEVELOPING SUPPORTIVE AND ADDITIONAL SKILLS

The fifth objective under Section B (Reading Comprehension Skills) of the reading skills area is concerned with supportive and additional reading skills. This section is actually a reminder that the teacher may expand the reading area as best suits the individual learner. No objectives per se are given, but the suggestion is made that any of the additional language skills may be used as reading material, as appropriate. For example, if a student learns the concepts of "left" and "right," "next to," and "big" and "little" through the work activity situation and the use of task materials, these words may be included in his reading vocabulary. Or, if a student is capable of using a more varied vocabulary than that presented in the curriculum unit, the teacher may add or substitute vocabulary words. For example, "Fill the tub with water" could be substituted for "Put water in the tub," which is simpler and more concrete language. "Put the tub away" is more abstract than "Put the tub in the closet." Depending on the individual learner's abilities, you may use the very concrete and repetitive language and reading material presented in the curriculum model or substitute more abstract and varied verbal and written material.

The teacher may also develop additional supportive activities not presented in the curriculum model, such as matching sentences to action pictures or answering questions with written words or phrases as cues. For example, I have a student who has difficulty answering questions. One method that has improved his ability to verbally answer questions involved asking a specific activity-related question and writing three responses, one of which was appropriate, on the blackboard. The student learned to select the appropriate response and read it. By providing a variety of appropriate written responses to the same question at different times, he eventually learned to answer the question in a variety of ways without the written responses as cues. Having mastered the correct sentence structure and the appropriate type of response, he was able to answer a variety of activity- and non-activity-related questions appropriately.

As in the supportive and additional language skills objective, the teacher should use the learner's skills and his own creative abilities to develop reading activities that can remediate areas of weakness or contribute to the learner's overall growth. The curriculum is presented as a model, and the principles and methods involved may serve as a basis for as wide a variety of learning opportunities as are appropriate to the student's abilities and needs.

EXAMPLES OF READING OBJECTIVES FOR INDIVIDUAL STUDENTS

The following examples of three students' work activity, language, and reading objectives are presented to illustrate how these areas of the curriculum may work together to support and reinforce each other in the students' programs.

Student A

Blackboard-Cleaning Work Activity Level 5:
    Learner will get a tub and sponge from appropriate place (e.g., closet), go to a sink and fill the tub with warm water, clean a blackboard, *empty the dirty water into the sink, and return sponge and tub to appropriate place.*
Language Unit Level 5, Condition D:
    Learner performs steps of the blackboard-cleaning activity in response to verbal commands given out of the activity sequence.
Variations of Language Program:
    Learner demonstrates ability to follow simple verbal directions by selecting the appropriate objects from a variety of objects (sponge, tub; and objects from previously learned units) and putting them in specific places (on/under a table, in a closet, on/under a chair, in the bathroom sink) in response to verbal directions ("Put the sponge in the bathroom sink").
Expressive Reading:
    Learner will read the following words from the blackboard-cleaning unit when presented on cards or on the blackboard: closet, tub, sponge, bathroom, sink, go, to, get, water, turn.

Student B

Table-Setting Work Activity Level 4:
    Learner places table-setting objects in correct positions on placemats *when two placemats are side by side on the table* and the appropriate number of objects are on a shelf near the table.
Language Unit Level 3, Condition G:
    Learner will express orally an appropriate descriptive phrase in imitation of the teacher's model before performing each step of the table-setting activity.
Variations of Language Program:
    Learner demonstrates ability to follow simple verbal directions by selecting the appropriate objects from a variety of objects provided by the teacher, and putting them in specific places in the classroom (on/under a table, in a tub, on/under a chair, in a closet, in a drawer), in response to verbal directions ("Put the napkin in a drawer").

Expressive Reading:
Learner will read the following words from the table-setting unit when presented on cards or on the blackboard: (plate, bowl, cup, napkin, fork, knife, spoon, table, placemat, get), put, chair, tub, in, on, drawer, closet, under.
Reading Comprehension:
Learner will get the correct object from a group of objects in response to the written phrase "get (object)."

Student C

Bed-Making Work Activity Level 4:
Learner puts a blanket on the bed, tucks it in, puts the pillow in the pillowcase and on the bed, and puts the bedspread on the bed properly, when provided with pillow, pillowcase, blanket, and bedspread.
Language — Object Identification:
Learner will identify through sign the following objects from the bed-making unit: bed, bedspread, pillow, pillowcase, blanket.
Variations of the Language Program:
Learner demonstrates ability to follow simple signed directions by selecting the appropriate objects from four different objects (bedspread, blanket, pillow, pillowcase) provided by the teacher and by putting them in specific places (on the bed, in the closet, on a chair) in response to signed directions ("Put the blanket on the chair").
Reading Readiness:
Learner will usually match the following words from the bed-making unit when presented with five of each word printed on cards: bed, pillow, blanket, bedspread, pillowcase.

    Student A is working on the blackboard-cleaning work activity at Level 5. His language unit level corresponds to the work activity level because he has achieved Condition I (expressing each step of the activity as he performs it) at Level 4 of the language program. This particular student's progress in language has closely followed his progress in performing the activity adequately and independently, although this is certainly not always the case. The language at Level 5 is the same as that at Level 4, with an additional nine phrases. If student A continues to progress as he has, he should learn to express these additional phrases relatively quickly, as he becomes familiar with them while performing the work activity.
    Note that his lesson in following verbal directions (Variations of the Language Program) includes previously learned objects and vocabulary. In addition, Student A is working on following verbal directions that involve movement outside the classroom ("... in the bathroom sink").

Although only an expressive reading goal is stated, a lesson in selecting written words in response to verbal words is conducted as a means of supporting and reinforcing the expressive task.

Student A does not yet have a reading comprehension objective, but one will be added as soon as he can read each of the words listed in his expressive reading objective. Because his language skills are relatively good and he is able to follow simple verbal directions, such as those in his language objectives, he should be able to read and follow written directions when he has acquired the necessary reading vocabulary.

Student B cannot yet set two place settings side by side correctly (Level 4). He is working on the language unit for Level 3 (which involves the same language as that of Level 4), so that he will not require interventions or correction for the placement of objects as he performs the language task.

The lesson in following simple verbal directions involves vocabulary that is also being introduced in his reading lesson. When he can consistently follow these directions correctly and can read each of the corresponding vocabulary words, the introduction of an objective for reading and following the corresponding written directions should be possible. The words in parentheses (under expressive reading) are those he has achieved; therefore, his current reading comprehension task involves reading those words in a simple two-word phrase ("get (object)") and performing the appropriate response.

Student C is at work activity Level 4 in the bed-making activity. He is nonverbal, and one of his language objectives is to identify five objects from the bed-making unit through sign. When he achieves this objective, several other objects from higher levels of the work activity may be introduced, or work on the language units may commence. I would probably begin at Level 3, since Levels 1 and 2 consist of only two and three phrases, respectively. It is possible that I might begin the language units at Level 4, if his only errors were in, perhaps, smoothing out the bedspread.

In Student C's lesson in following signed directions, the same objects that he is learning to identify expressively through sign are used. He must select these objects in response to signed directions, which should reinforce his work on identifying the objects through sign. In addition, he must then put them in specific places as directed, which involves signing vocabulary from higher levels of the activity that he may have learned in a previous unit (e.g., table-setting curriculum unit).

Reading vocabulary words from the bed-making curriculum unit are just being introduced, and Student C has difficulty discriminating some of these words because of similarity in appearance, sound, and sign. Because I will say and sign each word after he has correctly matched it, this task will again reinforce the language work (and vice versa).

CONCLUSION

The three students' programs discussed above illustrate several different combinations of objectives. There are as many possible programs as there are individual students. What is taught, the sequence in which it is taught, and how it is taught may be varied as best suits individual needs and abilities, using the curriculum model as a basis. As discussed in previous chapters, the curriculum does not have to be followed as a "recipe" but, rather, as a model. If educational programs are to meet the needs of individuals and be effective in teaching new skills and using existing skills, they must be highly individualized. The curriculum model presents a format, content, and methods that may be adapted as is appropriate.

Throughout this chapter, a sequence of reading objectives that build upon each previous objective have been presented. If a learner can perform on a given task, then he should be ready for the next step in the reading progression. For example, the learner who can read phrases like "get (object)," and who can get those objects in response to verbal directions, should be able to read the phrases and get the correct objects. However, learners with severe learning and behavior disorders do not always learn in such a logical fashion. Many factors, learning and behavioral, may interfere with achievement at any level of any task. The highly structured approach and methods of the reading program of the curriculum simplify the task of isolating and identifying problems as they appear. It is not always easy to overcome these problems, but the systematic structure of the reading program enables the teacher to determine where the problems exist and where, then, to focus remedial efforts.

The ability to read and follow directions can be a valuable tool for improving an individual's level of functioning within a structured environment. Few, if any, of the learners for whom the curriculum was originally developed will read for pleasure. It is not likely that they will pick up the evening news or read the latest best seller. However, it is realistic to believe that, even if each learner does not achieve the highest objective in reading, or in any other skill area, an appropriate educational program can help him reach his maximum potential.

Reading Readiness — Visual Matching

Objective: Learner places word cards on matching word cards.
Materials: task-related word cards from (activity) curriculum unit (see chart for specific words, number of different words)
Procedure:
1. Put out (number) of different word cards in a horizontal row, word-side up.
2. Using stacks of matching word cards, hold one card up at, or slightly above, the learner's eye level.
3. Learner takes card and places it on matching word card.
4. Teacher says/signs the word.
5. Continue holding up each card of that same word.
6. Learner matches word cards correctly.
7. Follow steps 2-5 with each of the other sets of word cards.
8. Follow steps 2-4, holding up different word cards each time, in random order.
9. Learner matches word cards correctly.
10. Say/sign each word as or after learner matches it correctly.
    If learner does not correctly match:
    a. Give learner a few seconds to self-correct.
    b. If learner does not self-correct, remind him (either verbally, by pointing to the cards, or by tapping the desk) to "look."
    c. If learner still does not respond correctly, point to correct word card.

Evaluation procedure: Count and record the number of word cards the learner matches correctly/incorrectly on the first try (steps 8-9).

Reading Readiness — Reception (1)

Objective: Learner selects correct word card in response to the verbal word.

Materials: five word cards of the word to be learned, one word card of each of two other words

Procedure:
1. Place all cards of the word to be learned, e.g., five "cup" word cards, on desk in a horizontal or vertical row or in any position (e.g., one word in each of the four corners of the desk, one in the center of desk, etc.).
2. Say/sign the word, e.g., "cup."
3. Learner picks up (selects) a word card and turns it facedown (word-side down). Initially, demonstrate, point to word card, or put learner through desired response.
4. Repeat until learner has selected each word card after you say/sign it and turned each facedown.
5. Repeat steps 1-4, varying position of word cards, until learner responds appropriately and independently (without nonverbal cues) at least five times consecutively (one trial presentation).
6. Place all cards of the word to be learned, e.g., five "cup" word cards, and one of another word card, e.g., "spoon," on the desk in any configuration.
7. Say/sign the word to be learned, e.g., "cup."
8. Learner picks up (selects) correct word card and turns it facedown.
   If learner does not respond, or responds incorrectly:
   a. Say "No."
   b. Say/sign word again.
   c. Point to correct word card (if learner has not self-corrected).
   d. Learner picks up correct word card and turns it facedown.
9. Repeat steps 7-8 until learner has selected and turned over each of the five word cards in response to the verbal words, e.g., "cup."
10. Remove the other word card, e.g., "spoon."
11. Place all of the word to be learned, e.g., five "cup" word cards, and one of another word card, e.g., "bowl," on the desk in any configuration.
12. Follow steps 7-9.

Evaluation procedure: Count and record the number of times learner selects correct/incorrect word card, in response to verbal word (steps 6-12) on two test trials (five cards of word to be learned are presented on each trial).

Reading Readiness — Reception (2)

Objective: Learner selects correct word card in response to the verbal word.
Materials: several word cards of the word to be learned, one word card of each of two or three other words
Procedure:
1. Place three word cards of the word to be learned and one each of two other words in any configuration on the desk, e.g., three "cup" word cards, one "spoon" card, one "bowl" card.
2. Say/sign the word to be learned, e.g., "cup."
3. Learner selects correct word and turns it facedown. If learner does not respond, or responds incorrectly:
   a. Say "No."
   b. Say/sign word.
   c. Point to word card (if learner has not self-corrected).
   d. Learner picks up correct word card and turns it facedown.
4. Repeat steps 2-3 until learner has selected and turned over each of the three word cards, e.g., "cup," in response to the verbal words.
5. Follow steps 1-4, changing the positions of the word cards.
   When the learner consistently selects correct word cards (steps 1-5):
6. Place two word cards of the word to be learned and one each of two other words in any configuration on the desk, e.g., two "cup" word cards, one "spoon" card, one "bowl" card.
7. Follow steps 2-5.
   When the learner consistently selects correct word cards (steps 6-7):
8. Place one card of the word to be learned, and one card of each of two or three other words, in any configuration on the desk, e.g., one "cup" card, one "spoon" card, one "bowl" card, and one "knife" card.
9. Say/sign the word to be learned, e.g., "cup."
10. Learner selects correct word card and turns it facedown. If learner does not respond, or responds incorrectly, follow procedure in steps 3 (a-d).
11. Turn over word card so it is faceup, and change position of word cards.
12. Say/sign the word to be learned, e.g., "cup."
13. Learner selects correct word card and turns it facedown.
14. Follow steps 8-13 at least 10 times, changing the position of the word cards each time.

Evaluation procedure: Count and record the number of times learner selects correct/incorrect word card in response to verbal word (step 14) on 10 test trials.

Reading Readiness — Reception (3)

Objective: Learner selects correct word cards in response to the verbal words.
Materials: ten word cards of each word
Procedure:
1. Place one of each word card on learner's desk word-side up, e.g., "cup," "spoon."
2. Using remaining word cards, hold each word card up one at a time.
3. Learner matches each word card to appropriate word cards.
4. As learner matches each word card, say/sign the word.
5. When learner has correctly matched all the word cards, and they are in stacks on learner's desk, say/sign one of the words, e.g., "cup."
6. Learner selects correct word card and turns it over (point to correct word card, if necessary).
7. Say/sign the same word, e.g., "cup."
8. Learner selects correct word and turns it over.
9. Continue as in steps 5-8, until learner has turned over all the cards of one word, e.g., "cup," in response to the verbal word.
10. Place the words in a faceup stack on the desk. (The other stack(s) of word cards have remained on desk throughout steps 5-9.)
11. Follow steps 1-9 with each of the remaining stacks of word cards.
12. Place one of each word card on learner's desk word-side up and follow steps 1-4 again.
13. When learner has correctly matched all the word cards, and they are in stacks on learner's desk, say/sign each of the different words one at a time, in random order.
14. Learner selects correct word card and turns it over.
    If learner does not respond or responds incorrectly:
    a. Say "No."
    b. Say/sign word.
    c. Point to word card (if learner has not self-corrected).
    d. Learner picks up correct word card and turns it over.
    e. Repeat same word on next trial.
15. Continue until learner has selected and turned over each word card in response to the verbal word (2 words, 10 cards of each — 20 word cards; 3 words, 10 cards of each — 30 word cards).

Evaluation procedure: Count and record the number of times learner selects correct/incorrect word card in response to the verbal word (steps 13-15).

Reading — Expression (1)

Objective: Learner will say/sign the correct word in response to a written word.
Materials: at least five word cards of each different word
Procedure:
1. Begin with one of the words, e.g., "cup."
2. Place a stack of five word cards ("cup") faceup on desk.
3. Point to the first word card (or hold it up).
4. Learner says/signs correct word.
   If learner does not respond, or responds incorrectly:
   a. Say/sign word.
   b. Learner imitates word (help him to imitate as needed).
   c. Point to word (or hold it up) again.
   d. Learner says/signs correct word.
5. Turn word card facedown.
6. Follow steps 3-5 with remaining word cards of that word, e.g., four "cup" cards.
7. Follow steps 1-6 with stacks of each word, e.g., five "spoon" cards, then five "bowl" cards.
8. Mix up all of the word cards so that both (or all three) of the different sets of word cards are together in a stack (e.g., ten word cards — five "cup," five "spoon"; 15 word cards — five "cup," five "spoon," five "bowl").
9. Place stack of word cards faceup on desk.
10. Point to first word card (or hold it up).
11. Learner says/signs correct word.
    If learner does not respond, or responds incorrectly, follow procedure as in step 4, a-d.
12. Turn word card facedown.
13. Continue with remainder of word cards.

Evaluation procedure: Count and record the number of words the learner reads (says/signs) correctly/incorrectly (steps 8-13), as presented.

Reading — Reception

Objective: Learner selects correct words in response to verbal words.
Materials: word cards
Procedure:
1. Place three or four words on the learner's desk at one time: two or three learned words and one new word (e.g., "cup," "spoon," "bowl"), in any configuration.
2. Say/sign each of the learned words (e.g., "cup," "spoon").
3. Learner selects each card and turns it facedown.
4. Say/sign the new word (e.g., "bowl").
5. Learner turns word card facedown.
6. Repeat steps 1-5 several times, varying the position of the word cards on the desk.
7. Place word cards on desk as in step 1.
8. Say/sign each of the words *in any order.*
9. Learner selects correct word card and turns it facedown.
   If the learner consistently responds incorrectly to the new word:
   a. Place word cards on desk as in step 1.
   b. Say/sign new word (e.g., "bowl").
   c. Point to correct word card.
   d. Learner turns word card over.
   e. Turn word card faceup and change position of word cards.
   f. Repeat steps b-e until the learner independently selects the new word on 10 consecutive trials.
10. Repeat steps 7-9 several times.

Evaluation procedure: Count and record the number of times learner selects correct/incorrect words in response to verbal words (steps 7-9) on a given number of trials.

Reading — Expression (2)

Objective: Learner reads each word presented.
Materials: word cards
Procedure:
1. Present each word card.
2. Learner says/signs correct word.
    If learner does not respond, or responds incorrectly:
    a. Say/sign word.
    b. Learner imitates word (help him to imitate as needed).
    c. Present word again.
    d. Learner says/signs correct word.
3. Continue as in steps 1-2, presenting each word several times.

Evaluation procedure: Count and record the number of words learner reads (says/signs) correctly/incorrectly as presented.

Reading Comprehension — Words

Objective: Learner will select an object or picture of an object in response to the written word.
Materials: word cards and corresponding objects/pictures
Procedure:
1. Place the objects/pictures on the learner's desk.
2. Place a tub on a chair next to the desk within the learner's reach.
3. Put the stack of word cards faceup on the learner's desk.
4. Point to top word card.
5. Learner says/signs the word.
6. Learner picks up appropriate object/picture and puts in the tub.
    If learner does not respond, or responds incorrectly:
    a. Point to card again. If necessary, tell learner to "read" it.
    b. Learner reads card (says/signs word).
    c. Tell learner to "get the _____."
        If learner does not pick up the correct object/picture, point to it or put him through correct response.
    d. Learner picks up correct object.
    e. Learner puts object/picture in tub. If learner does not put object/picture in tub, point to tub or put learner through correct response.
7. Turn word card facedown, and put object/picture back on the desk. (Eventually, learner should turn over each card himself after selecting the object, in preparation for reading and following a sequence of direction cards independently.)
8. Learner says/signs next word.
9. Learner picks up appropriate object/picture and puts it in the tub.
10. Follow steps 4-9 with each word card.

Evaluation procedure: Count and record number of times learner reads word correctly/incorrectly and gets correct/incorrect object/picture.

Reading Comprehension — Simple Phrases

Objective: Learner will get the correct object in response to the written phrase "get (the) (object)."

Materials: phrase cards, one direction per card; appropriate objects/pictures

Procedure:
1. Place objects/pictures on a chair or table next to learner's desk, within his reach. (You may also place a tub on learner's desk.)
2. Place stack of direction cards faceup on desk.
3. Learner says/signs (reads) first direction.
4. Learner gets correct object/picture and places it on the desk (or in the tub).
   If learner does not respond, or responds incorrectly:
   a. Point to each word in the phrase (if needed).
   b. Learner reads phrase.
   c. Tell learner to "do it," or repeat the phrase (e.g., "get the (object)").
   d. Learner gets correct object/picture and puts it in designated place.
5. Learner turns phrase card facedown (help him as needed).
6. Learner says/signs (reads) next phrase card.
7. Learner gets correct object/picture and places it on the desk (or in the tub).
8. Follow steps 3-7 with each phrase card.

Evaluation procedure: Count and record the number of times learner independently reads phrase correctly/incorrectly and gets correct/incorrect object/picture.

Reading Comprehension — Longer Phrases

Objective: Learner will perform an action in response to the written direction.
Materials: direction (phrase) cards
Procedure:
1. Arrange the immediate environment as needed, according to the directions that learner will read and follow. For example, if he will read and follow directions involving putting objects into a tub, make sure those objects and a tub are available.
2. Place objects/pictures on learner's desk.
3. Place stack of direction cards faceup on desk.
4. Learner says/signs (reads) first direction, e.g., "Put (the) plate on (the) table."
5. Learner follows the direction by performing the appropriate action, e.g., gets the plate and puts it on a table.
   If the learner does not respond, or responds incorrectly:
   a. Point to each word in phrase (if needed).
   b. Learner reads phrase.
   c. Tell learner to "do it," or repeat the phrase (e.g., "Put (the) plate on (the) table").
      If learner does not perform correct response action, provide a verbal or nonverbal cue, demonstrate, or put him through the appropriate response.
   d. Learner performs appropriate action (e.g., gets the plate and puts it on a table).
6. Learner turns phrase card facedown (help him as needed).
7. Learner says/signs (reads) next direction.
8. Learner follows the direction by performing the appropriate action.
9. Follow steps 4-8 with each phrase card.

Evaluation procedure: Count and record number of directions (phrase cards) learner reads and follows correctly/incorrectly.

9

IMPLEMENTING THE NUMBER SKILLS AREA OF A CURRICULUM UNIT

The primary objective of the number skills area of the curriculum is to teach the learner number skills and concepts that will be helpful in practical situations. As in the other skill areas of the curriculum units, the goal is to provide the learner with a useful skill that will improve and expand his level of functioning. The number skills and objectives presented in the curriculum units (see the appendices, Part IV) are divided into three basic skills: counting, numeral identification, and numeral/quantity association. Higher level operations and skills, such as addition, subtraction, multiplication, division, working with fractions, learning monetary equivalents, telling time, and solving word problems, are not a part of this curriculum model. Some of these skills may be taught to students for whom they are appropriate, but the curriculum model presents only the most basic and functional number skills. For most of the students for whom the curriculum was developed, the acquisition of these basic skills is a useful and important achievement.

Some of the curriculum units are not as well suited as others for work in numbers. The format is included in each curriculum unit, but number skills should be taught through the unit that can most easily be adapted to develop these skills (e.g., the table-setting unit). Acquired number skills may then be applied to any of the activities for which they might prove useful (e.g., sandwich making — making a specific number of sandwiches for a group; bed making — getting an appropriate number of linens, blankets).

COUNTING

The first objective in the number skills area states: "Learner demonstrates one-to-one correspondence by counting out a number of task-related objects presented." One-to-one correspondence means that for every object that the learner counts, he says/signs an appropriate number. Many of my verbal students, when initially evaluated, could say a sequence of numbers in the correct numerical order. However, few of them could relate this rote recitation to counting out a number of objects. Being able to say the numbers in their proper sequence can be helpful in teaching one-to-one correspondence, or it can interfere with teaching. A lesson plan for teaching the learner that for every object he counts there is a corresponding verbal number is presented below, and ways to prevent the learner from saying numbers without relating them to the objects being counted are discussed.

Although the task of seeing three objects and counting them, "one, two, three," appears to be a demonstrable operation, it is often a very difficult concept to teach. The learner must learn that, although the objects in front of him are, for example, "cups," they are also "three cups." Many learners are confused when something that has been labeled "cup" must now be called "one, two, three" cups. For those students who do not appear to understand the concept involved, the mechanics of counting must be taught with the hope that repeated, correct performance will eventually concretize the concept.

I usually begin teaching the learner to count out objects rather than to recognize groupings of objects. The skill of counting gives the learner more flexibility, in that once he learns to count he may be taught to count out any number of objects (unless attention or other problems interfere). Using a grouping method, the learner is shown clusters of objects, for example, 2 blocks, chips, or objects, 3 blocks, chips, or objects, and so forth. He learns to associate these groupings with the verbal number and/or written numeral and may:

1. Select a grouping in response to the verbal number
2. Identify a grouping with the appropriate verbal number
3. Select a grouping in response to the verbal and/or written numeral
4. Match a written numeral to the appropriate grouping

The learner who is taught to recognize or identify a visual configuration of objects may have difficulty with larger numbers of objects or with larger objects, themselves. For example, a student who learns to group objects may have problems getting a number of objects that cannot conveniently be grouped. Blocks, or even cups, forks, knives, and spoons, can be grouped in a visual pattern. However, many activities may involve counting items that cannot be conveniently arranged in sets. Some students, after learning to count, may be able to look at a pile of plates, a stack of cartons, or a loaf of bread and state a particular number without appearing to count out each item. But knowing how to count prepares the learner to use this skill in a wider range of activities than is possible by grouping. In cooking, for example, counting enables the learner to get 3 teaspoons of baking powder or 4 scoops of flour. The learner who must see objects in a group in order to associate the quantity with a given number will be limited in the kinds of activities involving numbers that he can perform. If, however, grouping appears to be an appropriate method for particular learners, lessons in counting out objects should also be a part of the number skills program.

The lesson plan presented on page 162 illustrates the basic format for a lesson designed to teach the learner to count out a group of objects presented by the teacher. It is likely that modifications in lesson presentation will be necessary, depending on the types of difficulty the learner demonstrates. The primary objective of the lesson is for the learner to say/sign the appropriate number as he picks up each object in a set of objects.

The learner may say/sign the incorrect number, say/sign the sequence of numbers incorrectly, or not associate the verbal number with the action of picking up the object. If he cannot correctly count out a number of objects presented, begin with as few as two or three objects. Whether the learner is to say each number or sign each number, the teacher should present the verbal model as the learner picks up each object. The learner who does not associate the verbal number with the objects as he counts each may require further assistance. It may be necessary to hand him each object one at a time, withholding the next object until he has said/signed the correct number. Or it may be necessary to pace the learner by pointing to each object for the learner to take as he counts (says/signs each number). Saying/signing each number after the learners says/signs it may also improve the learner's performance. This may cue him for the next number, if he is able to say/sign the correct sequence of numbers. One of my students needed only a sound, such as "hmmm," after he said each number in order to count out a number of objects correctly. Saying the number after the learner says/signs the number may also help if difficulties are attributable to attentional problems. All of these extra cues, verbal and nonverbal, should be gradually eliminated, so that the learner is counting out a number of objects independently. For example, if you must hand the learner each object one at a time, record the number of times (within a given number of trials, e.g., 10) he correctly counts out the objects presented. When he performs with only one or two incorrect trials, try merely pointing to each object before he picks each up and counts. When he can perform with only one or two incorrect trials as you point, eliminate this cue.

The primary principle involved in this sample lesson is repetition. In order for repetition to be effective, the learner must repeatedly count out a number of objects *correctly*. Therefore, instructional cues must be provided in order for the learner to perform correctly and then be systematically removed. If the learner can say/sign a rote sequence of numbers correctly, but does not associate the act of counting with a quantity of objects, it may be necessary to do more than physically coordinate the verbal number with the counting of objects. I had a student who would recite a sequence of numbers but would continue the sequence after each object had been picked up and put in its designated place. That is, he would say numbers 1-10 even if I had presented only three objects. Attempts to correct his continued counting by having him match a given number of objects to their outlines on a piece of paper were unsuccessful. The effective corrective measure proved to be simple: after several weeks, by putting my hand over his mouth after he had picked up the last object and said the correct number, he finally came to recognize the association. This example illustrates the degree to which individual problems may require very specific intervention procedures.

When presenting a number of objects for the learner to count, I may make use of the learner's ability to count by rote. I present the same number of objects each time, until the learner consistently counts out the objects correctly. For example, if I am teaching a learner to count out five objects, I present five objects each time. When he consistently performs correctly, I may then present one, two, three, four, or five objects during the lesson, varying the number with each presentation. When the learner can correctly count out any number of objects up to five, I can then begin work on counting out six objects, in the same manner. Usually, once the learner understands that he only says/signs a specific number as he picks up each object, it is fairly easy to increase the number of objects presented. However, difficulties may arise with increased numbers of objects if the learner cannot maintain his attention long enough to count out a larger number of objects. It is therefore extremely important that the learner master counting a given number of objects before any more are added.

How the objects themselves are presented must also be considered in lesson presentation. Whether they are presented in a horizontal row, in a pile or group, or in a stack may affect the learner's performance. I usually begin by presenting them in a row, so that each object is viewed as a separate object. When the learner consistently performs correctly, I may then present them in a pile or stack or in a container. These different ways of presenting the objects should be planned, and variations introduced only after mastery of a particular presentation.

Another factor that may influence performance is the time of day when the lesson is conducted in relation to the other lessons. In an activity like counting, which is very repetitive, the learner may perform better on the first few trials than on the last few; thus, it may help if the counting lesson is the first lesson presented within a lesson period. For example, one of my students consistently performed poorly on the counting task, which was his last lesson before lunch. We re-scheduled the counting lesson as the first task of several during that period, and his performance immediately improved.

NUMERAL IDENTIFICATION

As in the other curriculum skill areas, each number skills objective does not necessarily have to be achieved before moving on to the next objective. A learner may work on more than one objective in the same skill area at a time, providing he has demonstrated the prerequisite skills. I usually begin teaching identification of numerals when the learner can correctly count out at least three objects. In this way, although they may still be abstract, the numerals assume some meaning for the learner. Similarly, I do not usually teach the learner to read a numeral before the corresponding number of objects has been introduced in the counting lesson.

Receptive Identification of Numerals

The second objective in the number skills area states: "Learner demonstrates recognition of numerals by selecting/circling numerals in response to verbal numbers" and "Learner verbally identifies numerals when presented (on cards, blackboard, paper)." Lessons to teach numeral identification may follow a format similar to that used in word recognition lessons. Unfortunately, it may be more difficult to teach numeral identification than word recognition; "cup" or "sandwich," for example, usually have more meaning for the learner than the symbols "1" or "2."

Before beginning work on numeral identification, determine whether the learner can visually discriminate them by presenting a matching task. As in the word matching activity, begin by presenting two or three dissimilar numerals such as "1," "3," and "4." Prepare several numeral cards for each numeral to be matched. Place two or three different numeral cards on the desk, and hold up the cards to be matched. As in word matching, you may hold each card in a different position (at, slightly above, or below eye level) in order to observe whether the learner is making sufficient eye contact. If the learner matches numerals correctly, you may increase the number of different numerals he must match and include more similar-looking numerals (e.g., "2" and "3"). Say/sign each numeral after the learner has matched it so that he hears the verbal number (or sees the signed number) but does not use them as an auditory (or visual) cue in matching. If the learner performs well, you might give him a stack of numeral cards faceup and allow him to look at each and match them to the appropriate cards on the desk.

When the learner consistently matches a number of numeral cards correctly, begin work on selecting/circling a numeral in response to the verbal number. Three Numeral Identification Readiness — Reception lesson plans are provided at the end of this chapter; they follow the same format as that of the word recognition lessons in Chapter 8. The learner who has learned to read words may have less difficulty with numeral identification than the learner who has not demonstrated the ability to recognize written words. He should, at least, be familiar with the lesson format.

In Numeral Identification Readiness — Reception (1) (page 163), the learner is using the concept of *sameness* to select the correct numeral cards; the *different* numeral is never requested or selected. Steps 1-5 teach the learner the appropriate way of responding. These steps may usually be eliminated after a few sessions. If the learner has performed similar word recognition tasks, he probably has learned that he will hear a number (or see a sign) and must pick up a card and turn it facedown.

As in the reading activities, observe the learner's performance and try to identify any problems he may demonstrate. A lesson such as this is designed to minimize errors. It should be relatively easy to determine whether he is listening, looking, and generally attending to the task, or if he is engaging in off-task behaviors that may interfere with performance. It may be necessary to intervene, provide an extra cue for attention (e.g., tap the desk), or speed up the pace of the lesson. For example, if the learner reaches for a numeral card before you have said/signed a number, it may be necessary to remind him to "wait" or to direct him to keep his hands in his lap, on the desk, or folded. It is important in designing an effective lesson presentation, and appropriate behavioral procedures, to determine as much as possible the reasons for a poor performance — whether primarily attributable to the learning problem itself or to specific behaviors. You may then design modifications of presentation or intervention procedures that focus on the specific problems.

In order for the learner to benefit from a drill, he should perform the correct responses repeatedly. It is usually detrimental to the learning process, and certainly frustrating, for the learner to repeatedly make an incorrect response on an item. Therefore, unless the learner demonstrates the ability to self-correct, it is probably best to provide an extra cue to allow the learner to correct his error.

With a nonverbal learner, you may initially present this lesson by saying and signing the number to be selected. When he consistently performs correctly, you may eliminate the oral cue so that he must respond to the signed number alone. This ability becomes necessary when the learner is required to identify a numeral through sign, without the oral number as a cue. However, you should provide oral feedback after every response to reinforce the association between the written numeral and the verbal number. The oral number should also be provided when correcting the learner.

The second Numeral Identification Readiness — Reception lesson plan (page 164) is based on the previous one and should not be presented until the learner achieves the first objective. In this lesson, the learner must consistently select a specific numeral in response to the verbal word from a group of several other numerals. If an evaluation of performance shows that the learner consistently performs with 50% accuracy or less, it may be necessary to modify the lesson. Another numeral card of the numeral that is being taught can be used as a visual cue. The learner may then exercise his ability to match in selecting the correct (matching) numeral. When he consistently performs correctly with the matching numeral as a cue, eliminate it. At this point, his performance should have improved from the initial evaluation.

As in word recognition lessons, placing the numerals far apart on the desk may help the learner to look at each card. Sometimes placing the cards in each of the four corners of the desk, and directing him (by pointing) to look at each in a specific pattern every time will help improve performance.

In any task that requires the learner to respond to a verbal word, number, letter, etc., remember to minimize verbalizations other than that to which the learner must respond. Extra verbal input and directions may confuse the learner and make the association between the written symbol and the verbal word less clear and definite. Use nonverbal cues whenever possible, and make any necessary verbalizations clear and brief. Each lesson is designed so that the learner responds in the same manner throughout; therefore, he should learn how he is expected to respond through repetition of the task, rather than through repeated verbal directions.

Any of the lessons presented may be adapted to the blackboard, if the learner demonstrates the required fine motor skills (e.g., can circle a numeral). The learner should, at some point, perform lessons that require selecting a numeral from several numerals, or verbally identifying numerals, on the blackboard. He must learn to recognize written symbols presented on a variety of media (e.g., cards, blackboard, paper) in order for the skill to be most useful. Do not, however, introduce a new medium until the learner has mastered the task on one medium.

The first two Numeral Identification Readiness — Reception lessons presented are designed to introduce only one numeral at a time. When the learner consistently selects that numeral in response to the verbal number as described in the lessons, you may teach another numeral. The learned numeral should be periodically reviewed, but, in these two particular lessons, each new numeral is introduced and drilled separately. If the learner can consistently select "1" from several other numerals, review "1" but introduce the next new numeral (e.g., "2") in a separate lesson. Numerals "1" and "2" would not appear on the learner's desk at the same time until each numeral was overlearned in separate lessons.

The third lesson plan (page 165) presents two learned numerals at the same time. It should be used after the learner can select two or three numerals in response to the verbal numbers, in separate lessons; that is, after the learner can consistently select "1" when presented with numerals "4," "5," and "6," and can consistently select 2 when presented with "4," "5," and "6." In Numeral Identification Readiness — Reception (3), the learner must select each of the numerals (e.g., "1," "2") in response to the verbal numbers, when "1" and "2" are presented together. In this lesson, as in the first two lessons presented, the first steps (which are not part of the evaluation procedure) may be necessary for many sessions or only the first few sessions. With some learners, I conduct the lesson by first evaluating performance on steps 13-15 and then spend the remainder of the session drilling the numerals as in steps 1-11 or drilling a specific problem-numeral(s).

If a learner does not perform steps 13-15 with more than 50% accuracy, but has achieved the prerequisite objectives (e.g., matching, and the first two lesson plan objectives), you may need to provide an extra visual cue by holding up a matching numeral as you say/sign a number. For example, as you say/sign "one," hold up the numeral card "1." The learner then selects "1" from his stacks of numeral cards. When you say/sign "two," hold up a numeral card "2." The learner looks at the stacks of numeral cards and selects "2." When the learner consistently performs correctly with the visual cue of a matching numeral, eliminate it.

As in word recognition tasks, timing is very important in the lesson presentation. The learner must select the written numeral after you say/sign it. Do not let the learner begin to respond until you have said/signed the number. In the matching part of this lesson, as well (steps 1-4), be sure to say/sign the word as, or immediately after, the learner matches it. If your timing is off, you may appear (to the learner) to be saying/signing "one" as you are getting ready for the next number and holding up "2."

Expressive Identification of Numerals

When the learner consistently selects two or three different numerals in response to the verbal numbers, individually in the first two lessons, and/or together as in the third lesson, he may be ready to begin work on the expressive level of identifying numerals. I usually teach the learner to identify the two or three numerals he can select, before adding more numerals.

For maximum effectiveness, the lesson for teaching and testing expressive identification of written numerals should initially be conducted immediately after a receptive lesson. For example, follow the lesson procedure described in Numeral Identification Readiness — Reception (3) (page 165), steps 13-15, before going on to the expressive identification lesson presented on page 166. Keep in mind that each of these lessons is designed primarily for the first stages of numeral recognition and identification (beginning acquisition). Once the learner can identify two or three numerals consistently, a simpler format with less repetitive drill may be used.

When the learner demonstrates the ability to identify (expressively) two or three different numerals, you may add more numerals. Usually, a numeral should not be introduced until the learner can count out the corresponding number of objects or, at least, is working on it in his counting lesson. That is, do not introduce the written numerals "5" and "6" until the learner is counting out five or six objects during the counting lesson. When adding more numerals to the original two or three acquired by the learner, it should not be necessary to introduce the new numerals separately as in the previous readiness lesson plans for receptive identification. Instead, the teacher can present one new numeral at a time, grouping it with previously learned written numerals. The learner should be able to select the new numeral in response to the verbal number by a process of elimination. In other words, if he has learned to select "1" and "2" from a group of three or four numerals, and can read "1" and "2" orally or through sign when presented, introduce "3" in the manner described in Numeral Identification — Reception (page 167).

As stated before, once the learner can identify three or four numerals, any new numeral may be presented with the learned numerals. The learner should then select it in response to the verbal number by a process of elimination. When the learner has acquired more than five numerals, present only four or five at a time (following steps 7-10 of the reception lesson plan on page 167). As the learner selects a numeral in response to the verbal number and turns it over, replace it with another numeral (faceup). The procedure continues until the learner has selected each of the numerals presented.

It is possible that the learner may respond incorrectly to the learned numerals when they are grouped with a new numeral. This is especially true as numerals that are similar in appearance (e.g., "2," "3"; "6," "9") are presented. When this happens, you may use any of the receptive lessons or variations to drill the problem numerals. It may be necessary, however, to make modifications in the lesson presentation or in the materials. For example, a numeral with which the learner has difficulty may be color coded or printed larger than the other numerals presented. Remember to gradually phase out any color-coding cues by going from, perhaps, red to blue to purple to black. Similarly, variations in size should be gradually phased out over a period of time so that all numerals are eventually the same size. Printing the word (e.g., "three") on each numeral card ("3") may also be a successful training cue. This helped one of my students discriminate between "2" and "3," and I was able to eliminate the cue after several weeks. As you add more numerals to the initial three or four mastered numerals, steps 1-6 of Numeral Identification — Reception may be omitted and used as a drill for problem numerals.

An expressive lesson plan that can be used once the learner can identify three or four numerals correctly is provided on page 168.

When the learner has acquired eight to ten different numerals, you may evaluate his performance by presenting each numeral once. Until he has acquired eight to ten numerals, each numeral should be presented several times, so that he is evaluated on the basis of at least ten presentations. For example, if he is working on five different numerals, present each twice for a total of ten trials. This reduces the possibility of chance, or guessing, influencing the learner's recorded performance.

NUMERAL/QUANTITY ASSOCIATION

Association of Verbal Number and Quantity

The first objective in the last basic skill category in the number skills area states: "Learner demonstrates association of verbal number and quantity by getting correct number of task-related objects in response to the verbal number." To achieve this objective, the learner must hear a number (or see a signed number) and get the corresponding number of objects from a group of objects. Of course, he must first demonstrate the ability to count out objects. However, this objective may be introduced when the learner can count out as few as three objects correctly.

An important consideration, in determining when to implement tasks to achieve this objective, is the learner's memory and, closely related to memory, his attention. Many learners cannot perform this task because they cannot "hold" a given number in their heads and stop counting out objects when they have reached that number. Therefore, it may be necessary to teach the association of a written numeral and quantity of objects before expecting the learner to get a number of objects in response to the verbal number alone. However, some learners are able to perform this task without the written numeral as a cue; the lesson plan on page 169 is a basic procedure for teaching a learner to get a number of objects in response to the verbal number. (If a learner does not progress within a reasonable amount of time, move on to the next objective, discussed later in this chapter.) The format of this lesson is very similar to the counting lesson presented on page 162. This simplifies the task for the teacher conducting the lessons as well as for the learner. The learner should have mastered counting out a number of objects presented before the teacher asks him to get that number of objects from a group. For example, he must be able to consistently count out 1-5 objects before you ask him to get one to five objects from a group of six or more objects. In this lesson, then, the learner is developing an acquired skill (counting) into a practical skill (getting a number of objects as directed).

The nonverbal learner performing this task should first learn to get a number of objects in response to an oral/signed number. When he consistently performs correctly, the teacher may eliminate the oral number so that the learner is responding to the signed number alone. It is important that the learner who must communicate through sign language not become dependent on oral cues. Those oral cues will not be present when he must express a word, phrase, or number. For example, he may learn to count out a number of objects through sign and to respond to the question "How many?" This task requires him to associate the number of objects with a verbal number and to express that number through sign. To do this he must develop his own internal cues, rather than depend on the external cues provided by the teacher.

There are several ways in which the teacher may vary this task so that it more closely approximates a real work situation. Again, the learner must first demonstrate the ability to perform the task correctly as it has been presented. The teacher may then move the objects a few feet from the desk, requiring the learner to get the objects and bring them back to his desk. The learner must be able to remember the verbal number, count out the correct number of objects, and bring them to a designated place (e.g., desk). Or, working seated at the desk, the teacher may present two different sets of objects and ask the learner to get a number of one object. He must then listen to (or, if responding to sign, look at) a phrase, "Get (number) (object)." The teacher may gradually increase the number of different objects from which the learner must choose. Before introducing this variation of the task, the learner must demonstrate the ability to follow a simple verbal phrase by selecting an object or objects from a variety of objects. The task may be made systematically more complex, by requiring the learner to get a number of objects from a number of different objects placed several feet from the work area. When the learner consistently performs correctly, the objects may be moved farther away, or even placed out of view (e.g., in a drawer, closet, container, etc.).

Each variation must be introduced only after the learner demonstrates the prerequisite skills. The teacher should not expect the learner to get a number of specific objects from a "mixed" group of objects in a drawer (e.g., forks, spoons, knives), until he can perform correctly when a variety of objects are placed on his desk. The learner must first demonstrate the appropriate language and numbers skills in order to perform a number task that requires responding to a verbal direction. These variations and expansions of a basic number lesson bring together the learner's skills from several areas. It is extremely important, however, that the learner demonstrate each individual skill and that each "combination" of skills be introduced gradually and systematically. In this way, the learner works on one new aspect of a task at a time, and the teacher can more clearly evaluate problem areas as they appear.

What about the learner who can count out a number of objects presented, but cannot get a number of objects in response to a verbal number? Again, it is important to try and assess where the learner "breaks down." Does he keep counting out objects beyond the number asked for? Does he appear to "forget" the verbal number? Does he become distracted, or engage in off-task behaviors as he is counting, and lose count? If behaviors seem to interfere, a procedure for reducing the frequency of the behaviors or eliminating them must be developed and implemented. Sometimes, increasing the pace of the lesson by counting along with the learner at the desired speed and then phasing yourself out may improve performance. If, however, the learner does not appear to understand that he must count out only a specific number of objects, rather than all the objects presented, a modification of the lesson may be necessary. One possible method is provided on page 170. When the learner can consistently perform the task when asked to get the same number of objects each time, the teacher may ask for a different number of objects. It may be necessary to go through the procedure (steps 1-8) of the modified lesson plan for each different number of objects. If a learner's performance does not improve on any or all of the steps of the modified procedure, his difficulty may be primarily an attentional or memory problem. If such is the case, it may be more effective to teach him to get a number of objects in response to a written numeral. When he achieves this objective, you may again evaluate his performance in response to the verbal number.

Receptive Association of Written Numeral and Quantity

Before the learner can get a number of objects in response to a written numeral, he must be able to count out a number of objects presented and identify the corresponding written numerals. This is the second objective under number/quantity association in the number skills area, which states: "Learner demonstrates association of numeral and quantity by selecting/circling the appropriate numeral after counting out a group of objects." The first lesson designed to achieve this objective is a receptive task, presented on page 171. This lesson involves three different skills: counting, identifying numerals, and matching the correct numeral to the corresponding number of objects. The learner should have already mastered counting and identifying the numerals presented in this lesson. Theoretically, therefore, his incorrect responses should be related to the new aspect of the task: selecting the numeral after counting out the objects. Unfortunately, not every learner learns in such a logical fashion. The teacher must observe where the learner makes errors and either modify the lesson or review the skills that are presenting problems.

The learner should remain at steps 1-7 until he consistently performs correctly with the verbal cue of the number provided by the teacher. Next, he should move to steps 8-9 (no verbal cue provided, except to correct an incorrect response). Only after he demonstrates the ability to count out the objects and select the correct numeral from two different numerals, should the number of different numerals presented at one time be increased. When evaluating the learner's performance, note should be made on the learner's data chart of which steps in the procedure are being evaluated.

Demonstration of Numeral/Quantity Association

When the learner can select the correct numeral from several, after counting out a number of objects (even as few as three), the next final objective in number/quantity association may be introduced: "Learner demonstrates association of numeral and quantity by getting the correct number of task-related objects in response to the numeral (on cards, blackboard, paper)." The learner must read a numeral and count out the appropriate number of objects from a group of objects. The basic lesson plan to achieve this objective is provided on page 172.

As in every other lesson plan that involves a combination of prerequisite skills, the teacher must analyze errors as they occur in order to determine which aspect of the task is presenting problems. Although the learner should be able to identify each numeral presented, count out a number of objects, and select a numeral after counting out a number of objects before this lesson is introduced, few learners perform with 100% accuracy when any new lesson is presented. Therefore, when problems occur, intervention procedures or lesson modifications should be developed and implemented as necessary. For example, the student, discussed above, who had difficulty discriminating the numerals "2" and "3" was unable to get the correct number of objects in response to those numerals. As in the previous tasks involving numeral discrimination and identification, I wrote the word "three" in small letters below the numeral "3." He can now perform the task correctly, with the written word as a cue. It is possible that he may never perform such an activity successfully without that additional cue. If, after a period of time, eliminating the written word still interferes with performance, then we will continue providing the cue for him. The primary objective is for the learner to perform the task independently; if an additional cue enables him to do so, it should be provided as long as it is necessary.

Another student was able to identify numerals, count out objects, and select the correct numeral after counting out a number of objects. However, he was apparently unable to get a number of objects in response to a written numeral. I modified the lesson by drawing the outlines of the appropriate number of objects next to the corresponding numerals. The learner could then read each numeral and match the correct number of objects to the outlines while counting. The disadvantage of this method is that the learner may merely match the objects to their outlines without counting. Therefore, the teacher must require the learner to count out each object as he matches it, providing the verbal model if necessary. When the learner consistently counts out each object appropriately, some of the numeral cards can be presented without the object outlines and performance then reevaluated. Gradually eliminate the object outlines so that the learner is counting out the correct number of objects in response to the numerals alone. If the learner is unable to make the transition from outlines to numerals alone, you might substitute lines or dots for the outlines. For example, the card with numeral "3" would also have three lines or three dots. These cues should then be gradually eliminated, as were the outlines.

In any number lesson, the objects used may affect performance. Some learners demonstrate no difference in performance whether they are counting out spoons, forks, knives, cups, plates, bowls, toothbrushes, sponges, and so on. However, if a learner does have difficulty transferring learning from one set of objects to the next, the lesson should be conducted with a variety of different objects. One set of objects should be worked on until the learner consistently performs correctly before a new set of objects is introduced.

The basic lesson for reading a numeral and getting the correct number of objects may be varied once the learner achieves the stated objective. Objects may be gradually moved farther from the learner's desk, to a table a few feet away, across the room, or even put in designated places (e.g., closet, drawer). Again, these changes may affect performance, even though the learner can perform the task when seated at his desk. He must learn to take the numeral card, go to the appropriate place, count out the objects (I usually provide him with a container in which to put the objects, such as a plastic tub), and bring them back to his desk. This requires a greater degree of behavioral control, attention, and independence. As in other tasks requiring movement from one place to another, the activity itself may be used to foster better work behaviors. The teacher may observe off-task behaviors or other factors interfering with performance (e.g., moving through the task too slowly), and should implement procedures to improve specific work behaviors.

The basic lesson may also be modified by presenting a set of numeral cards in a stack. The learner must take the first card, get the correct number of objects (from a place other than his desk), bring the objects back, take them out of the container, turn the numeral card facedown, pick up the next numeral card in the stack, and continue, until all the numeral cards are facedown (indicating to him that he has finished). Again, taking a basic lesson task that the learner can perform, the teacher may increase the number of variables in the task situation. These changes may require a higher degree of independence and be designed to gradually more closely approximate a work activity involving the basic skills.

COMBINING READING AND NUMBER SKILLS

Once the learner demonstrates the necessary number skills and reading skills, tasks may be designed that combine the two areas. For example, the learner who can read a phrase and perform the appropriate action (e.g., "get a plate"), and count out a number of objects in response to a written numeral, may learn to follow written directions like "get 5 plates," "get 8 forks," "get 4 slices of bread," and so forth. If he can read and follow a sequence of directions, the teacher may include numbers in these directions, for example:

> go to (the) closet
> get 2 tubs
> get 2 sponges
> put (the) sponges in (the) tubs

Depending on the learner's skills and work behavior, reading/number tasks may be designed that require movement through the environment and a high degree of independence. For example, one of my students has been diagnosed autistic and is deaf and nonverbal. When left alone in an unstructured situation, he would engage in ritualistic behaviors, such as twiddling objects and slapping his head (not in an abusive manner). He was taught to read and follow directions, and acquired the number skills described in this chapter. To illustrate, he learned the following sequence of directions:

> go to kitchen
> get 8 plates
> get 6 forks
> get 5 napkins
> get 9 spoons

He would take a tub, go downstairs to the school kitchen, get the correct number of appropriate objects, bring them back to the classroom, empty the tub, take the next list of directions, and follow them. He was also given the job of filling each of seven tubs (one for each lunchroom of the school) with the correct number of appropriate objects (plates, napkins, cups, forks, knives, spoons, pitcher), according to lists on each tub. Initially, it was necessary for him to be supervised in order to remain on-task, and occasional correction was also needed. Gradually the supervisor moved out of the learner's view and observed him unseen. When the learner consistently performed the job correctly, with few if any off-task behaviors, the supervisor left him alone and merely checked his work when the learner had completed the task. This is a student whom many professionals thought incapable of learning and, certainly, unable to perform a useful task without constant supervision. The important and exciting element of this story is that he has learned to perform many useful activities independently or with minimal supervision. His case is not an isolated example. The process may be slow and difficult, but the results are well worth the effort.

RELATION OF NUMBER SKILLS, LANGUAGE SKILLS, AND READING SKILLS TO THE WORK ACTIVITY

The combination of language and number skills may be integrated into the work activity itself. For example, Level 11 of the table-setting activity states that the learner will get the correct number of table-setting objects from the appropriate place (e.g., cupboards, drawers) and set a table *in response to verbal directions*. In this activity, the teacher may say/sign, "Set the table for (number of settings)." The learner should count out the correct number of each object and set the table properly. Before reaching this level of the activity, the learner should be able to correctly set a table and to get a number of objects in response to the verbal number. If most errors occur in the counting aspect of the task, a drill to review getting a number of objects in response to the verbal numbers may be done in addition to the task itself. This activity allows the learner to apply his acquired skills to the performance of a useful activity, which is the primary objective of the curriculum.

The learner who demonstrates the appropriate reading and number skills may learn to perform an activity such as table-setting at Level 12 (Learner gets correct number of table-setting objects from appropriate place (cupboard, drawer), and sets a table *in response to written directions*). The teacher's long term objective should be to set up tasks that require the learner to use his acquired skills in performing a work activity. Work activities, themselves, may be expanded to approximate real-life work situations. For example, a learner may be taught to set a number of tables correctly in a school lunchroom, following verbal or written directions. He may learn to clean blackboards, tables, or windows by following a list of written directions that specify different areas in the school (e.g., specific classrooms, kitchen, bathrooms, etc.). Once the learner demonstrates some basic functional language skills (e.g., following verbal directions), reading skills (e.g., reading and following directions), and number skills (reading and following directions involving numbers), through which appropriate work behaviors may be developed, these skills can be applied to a variety of work situations. Although the process may be long and the obstacles many, students' accomplishments have demonstrated that the objectives are realistic, and worth the energy and effort needed to achieve them.

Counting

Objective: Learner will demonstrate one-to-one correspondence by counting out a number of objects presented.

Materials: paper plate, shallow container, or piece of construction paper; variety of objects

Procedure:
1. Put paper plate, container, or paper on learner's desk.
2. Put a number of identical objects to the left or right of the plate/container.
3. Say/sign, "Count."
4. Learner picks up each object, one at a time, and says/signs correct number as he puts it on the plate or in the container.
   If learner does not say/sign correct number:
   a. Say/sign correct number.
   b. Learner imitates.
   c. Repeat the trial (present the objects).
   d. Count along with learner, if necessary.
5. Repeat steps 2-4, presenting the same set of objects or sets of different objects.

Evaluation procedure: Count and record the number of times learner counts out objects presented correctly/incorrectly in 10 trials.

Numeral Identification Readiness — Reception (1)

Objective: Learner selects correct numeral card in response to verbal number.

Materials: five numeral cards of numeral to be learned; one numeral card of each of two other numerals

Procedure:
1. Place all of the numerals to be learned (e.g., five "1"s) on desk in horizontal or vertical row, or any position (e.g., one numeral in each of the four corners of the desk, one in the center of the desk, etc.).
2. Say/sign numeral (e.g., "one").
3. Learner picks up (selects) a numeral card and turns it facedown. Initially, demonstrate, point to numeral card, or put learner through desired response.
4. Repeat until learner has selected each numeral card after you say/sign it and has turned each facedown.
5. Repeat steps 1-4, varying position of numeral cards, until learner responds appropriately and independently (without nonverbal cues) at least five times consecutively (one trial presentation).
6. Place all of the numerals to be learned (e.g., five "1"s) and one of another numeral card (e.g., "2") on desk in any configuration.
7. Say/sign the numeral to be learned (e.g., "1 (one)").
8. Learner picks up (selects) correct numeral card and turns it facedown.
   If learner does not respond or responds incorrectly:
   a. Say, "No."
   b. Say/sign numeral again.
   c. Point to correct card (if learner has not self-corrected).
   d. Learner picks up correct numeral card and turns it facedown.
9. Repeat steps 7-8 until learner has selected and turned over each of the five numeral cards in response to the verbal numbers (e.g., "one").
10. Remove the other numeral card (e.g., "2").
11. Place all of the numerals to be learned (e.g., five "1"s) and one of another numeral card (e.g., "3") on desk in any configuration.
12. Follow steps 7-9.

Evaluation procedure: Count and record the number of times learner selects correct/incorrect numeral card in response to verbal number (steps 6-12) on two test trials (five cards of numeral to be learned presented on each trial).

Numeral Identification Readiness — Reception (2)

Objective: Learner selects correct numeral in response to the verbal number.

Materials: several numeral cards of the numeral to be learned; one numeral card of each of two or three other numerals

Procedure:
1. Place three numeral cards of the numeral to be learned and one each of two other numerals in any configuration on the desk (e.g., three "1"s, one "2," one "3").
2. Say/sign the numeral to be learned (e.g., "one").
3. Learner selects correct card and turns it facedown.
   If learner does not respond, or responds incorrectly:
   a. Say, "No."
   b. Say/sign number.
   c. Point to numeral card (if learner has not self-corrected).
   d. Learner picks up correct word card and turns it facedown.
4. Repeat steps 2-3 until learner has selected and turned over each of the three numeral cards in response to the verbal numbers (e.g., "one").
5. Follow steps 1-4, changing the positions of the numeral cards.
   When the learner consistently selects correct numeral cards (steps 1-5):
6. Place two numeral cards of the numeral to be learned, and one each of two other numerals, in any configuration on the desk (e.g., two "1"s, one "2," one "3" card).
7. Follow steps 2-5.
   When the learner consistently selects correct numeral cards (steps 6-7):
8. Place one card of the numeral to be learned, and one card of each of two or three other numerals in any configuration on the desk (e.g., one "1," one "2," one "3," and one "4").
9. Say/sign the numeral to be learned (e.g., "one").
10. Learner selects correct numeral and turns card facedown.
    If learner does not respond or responds incorrectly, follow procedure in step 3 (a-d).
11. Turn over numeral card so it is faceup, and change position of numeral cards.
12. Say/sign the numeral to be learned (e.g., "one").
13. Learner selects correct numeral and turns card facedown.
14. Follow steps 8-13 at least 10 times, changing position of the numeral cards each time.

Evaluation procedure: Count and record number of times learner selects correct/incorrect numeral (card) in response to verbal number (step 14) on 10 test trials.

Numeral Identification Readiness — Reception (3)

Objective: Learner selects correct numeral cards in response to the verbal numbers.
Materials: ten numeral cards of each numeral
Procedure:
1. Place one of each numeral card on learner's desk, numeral side up (e.g., "1," "2").
2. Using remaining numeral cards, hold each numeral card up one at a time.
3. Learner matches each numeral card to appropriate numeral cards.
4. As learner matches each numeral card, say/sign the number.
5. When learner has correctly matched all the numeral cards, and they are in stacks on learner's desk, say/sign one of the numerals (e.g., "one").
6. Learner selects correct numeral and turns card over (point to correct numeral card, if necessary).
7. Say/sign the same number (e.g., "one").
8. Learner selects correct numeral card and turns it over.
9. Continue as in steps 5-8 until learner has turned over all the cards of one numeral (e.g., "1") in response to the verbal number.
10. Place the numeral cards in a faceup stack on the desk (the other stack(s) of numeral cards have remained on desk throughout steps 5-9).
11. Follow steps 1-9 with each of the remaining stacks of numeral cards.
12. Place one of each numeral card on learner's desk numeral side up, and follow steps 1-4 again.
13. When learner has correctly matched all the numeral cards, and they are in stacks on learner's desk, say/sign each of the different numerals one at a time in random order.
14. Learner selects correct numeral card and turns it over.
    If learner does not respond or responds incorrectly:
    a. Say, "No."
    b. Say/sign the number.
    c. Point to numeral card (if learner has not self-corrected).
    d. Learner picks up correct numeral card and turns it over.
    e. Repeat same word on next trial.
15. Continue until learner has selected and turned over each numeral card in response to the verbal number (2 numerals, 10 cards of each — 20 numeral cards; 3 numerals, 10 cards of each — 30 numeral cards).

Evaluation procedure: Count and record the number of times learner selects correct/incorrect numeral card in response to the verbal word (steps 13-15).

Numeral Identification — Expressive

Objective: Learner will say/sign the correct number in response to a written numeral.
Materials: at least five numeral cards of each different numeral
Procedure:
1. Begin with one of the numerals (e.g., "1").
2. Place stack of five numeral cards ("1") faceup on desk.
3. Point to first card (or hold it up).
4. Learner says/signs correct numeral.
   If learner does not respond or responds incorrectly:
   a. Say/sign number.
   b. Learner imitates number (help him to imitate as needed).
   c. Point to numeral (or hold it up) again.
   d. Learner says/signs correct number.
5. Turn numeral card facedown.
6. Follow steps 3-5 with remaining numeral cards of that numeral (e.g., four "1"s).
7. Follow steps 1-6 with stacks of each numeral (e.g., five "2" cards, then five "3" cards).
8. Mix up all of the numeral cards so that both (or all three) of the different sets of numeral cards are together in a stack (e.g., five "1"s, five "2"s, five "3"s — 15 cards).
9. Place stack of numeral cards faceup on desk.
10. Point to first card (or hold it up).
11. Learner says/signs correct number.
    If learner does not respond or responds incorrectly, follow procedure as in step 4, a-d.
12. Turn numeral card facedown.
13. Continue with remainder of numeral cards.

Evaluation procedure: Count and record the number of numerals the learner identifies (says/signs) correctly/incorrectly (steps 8-13) as presented.

Numeral Identification — Reception

Objective: Learner selects correct numeral cards in response to verbal numbers.
Materials: numeral cards
Procedure:
1. Place three or four numeral cards on the learner's desk at one time; two or three *learned* numerals, and one *new* numeral (e.g., "1," "2," "3") in any configuration.
2. Say/sign each of the learned numbers (e.g., "one," "2 (two)"):
3. Learner selects each and turns card facedown.
4. Say/sign new numeral (e.g., "three").
5. Learner turns numeral card facedown.
6. Repeat steps 1-5 several times, varying the position of the numeral cards on the desk.
7. Place numeral cards on desk as in step 1.
8. Say/sign each of the numbers *in any order.*
9. Learner selects correct numeral card and turns it facedown.
    If the learner consistently responds incorrectly to the new number:
    a. Place numeral cards on desk as in step 1.
    b. Say/sign new number (e.g., "three").
    c. Point to correct numeral card.
    d. Learner turns card over.
    e. Turn numeral card faceup and change position of numeral cards.
    f. Repeat steps b-e until the learner independently selects the new numeral on 10 consecutive trials.
10. Repeat steps 7-9 several times.

Evaluation procedure: Count and record the number of times learner selects correct/incorrect numerals in response to verbal numbers (steps 7-9) on a given number of trials.

Numeral Identification — Expression

Objective: Learner identifies each numeral, presented orally or through sign.
Materials: numeral cards
Procedure:
1. Present each numeral card.
2. Learner says/signs correct number.
   If learner does not respond or responds incorrectly:
   a. Say/sign number.
   b. Learner imitates number (help him to imitate as needed).
   c. Present numeral card again.
   d. Learner says/signs correct number.
3. Continue as in steps 1-2, presenting each numeral several times.

Evaluation procedure: Count and record number of numerals the learner reads (says/signs) correctly/incorrectly as presented.

Number/Quantity Association

Objective: Learner will get the correct number of objects in response to the verbal number.
Materials: several different objects; paper plate or shallow container
Procedure:
1. Put plate or container on desk.
2. Put a number of objects to the left or right of the plate.
3. Say/sign, "Get (number) (object)."
4. Learner counts out correct number of objects.
   If learner does not respond or responds incorrectly:
   a. Say/sign the number.
   b. Count out the objects with the learner.
   c. Repeat a and b until learner counts out the correct number of objects independently.
5. Present the same objects or a group of different objects.
6. Say/sign, "Get (number) (object)."
7. Learner counts out correct number of objects.
8. Continue as in steps 2-7, asking for different numbers of objects.

Evaluation procedure: Count and record the number of times learner gets correct/incorrect number of objects in response to verbal number in 10 trials.

Number/Quantity Association —
Modification to Eliminate "Extra" Counting

Objective: Learner will get the correct number of objects in response to the verbal number.

Materials: several different objects; paper plate or shallow container

Procedure:
1. Present the number of objects that the learner must get, and one additional object a few inches apart from the others. For example, present five forks in a row and one fork a few inches away.
2. Say/sign, "Get (<u>number</u>)" (e.g., "five").
3. When learner has counted out five objects, say/sign, "five," and intervene to prevent the learner from picking up the sixth object if necessary (e.g., move the object farther away on the desk, hold it on the desk, or take the learner's hand and put it down).
4. Repeat steps 1-3, until the learner does not attempt to count the "extra" object, when the teacher does not intervene.

When the learner consistently performs correctly on step 4:

5. Present the objects as in step 1.
6. Say/sign, "Get (<u>number</u>)" (e.g., "five").
7. Learner counts out five objects independently (without teacher saying/signing the number after the learner counts out the correct number of objects).

When the learner consistently performs correctly on steps 5-7:

8. Follow step 1-7, presenting the group of objects together (e.g., all six objects in a row).

Evaluation procedure: Count and record the number of times learner gets correct/incorrect number of objects in response to verbal number in 10 trials.

Numeral/Quantity Association — Receptive

Objective: Learner selects the correct numeral from several numerals after counting out a number of objects.
Materials: several different objects; paper plate or shallow container
Procedure:
1. Put plate or container on desk.
2. Put two different numeral cards above the plate/container.
3. Put a number of objects to the left or right of the plate; the number of objects should correspond to one of the numeral cards.
4. Tell the learner to "count."
5. Learner counts out objects.
6. Initially, say/sign the number (of objects counted) and point to numeral cards.
7. Learner selects correct numeral card and puts it on the plate/in the container.
   If learner does not respond or responds incorrectly:
   a. Direct learner to "count" again.
   b. Say/sign the number (of objects counted).
   c. Point to correct numeral, demonstrate, or put learner through desired response.
   d. Repeat steps 1-7 with same number of objects and numerals.
8. Follow steps 1-5, presenting different numbers of objects (to be counted) and two numeral cards (one of which corresponds to number of objects presented).
9. Learner selects correct numeral card and puts it on the plate or in the container.
   If learner does not respond or responds incorrectly, follow procedure step 7, a-d.

When learner consistently performs correctly on steps 8-9, increase the number of numerals from which he selects the correct numeral, and follow steps 8-9.

Evaluation procedure: Count and record the number of times learner selects correct/incorrect numeral after counting out a number of objects on 10 trials (steps 8-9). Note the number of numeral cards from which he selects.

Numeral/Quantity Association — *Expressive*

Objective: Learner reads each numeral presented, and gets the correct number of objects.

Materials: written numerals; several different objects; paper plate or shallow container

Procedure:
1. Place paper plate/container on learner's desk.
2. Place a group of objects (all the same) to the left or right of the plate/container.
3. Place a numeral card above, below, or on/in the plate/container.
4. Direct the learner to "read" the numeral, verbally or nonverbally (e.g., by pointing to the numeral).
5. Learner reads (identifies verbally) numeral.
6. Direct learner to "get (number)."
7. Learner counts out correct number of objects.
    If learner does not respond or responds incorrectly:
    a. Point to numeral again.
    b. Learner says/signs it.
    c. Direct learner to "get (number)."
    d. Help learner to count out correct number of objects by counting with him, demonstrating, or pointing to each object (as needed).
    e. Repeat steps a–d.
8. Follow steps 1–7, presenting a different numeral each time.

Evaluation procedure: Count and record the number of times learner gets correct/incorrect number of objects after reading each numeral.

10

IMPLEMENTING THE SUPPLEMENTARY SKILLS AREA OF A CURRICULUM UNIT

Fine motor skills are presented as a suggested supplement to the basic skill areas of work activity, language, reading, and numbers. This supplementary skills area differs from the other skill areas in that the curriculum does not provide a method for developing fine motor abilities but, rather, suggests meaningful ways of relating fine motor skills to the other skill areas. The learner must first demonstrate the ability to trace and copy simple line and curved forms before this area is introduced.

A primary objective of the supplementary skills area is to develop fine motor skills that can expand the variety of activities the learner is able to perform. A secondary objective is to reinforce and expand language and reading skills through written expression.

Objectives are broken down into tracing, copying, and writing skills. These skills may be applied to the curriculum units by teaching the learner to trace, copy, and write numerals, letters, and words (and phrases or sentences at a higher level) that correspond to the learner's work in the work activity, language, reading, and number skills areas. For example, the learner who can identify specific numerals or read particular words can be taught to write them. Once the learner can copy numerals, letters, and words, he may learn to write them in response to the verbal numbers, letters, and words.

When the learner is tracing, copying, or writing on a blackboard, remember to seat him (or have him stand) so that he is working at his own eye level (not yours). Check his position when he writes on paper so that his wrist is flat on the desk and he is holding the pencil properly. Some learners with good visual memories may learn to write numerals or words through drills. The teacher says/signs the numeral/word (or holds up an object), the learner copies a written model repeatedly, and then writes it from memory. Learners who read phonetically may learn to write regular words by decoding and irregular words by repeated drill.

The learner who can write a word in response to the verbal word or in response to an object may be trained to apply this skill to a work situation. For example, he may assist in, or perform, inventory-type tasks. The teacher may present a group of objects to the learner who can identify the objects, read the object words, and write the object words. The learner may be trained to write down each object when presented 1) one at a time, 2) in a group on his desk, 3) in a group on an open shelf, and 4) in a group in a closet, cupboard, drawer, etc.

The learner who demonstrates the appropriate number skills may be taught to count out a group of objects and write the correct numeral. When he can consistently count out a number of objects presented and write the correct numeral, the teacher may present more than one set of different objects. A list of the objects may be provided and the learner trained to count out each set of objects and record the correct number next to the appropriate object name listed. If the learner can also write each object name in response to the object, then he may record both the objects and the number of objects.

For learners who demonstrate good reading (whether sight or phonetic) and writing skills, it may be appropriate to use writing to reinforce language skills. For example, a learner may be taught to say/sign a sentence using a vocabulary word appropriately. The teacher may then have him write the sentence. Or the teacher might present an object or picture, or a picture of someone performing an action. If the learner is able to verbally describe the object or picture, the teacher might have him write his responses as well. The teacher might also develop a lesson in which he asks questions and the learner writes the appropriate responses. These types of activities are more conventional academic tasks and should be used only with students who demonstrate the appropriate language, reading, and writing skills.

As in the supportive and additional skills sections of the language and reading skills areas, the fine motor skills area is presented as an example of a supplementary skill that may be developed through, and applied to, the curriculum units. It should be viewed as a suggested area for work, in which the teacher may develop appropriate objectives and activities for individual learners. Lessons to develop other supplementary skills can be developed according to individual needs and abilities.

11
INTEGRATING CURRICULUM UNITS

The curriculum units are all interrelated, in that each unit is composed of objectives and activities for the development and reinforcement of work activity, language, reading, number, and supplementary (e.g., fine motor) skills. They differ in the specific work activity upon which each skill area is focused.

As discussed under "Developing Individual Educational Programs within the Curriculum Model" in Chapter 5, a learner may be working on various skills from a number of different curriculum units. This may happen when a learner achieves each objective in a particular skill area faster than he progresses in other skill areas of that unit. Or the teacher may select one or more areas from a curriculum unit that may be richer in activities for the development of specific skills appropriate to a learner's program. A learner may be performing a work activity from a given unit and its corresponding language and reading activities, while working on number skills using task-related objects from another curriculum unit. Classroom time, as well, is a factor in the number of activities on which a learner may work at a given time. There may be enough class periods for a learner to be working at a high level of one activity and at an introductory level of another activity from a different curriculum unit.

It is hoped that skills learned through one curriculum unit will be transferred to other curriculum units. In a general sense, the learner who can follow simple directions from a curriculum unit should be able to follow similar verbal directions from another unit once he learns the new language components. More specifically, any learning of language or reading vocabulary from one curriculum unit should be demonstrated in other units that work with the same vocabulary. There may be work activities, as well, that involve similar skills, such as cleaning a blackboard, table, or counters, or washing hands and brushing teeth. Appropriate work behaviors that the learner has acquired, such as remaining on-task, working at a steady rate, completing a task, and working with minimal supervision, should be maintained when he is performing a variety of work activities.

Certain skills, such as reading a sequence of directions, once mastered, can be applied to any work activity or curriculum unit. As new vocabulary is acquired, it may be integrated into the directions that the learner reads and follows. Number skills, as well, may be applied to a variety of activities, from counting out spoons and forks to counting out linens, slices of bread, or teaspoons of sugar.

Another way in which the relation among curriculum units makes the curriculum an efficient as well as effective model is in the similarity of format among units. Both the learner and the teacher will become familiar with the progression of objectives and activities, the suggested methods of teaching, and patterns of responding. As the teacher becomes more familiar and comfortable with the structure of the curriculum and the process of teaching through the curriculum units, he should become more adept at determining appropriate objectives and designing activities to develop specific skills. The teacher's increased understanding of the curriculum and ability to implement it should, in turn, have a positive effect on the learner's progress.

Part III

Preparation and Assessment within the Curriculum Model

12

INTRODUCING THE CURRICULUM
Teacher and Materials Preparation

The value of any curriculum lies not only in its effectiveness as a teaching tool, but in its ease and efficiency of implementation as well. Once the teacher has prepared the necessary basic materials and trained staff members in the principles of effective teaching, the objectives of the curriculum, and the methods of carrying out lessons and evaluation procedures, the curriculum should promote more effective teaching, reduce paperwork, and simplify reporting.

TEACHER TRAINING

Teacher training is simplified because both the objectives and the methods for each curriculum unit follow the same structure and format; only the specific content changes, according to the curriculum unit. If a teacher has been trained to carry out the language program for the table-setting unit, he can follow the same format and use the same methods in the language program of any curriculum unit. Any variations in teaching method are in response to individual student needs and abilities rather than to the material being taught.

Training staff to implement the curriculum means more than discussions and training sessions in techniques and methods. Staff should understand the philosophy and rationale behind the structure and format of the curriculum. They should be familiar with the long term and short term objectives of the program, in order to most effectively carry out individual lessons. In addition, training should include sessions in observation and evaluation procedures. The instructors involved in training teachers should initially demonstrate and then supervise lessons, pointing out factors in learning and behavior that the teacher must learn to observe and identify.

Teacher training should begin with a presentation and discussion of learning and behavioral characteristics of the students, general principles of effective teaching (Chapter 4), and specific principles, structure, and format of the curriculum model (Chapter 2). Teachers then observe lessons from the various skill areas as they are conducted with students. They are encouraged to write down any observations and questions, to be discussed later. After the teachers have observed students engaged in a variety of lesson situations and discussed their observations and questions, sessions in role-playing may be helpful before they actually work with the students. The training supervisor may play the student roles, presenting a variety of learning and behavior styles and problems. Trainees may then identify these factors and discuss methods of dealing with them within the teaching situation.

When teachers begin working with the students, they should be carefully supervised so that problems and strengths in lesson presentation and evaluation can be identified early. When lesson or objective modifications are indicated, new teachers should participate in the process of determining, and then implementing, those changes.

Once the teacher becomes familiar with the format and methods of a curriculum unit, he should be able to carry out the program with any other curriculum unit. The subtleties and many possible variations in teaching will be determined by individual student needs and abilities, while the basic structure of the curriculum will remain consistent throughout the units.

MATERIALS

The first consideration in readying the classroom is preparing the teaching environment itself. Before implementing any curriculum unit, make sure that the environment can accommodate the performance of the work activity. For example, before beginning the table-setting unit, areas in the classroom should be set up with a table(s), closet (or cupboard), shelf, and drawer(s). The appropriate materials should be prepared, following the guidelines for safety and suitability of materials, discussed in Chapter 4.

The initial materials needed will be those required for 1) basic lesson plans at each performance level of the work activity or activities, 2) language programs (object identification, lessons for language Conditions A-K, following verbal directions), 3) reading lessons (matching, reception, expression, reading comprehension), 4) number skills lessons (counting, numeral identification, number and numeral/quantity association), and 5) fine motor and other supplementary and supportive skill area lessons. Keep a file of lessons for each skill, and add to it as new lessons and variations of basic lessons are developed. In this way, an appropriate lesson procedure can be pulled from the file as needed. Because specific variations can be described on the evaluation charts (see Chapter 13), new lesson plans do not need to be written up for each individual learner. However, a learner may present problems or a style of learning that requires a new lesson plan; this lesson may be designed, copies made, and the lesson added to the file.

The teacher will also need to prepare 1) the content of each language unit for a given curriculum unit, 2) a list of specific verbal cues for Condition H^a, and 3) a list of language and reading vocabulary words for each curriculum unit. These lists may be prepared as checklists and kept as records of progress and achievement. (Examples of these materials are included at the end of this chapter.)

The teacher will also need to prepare the following materials: 1) word cards (some sets with several of each word for matching lessons), 2) reading and number/reading phrase cards (one direction, sequence of directions), and 3) numeral cards. Phrase cards may be developed as needed, according to the learner's objectives. For example, you may develop a set of phrase cards (one direction or more per card), such as:

>   get the (object)
>   *or*
>   get (object)

and

>   Put the (object) in/on/under the (place).
>   *or*
>   (Object) in/on/under (place).

and any combination of appropriate directions:

>   Go to the (place).
>   Open the (   ).
>   Get (numeral) (objects).

Each of my students has a spring-clip notebook/folder containing his long term objectives for a 4-month period (from which reports are written for the school, school boards, and parents). Each basic lesson procedure for his program is included, followed by the evaluation chart for the specific lesson. Vocabulary lists are also provided in the notebook, in addition to reading lesson evaluation charts. Lessons may be added to this folder or removed at any time. I save all old data in manila envelopes on which I record the lessons and the period of time covered by each chart. Vocabulary lists should also be saved as a record of specific vocabulary achievement in the reading area.

Although the initial preparation of materials may indeed be time consuming, this amount of preparation is not necessary for each curriculum unit. Each curriculum unit does require the work activity lesson, language program phrases and corresponding verbal cues (for Condition H[a]), vocabulary lists, and word and phrase cards. However, the basic lesson plans for each skill area may be kept on file for use with any curriculum unit, with new lessons added as they are developed. The format of the curriculum and the use of evaluation charts in communicating changes in lesson procedures and objectives allow the teacher to individualize lessons and programs without necessarily having to write out new objectives and lessons or prepare new materials for each learner. In addition, the similarity in format and methods throughout each curriculum unit provides the teacher with a consistent framework within which to set objectives and implement lessons. This, in turn, should foster more effective and efficient teaching.

Content for Language Unit Level 3 in Table-Setting Activity
(to be used with appropriate teaching condition)

Basic	Expanded
get placemat	Get (the) placemat.
placemat on table	Put (the) placemat on (the) table.
get plate	Get (the) plate.
plate on table	Put (the) plate on (the) table/placemat.
get bowl	Get (the) bowl.
bowl on table	Put (the) bowl on (the) table/placemat.
get cup	Get (the) cup.
cup on table	Put (the) cup on (the) table/placemat.
get napkin	Get (the) napkin.
napkin on table	Put (the) napkin on (the) table/placemat.
get fork	Get (the) fork.
fork on table	Put (the) fork on (the) table/placemat.
get knife	Get (the) knife.
knife on table	Put (the) knife on (the) table/placemat.
get spoon	Get (the) spoon.
spoon on table	Put (the) spoon on (the) table/placemat.

Verbal Cues for Condition H[a] Language Unit Level 3 for Table-Setting Activity

1. What do you get?
2. Where do you put (the) placemat?
3. What do you get?
4. Where do you put (the) plate?
5. What do you get?
6. Where do you put (the) bowl?
7. What do you get?
8. Where do you put (the) cup?
9. What do you get?
10. Where do you put (the) napkin?
11. What do you get?
12. Where do you put (the) fork?
13. What do you get?
14. Where do you put (the) knife?
15. What do you get?
16. Where do you put (the) spoon?

Language/Reading Vocabulary for Table-Setting Activity
Check (✓) after three consecutive correct days, and date.

Word (word #)	Reads	Writes in response to verbal word	Uses appropriately in sentence
1. in			
2. on			
3. up			
4. cup			
5. tub			
6. get			
7. set			
8. go			
9. to			
10. pick			
11. the			
12. put			
13. napkin			
14. closet			
15. shelf			
16. room			
17. spoon			
18. open			
19. close			
20. table			
21. plate			
22. placemat			
23. knife			
24. fork			
25. bowl			
26. drawer			
27. chair			
28. dining			
29. kitchen			
30. cupboard			

Language/Reading Vocabulary for Blackboard-Cleaning Activity
Check (✓) after three consecutive correct days, and date.

Word (word #)	Reads	Writes in response to verbal word	Uses appropriately in sentence
1. in			
2. on			
3. up			
4. get			
5. wet			
6. tub			
7. put			
8. hot			
9. fill			
10. go			
11. to			
12. the			
13. into			
14. off			
15. pick			
16. with			
17. closet			
18. water			
19. sink			
20. cold			
21. down			
22. turn			
23. classroom			
24. bathroom			
25. empty			
26. dirty			
27. wash			
28. clean			
29. blackboard			
30. kitchen			
31. pour			
32. sponge			
33. squeeze			

Language/Reading Vocabulary for Bed-Making Activity
Check (✓) after three consecutive correct days, and date.

Word (word #)	Reads	Writes in response to verbal word	Uses appropriately in sentence
1. in			
2. on			
3. get			
4. bed			
5. top			
6. tuck			
7. put			
8. pull			
9. shelf			
10. closet			
11. pillow			
12. make			
13. pillowcase			
14. over			
15. smooth			
16. sheet			
17. down			
18. blanket			
19. bottom			
20. bedspread			
21. the			

Language/Reading Vocabulary for Sandwich-Making Activity
Check (✓) after three consecutive correct days, and date.

Word (word #)	Reads	Writes in response to verbal word	Uses appropriately in sentence
1. on			
2. in			
3. get			
4. cut			
5. put			
6. and			
7. with			
8. open			
9. close			
10. make			
11. table			
12. sandwich			
13. bread			
14. spread			
15. cover			
16. spoon			
17. knife			
18. slice			
19. of			
20. drawer			
21. refrigerator			
22. cupboard			
Sandwich fillings:			
23. ham			
24. butter			
25. jelly			
26. tuna fish			
27. peanut butter			
28. cheese			
29. mustard			
30. mayonnaise			

13

EVALUATING A PROGRAM AND MONITORING PROGRESS

Careful and ongoing evaluation procedures are necessary in order to measure the effectiveness of various teaching methods, monitor what is learned and the rate of learning, and identify any factors that may affect learning. There are many practical benefits to keeping data on each objective and activity that the learner performs. Accurate records enable the teacher to obtain a clear picture of progress or lack of progress. Based on this information, the teacher can modify lesson presentation, procedures, or objectives. The teacher may add new material or make any other indicated changes and monitor the effects of these changes on the learner's performance. It is also helpful for purposes of communication to other staff members, professionals, or parents to base reports on reliable, specific, and informative data.

Evaluation procedures and the recording of data do not have to be time consuming or complex. The simpler the evaluation procedure and method of recording, the easier it will be to maintain ongoing, reliable records of performance. Each lesson plan the teacher develops should include an evaluation procedure that defines precisely what, in terms of the lesson's objective, is to be evaluated. When appropriate, it should also indicate when the evaluation is to be conducted and specify the number of trials, minutes of observation, or any other pertinent conditions of testing.

EVALUATING AND RECORDING PERFORMANCE

A daily behavior chart (Figure 1),[1] which covers 20 weeks, or 140 days, can be used to record performance on each lesson. The vertical lines indicate the day of the week, with a heavier line every seventh line to indicate the end

---

[1] Daily behavior charts may be obtained by writing to Daily Behavior Chart, Behavior Research Co., Box 3351, Kansas City, Kansas 66103.

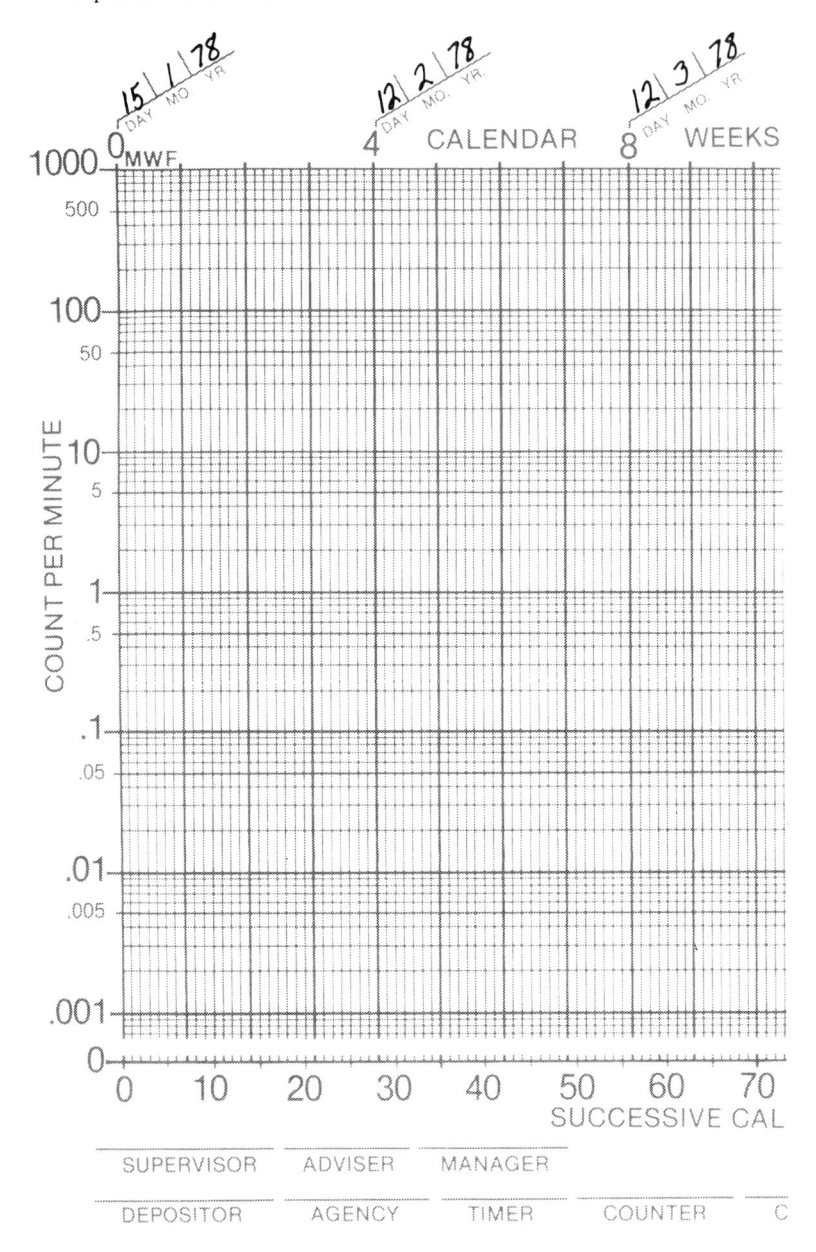

Figure 1. Sample daily behavior chart. (Chart developed by Ogden Lindsley.)

Evaluating and Monitoring 191

COUNTING PERIOD FLOORS

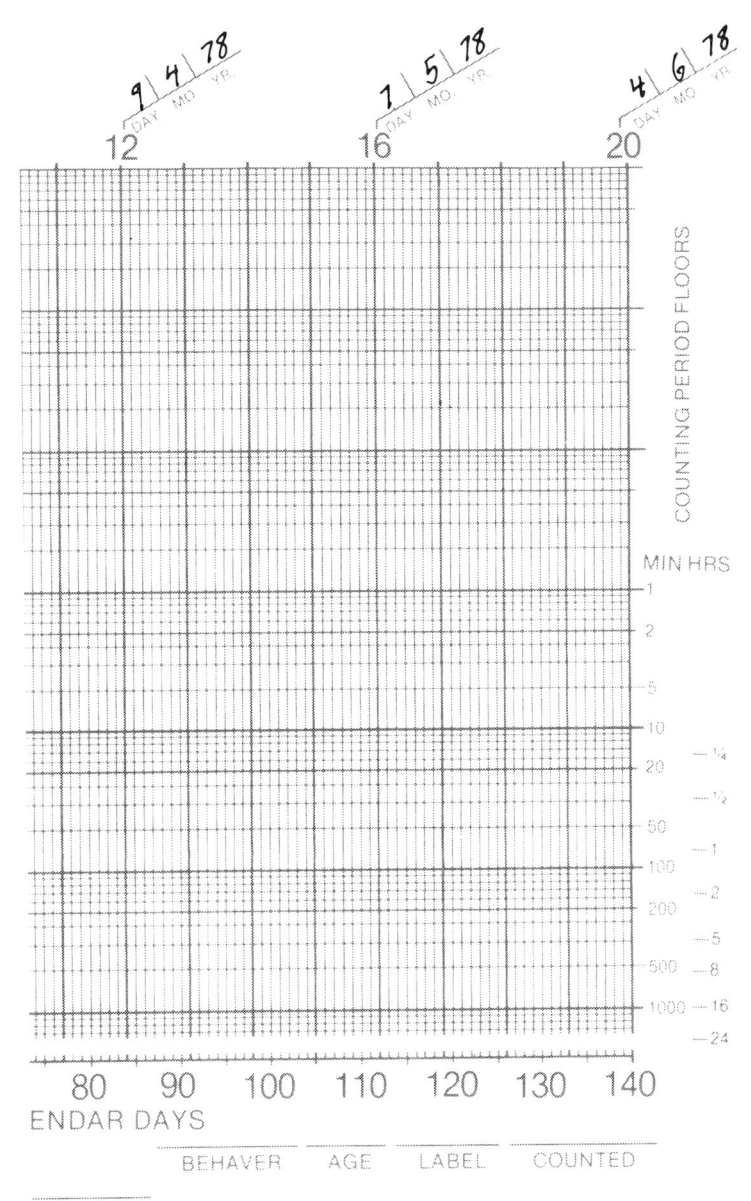

MIN HRS

BEHAVER   AGE   LABEL   COUNTED

HARTER

192 Preparation and Assessment within the Curriculum Model

of a week. The horizontal lines indicate the count per minute, or the number of times a given behavior(s) occurs. This chart may be used to record either the number of times a behavior occurs per minute or the number of times a behavior occurs during a lesson, in a given number of trials, or in the performance of an activity. If time is a relevant factor in performance, the chart may be used to include the number of minutes the learner is observed or the number of minutes needed to complete the activity. This can be done by charting your data on the basis of a given number of minutes using the horizontal lines as a "record floor" (or "counting period floor"). If the data are recorded on the basis of 1 minute of observation or performance, the record floor is drawn at 1 (see right and left sides of chart). If the time period is 2 minutes, the record floor is drawn at .5; for 5 minutes, .2; 10 minutes, .1, etc. Note that the chart allows you to record data for an observation period as long as 24 hours (see bottom right of chart). The record floor may be varied each day; for example, if you are recording the number of interventions needed for the learner to perform an activity correctly, and the number of minutes it takes him to complete the activity, this information may be recorded in the following manner (see Figures 2 and 3):

1. Using a second piece of chart paper, fold the left side ("count per minute") back so that the numbers are visible (from the bottom: 0–1000).
2. Cut this "marker" off (Figure 2).
3. On the daily behavior chart (Figure 3), find the appropriate day on which you are recording performance (e.g., Monday, June 5).
4. Draw a small line at the appropriate number to indicate how long it took the learner to perform the given activity (e.g., 10 minutes — draw line at .1).
5. Next, you may record the number of interventions needed for the learner to perform the activity adequately. Take the marker (made from the second piece of chart paper), and line up number 1 with the line you drew for the baseline (.1).
6. Now, following the numbers from 1–1000 on your marker, record the number of interventions (e.g., 10) with an X. Looking at the sample chart (Figure 3), 10 interventions within a 10-minute period falls on the 1 line.

Let's say that on Wednesday he completes the activity within 8 minutes, with five interventions (quite an improved performance!). Find the "Wednesday line" for June 7 on the chart. Draw in a baseline to indicate 8 minutes, at slightly above .1 (see right side of chart for number of minutes, and record on appropriate day). Match the marker's 1 to the baseline, and mark an X on the chart next to number 5 on the marker.

Evaluating and Monitoring 193

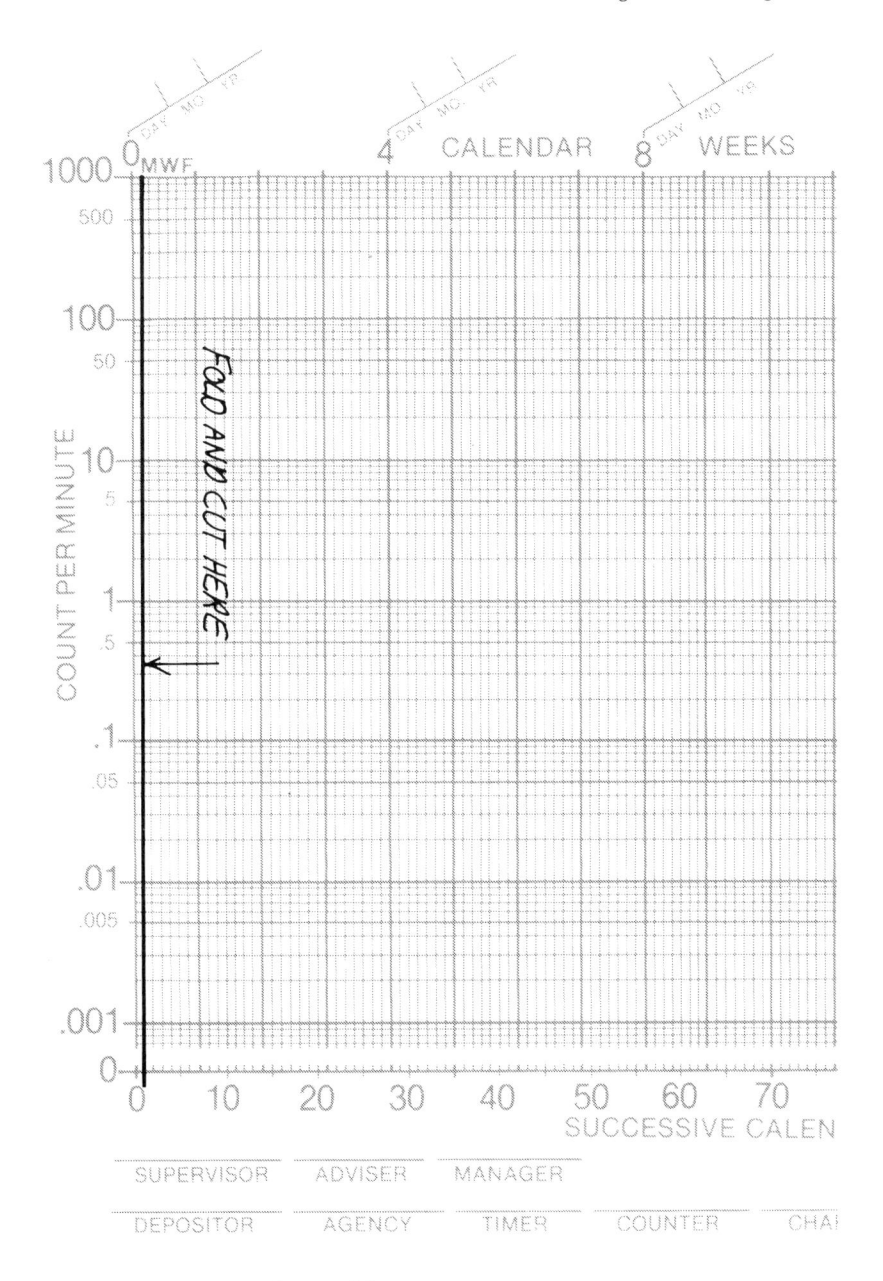

Figure 2. Establishing the record floor.

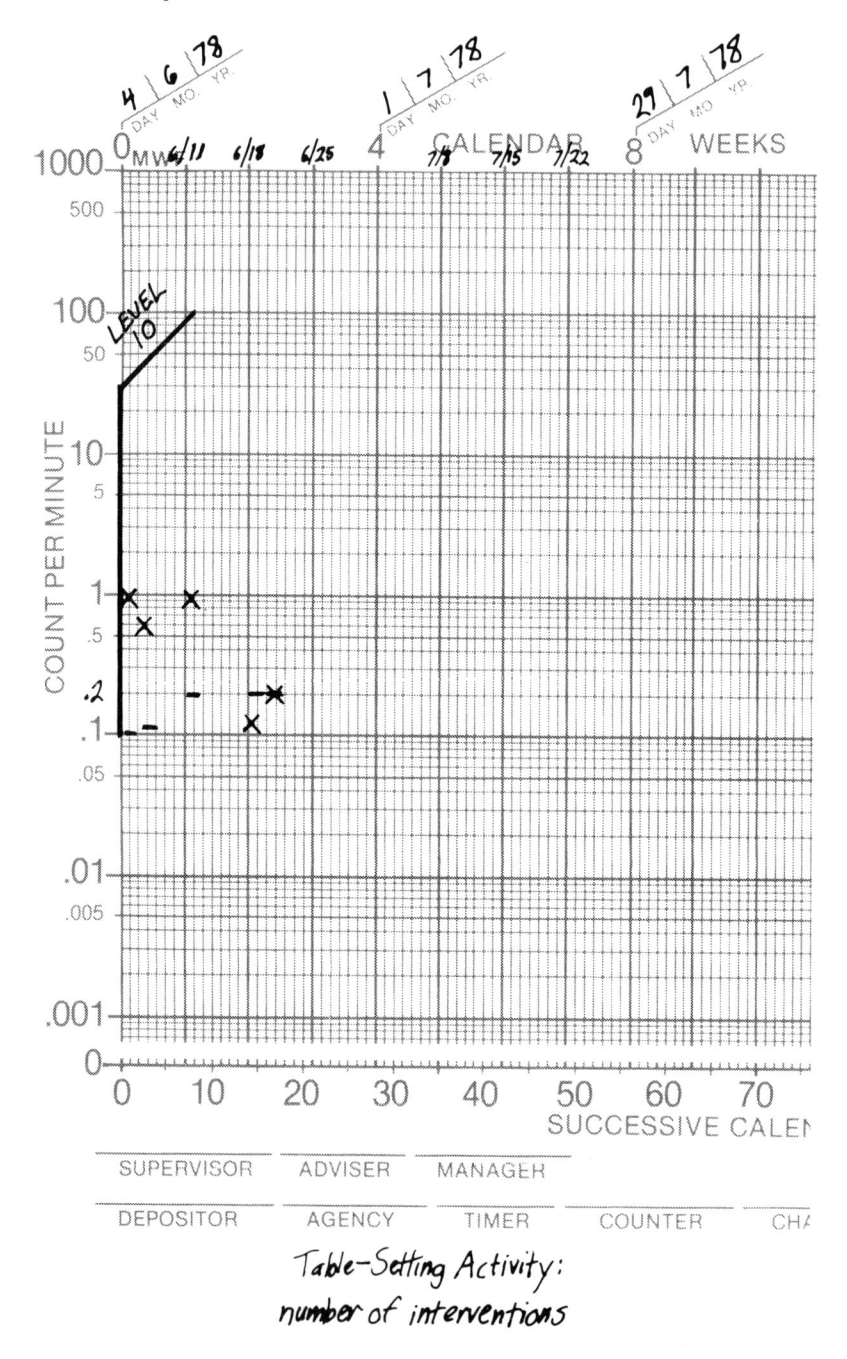

Figure 3. Recording the number of interventions necessary in a table-setting activity.

On Monday of the following week (June 12), the learner performs the activity within 5 minutes with five interventions. Draw in the baseline for 5 minutes (.2) for Monday, June 12. Match the marker's 1 to this baseline. Mark an X at number 5. By looking at the chart, you can see that the learner is performing at a faster rate of speed, without an increase in the need for interventions. For the sake of illustration, look at Monday, June 18. The baseline is still at .2, indicating that it took the learner 5 minutes to complete the activity. However, the X is marked below the baseline. This indicates that there were no interventions given. Any time you wish to indicate a "zero" count, that is, no interventions, no errors, no correct responses, etc., place an X slightly below the baseline.

Instead of recording the number of interventions, you may wish to record the number of correct and incorrect responses during a lesson. Incorrect responses, interventions, or any behavior that we want to decrease is indicated by an X. Any behavior to be increased, for example, correct responses, is indicated by a dot. Thus, if the learner is improving, the dots should slant upward from the baseline and the Xs should slant toward, and eventually continue below, the baseline. If the learner responds with an equal number of correct and incorrect responses, the dot and X will be on the same line.

At first reading, and without reference to the charts themselves, this recording procedure may seem complicated. However, the charts are very versatile and may be used in an even simpler way. If you are recording performance on the basis of the number of trials presented or if time is not significant to the task performance, you may simply draw in a baseline at 1. This eliminates the need for a marker. All you must do is find the correct day and record performance by finding the correct numbers on the left side of the chart. For example, in Figure 4, I am recording the learner's performance on a reading activity. I have indicated the activity and what I am evaluating (bottom right of chart). The baseline is drawn in at the 1 line, and I will record the number correct and incorrect within 10 trials, because the learner is working on 10 vocabulary words. I have also indicated that the words are presented on cards. In addition, I have written in, on the left side of the chart, "before practice." This specifies that I will test performance before reviewing and drilling the reading words. If you wish, the specific words may be listed somewhere on the chart or on a separate page preceding the chart. The lesson is conducted and performance recorded by marking the number of words read correctly and incorrectly on the appropriate day line. Looking at the chart (Figure 4), on Monday, June 5, the learner read six words correctly, and four words incorrectly. On Thursday and Friday, June 8 and 9, he performed with seven correct and three incorrect responses. After the weekend, he again made four incorrect and six correct responses. At the end of the third week (Friday, June 23), he made only one

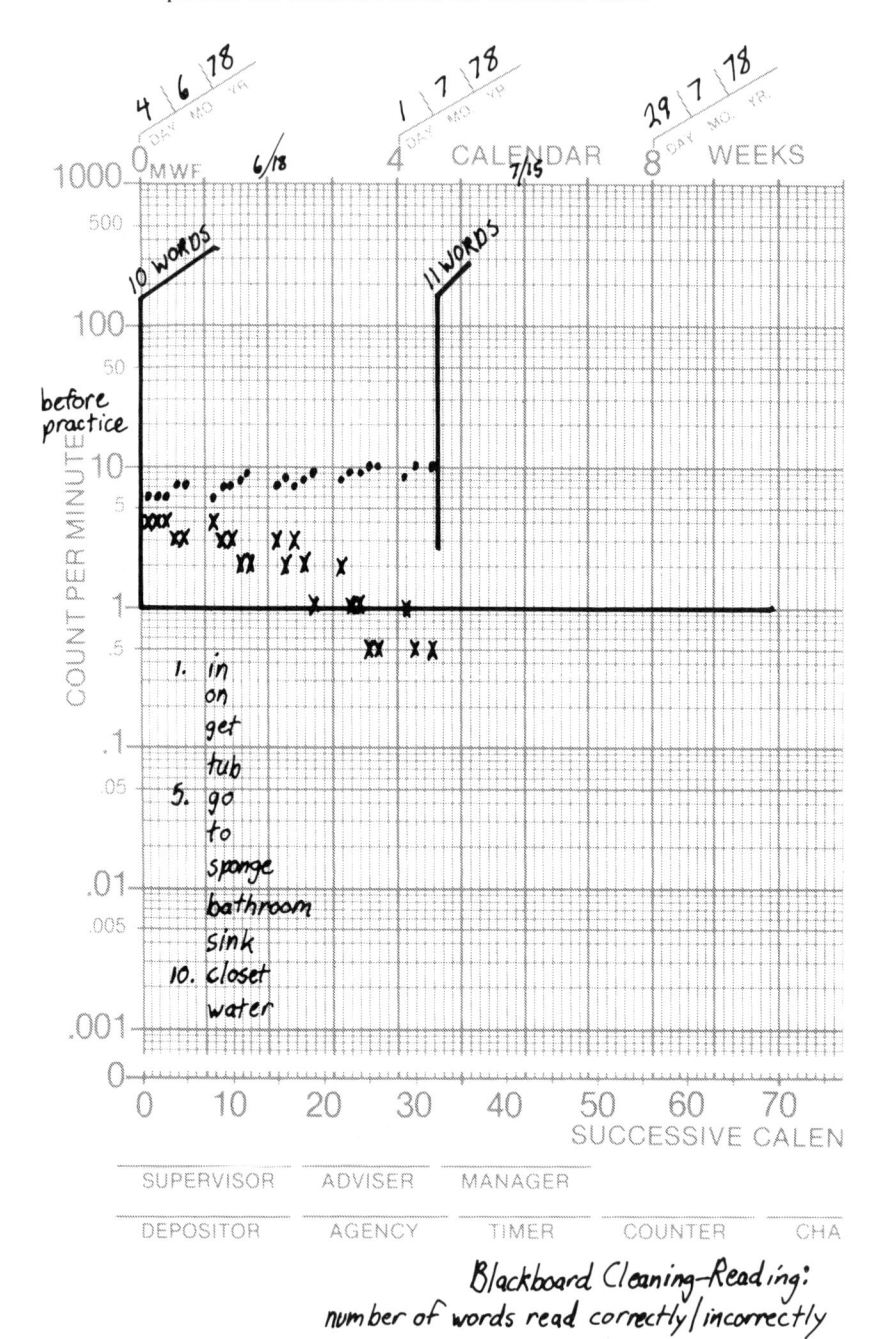

196   Preparation and Assessment within the Curriculum Model

Figure 4. Recording performance on a reading activity in the blackboard-cleaning curriculum unit.

error. By Thursday, July 5, he had responded with 100% accuracy on 4 days, and 2 days consecutively. Therefore, I decided to add another word. If, at any time, I had decided to modify the presentation, this, too, could have been written into the chart (e.g., recording after practice, color coding a word, drilling a problem word or words before testing, etc.). When reporting on progress, I have all the information needed to report accurately: the method of presentation (as described in the given lesson plan), the number of words presented and on what medium, the specific vocabulary words, conditions of evaluation ("before practice"), and the number of words read correctly/incorrectly.

The charts in Figures 5-9 are presented to illustrate the ways in which valuable information can be recorded directly on the chart. Lesson modifications, additions, and changes in procedures and objectives may all be recorded on the chart. This makes it unnecessary to write a new lesson procedure for every condition or individual. A basic lesson plan may be developed and individualized as needed, directly through information on the chart itself.

Figure 5 shows the progress of a learner performing a number/reading comprehension task. He must read a direction card with the phrase "get (number) (object)." Looking at the chart, the conditions of the lesson are identified: one direction per card, numerals 7-10, and objects placed in the classroom several feet from the work area. Within 3 weeks, the learner performed with 100% accuracy. The objects could then have been moved to a closet or adjoining room, but we decided to try putting the objects in the kitchen (on a different floor than the classroom). His performance was affected by this change, in that he made one or two errors on a series of 10 direction cards. Within 2 weeks, however, he was able to read a direction, go to the kitchen, and get the correct number of appropriate objects. The next lesson modification was to increase the number of directions on each card to two directions. We began back in the classroom, in order to have more control over his responses and to correct errors as they occurred. Within one week, he performed for 2 consecutive days with 100% accuracy, and the objects were then moved to the kitchen again. From this point on, the activity was complicated only by the number of directions presented on each card. Data collection allowed us to determine when to increase the complexity of the task and reflected the effect of these changes on performance.

Figure 6 shows the progress of a learner in performing the table-setting activity. His objective here is to set the table correctly, that is, to place each object in the correct position on a placemat. This chart does not reflect any interventions needed to improve work behavior, for instance, keeping the learner on the task. By indicating this on the chart, however, you may include such interventions in your recording. As discussed in previous chapters, I do not usually record interventions for behavior until the learner has

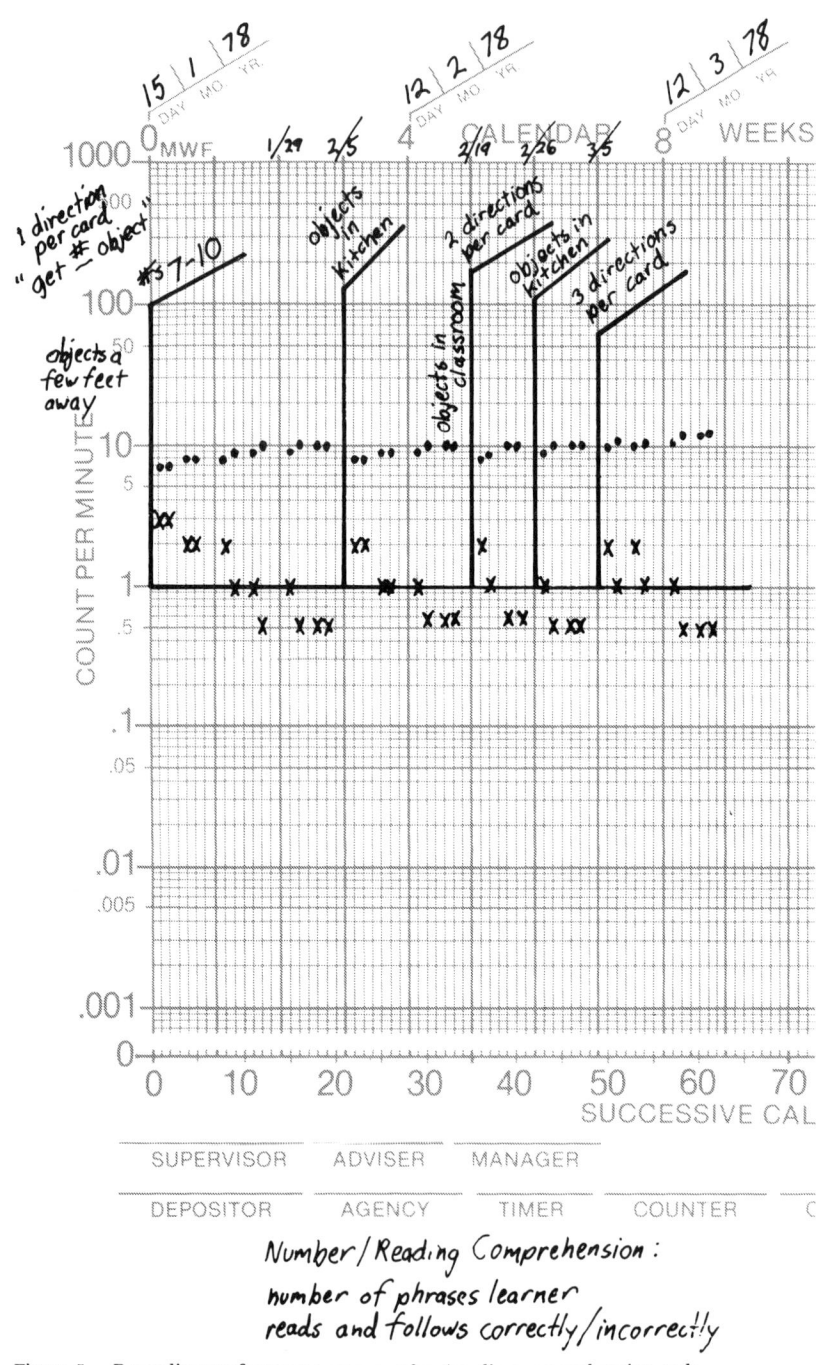

198   Preparation and Assessment within the Curriculum Model

Figure 5. Recording performance on a number/reading comprehension task.

ters, I do not usually record interventions for behavior until the learner has mastered the activity itself.

This learner progressed relatively smoothly, demonstrating the most difficulty at Level 3, which requires the learner to get each object from a shelf a few feet from the table to be set, and at Level 4, where two place settings are first introduced. In addition, the teacher introduced a lesson modification after the first week of training (pointing to each object in sequence). This nonverbal direction for getting each object in a specific sequence before placing it on the placemat immediately improved performance. It is written in on the chart and was eliminated when the learner consistently performed correctly (after 8 weeks). The removal of this intervention did not significantly affect his performance, and the learner was able to correctly set three place settings when this level change (from Level 6 to Level 7) was introduced.

Figure 7 charts the progress of a learner in following simple verbal directions. During the first week of training (January 16 to January 20), the learner was required to select the correct object from two sets of objects on his desk (forks, cups) and place them in a tub (also on his desk) or on a table (next to the desk) in response to the oral/signed direction ("Put cup/fork in/on tub/table"). During those 5 days, the learner followed only four of the ten directions correctly. Therefore, the lesson was modified so that the learner selected an object from the two sets of objects and put each object in one place (in the tub). This simplification immediately improved performance, so that the learner responded correctly to six of the ten directions. By the end of the 2nd week (January 27), the learner made only two incorrect responses. During the 4th week (February 6 to February 10), the learner responded with 100% accuracy for 3 consecutive days. The lesson was then made more difficult by requiring the learner to both select the correct object from two sets of objects, and put each in the correct place ("in tub" or "on table"). It took 4 weeks for the learner to achieve 100% accuracy, but progress was fairly steady. The next change procedure implemented was to eliminate the oral directions, so the learner would respond to the signed directions alone. As with other change procedures that increased the difficulty of the task, the number of incorrect responses initially increased. However, performance steadily improved, and the learner consistently performed correctly at the end of 2 weeks. The next change in the lesson could be to increase the number of different objects from which the learner selects or to add a third place in which to put the objects. The chart allows the teacher to determine how the learner performs, when to implement change, and the effect of that change on performance.

Figure 8 shows the progress of a learner performing Level 5 of the blackboard-cleaning activity, at language Condition H[a]. The objective of this condition is for the learner to express verbally each step of the activity as

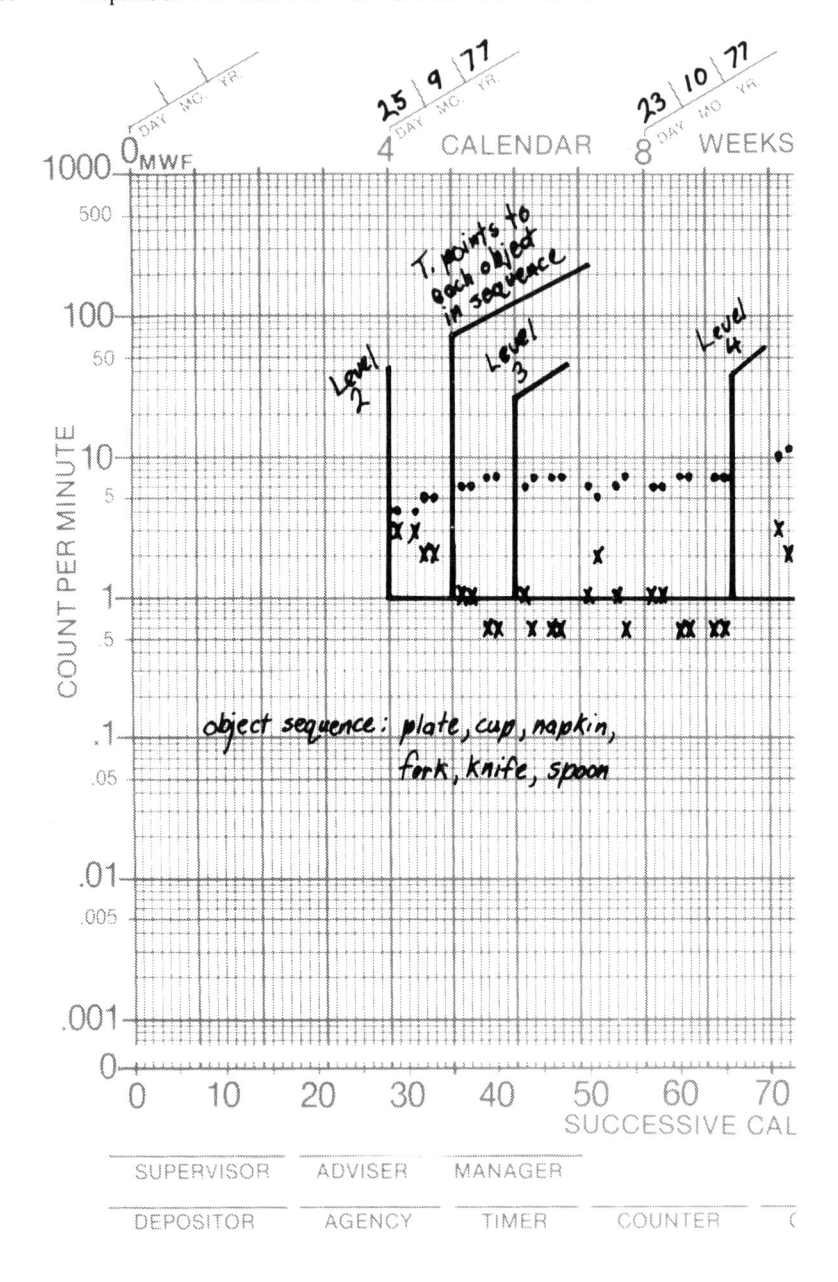

Figure 6. Recording a learner's progress in performing a table-setting activity.

Evaluating and Monitoring 201

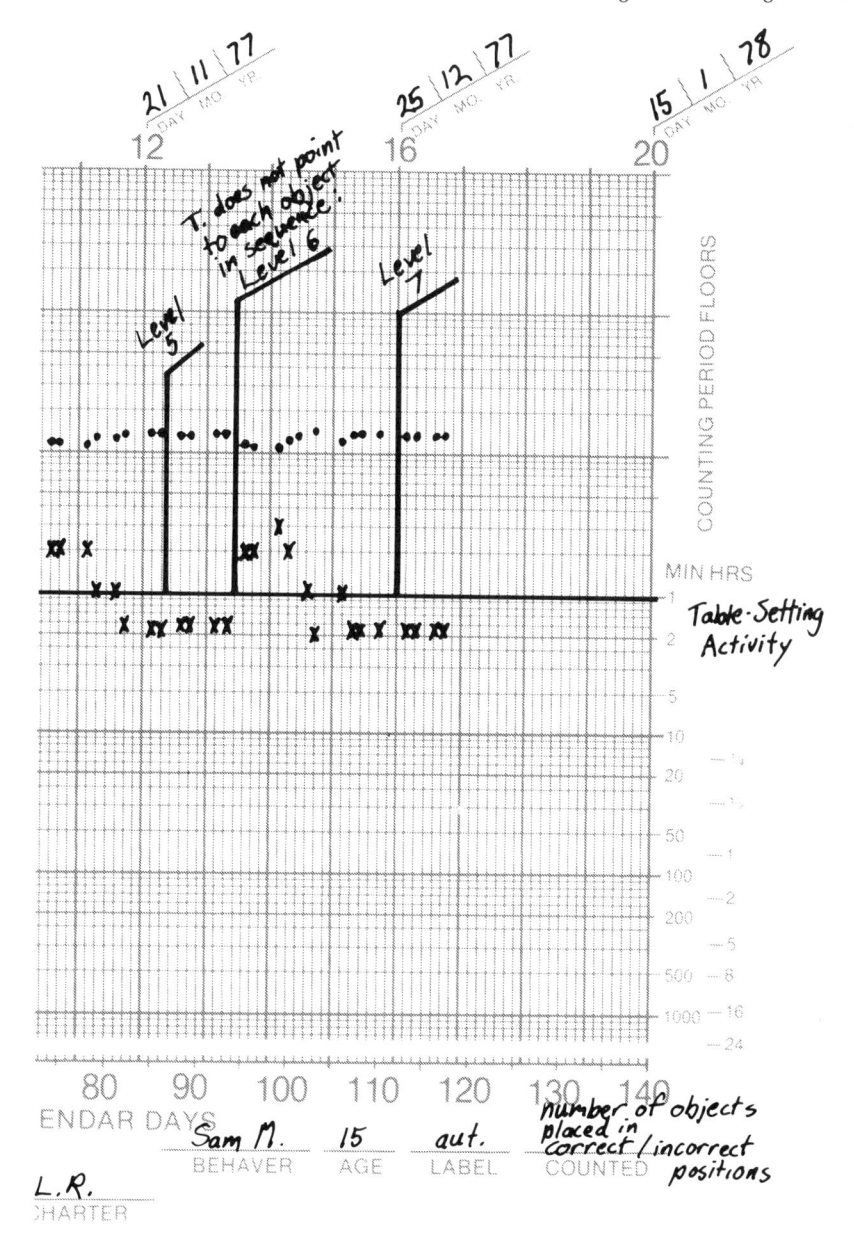

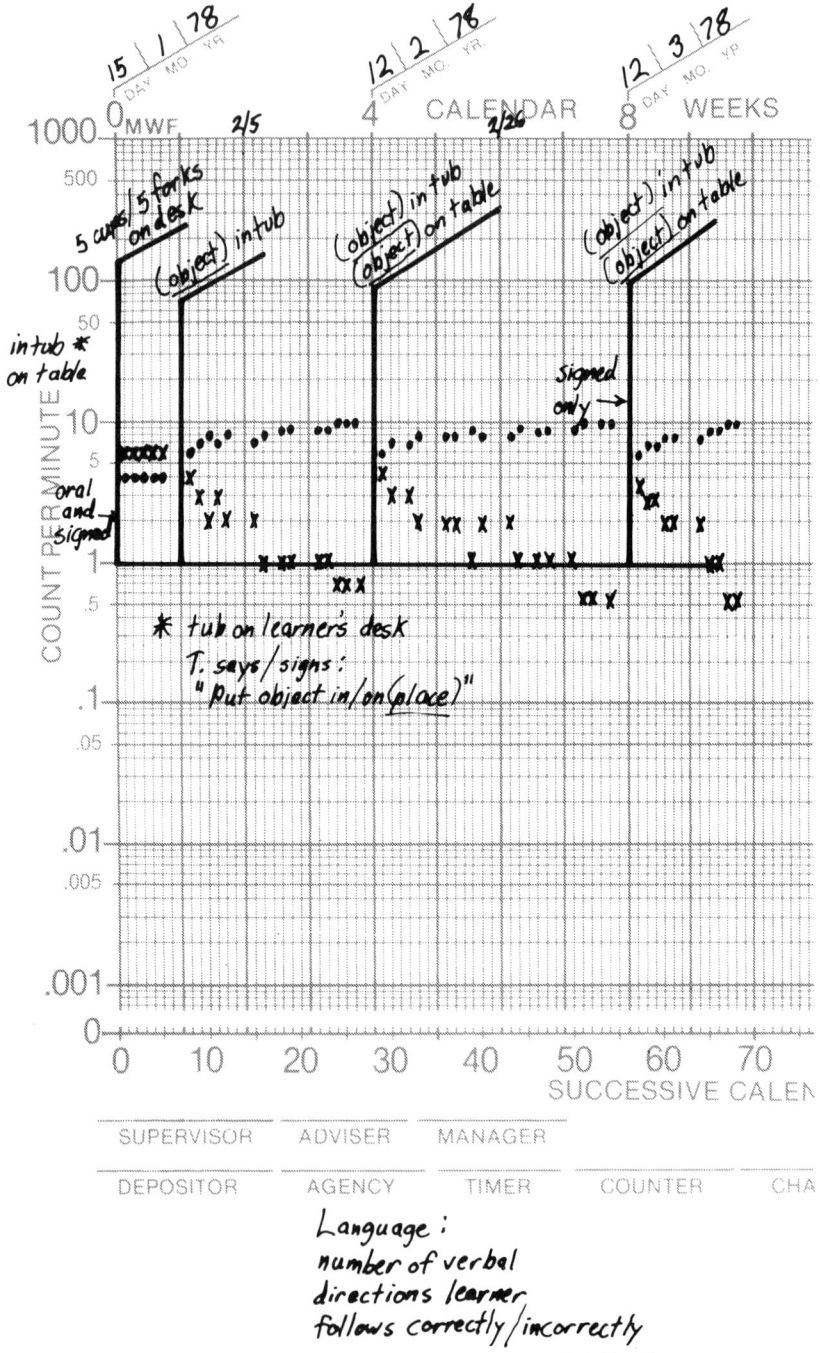

202   Preparation and Assessment within the Curriculum Model

Figure 7. Recording a learner's progress in following simple verbal directions.

Evaluating and Monitoring   203

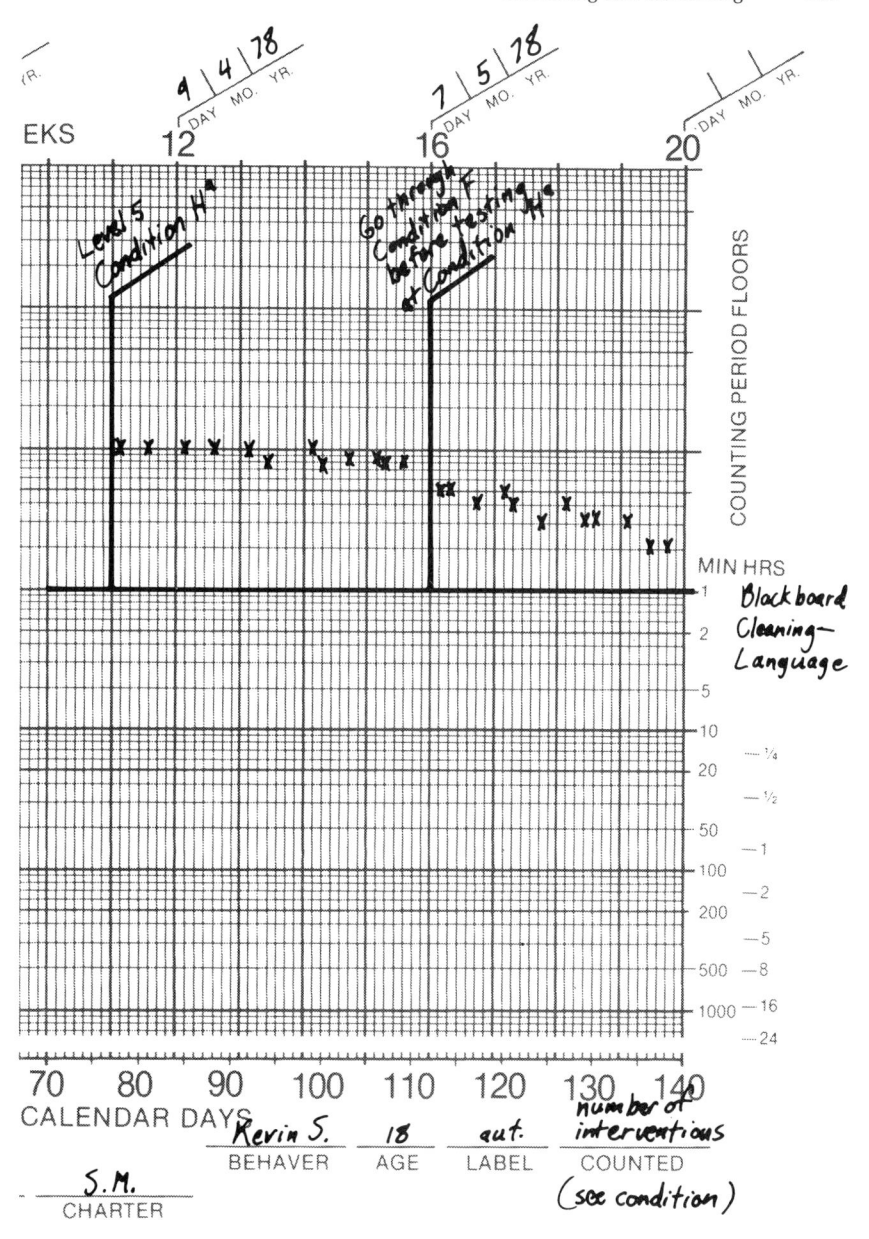

Figure 8. Recording a learner's progress at Level 5, Condition H[a] of the language skills area in the blackboard-cleaning curriculum unit.

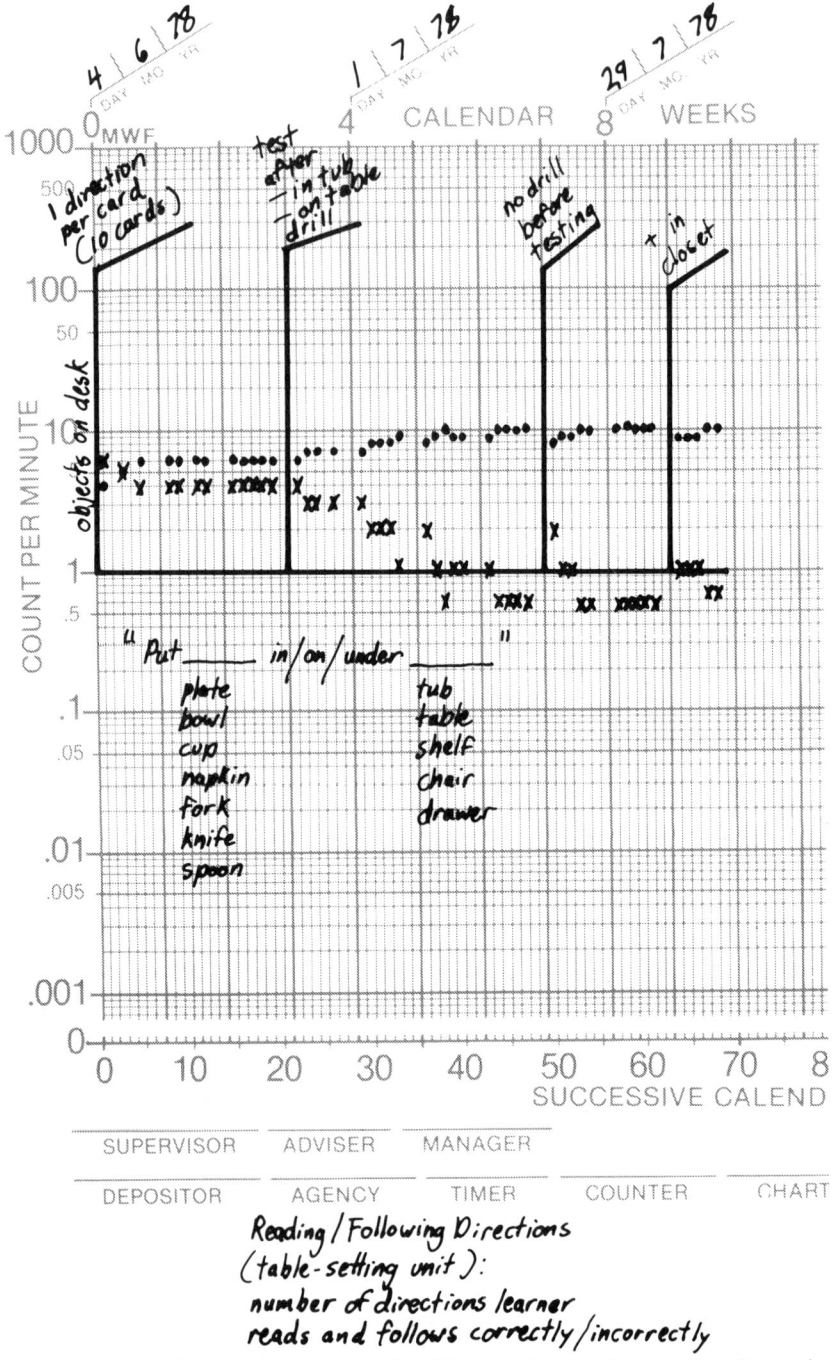

Figure 9. Recording performance on reading/following directions in the table-setting curriculum unit.

he performs it, in response to verbal cues (e.g., "Where do you go?" "What do you get?" "What do you turn on?" "What do you fill?" "What do you turn off?" "Where do you go?" "What do you clean?"). Interventions are recorded any time the teacher must provide the verbal model (e.g., "I go to the closet," "I get the tub and sponge," "I turn on the water," "I fill the tub," "I turn off the water," "I go to the classroom," "I clean the blackboard"). Over a 5-week period (April 3 to May 4), little progress was recorded. Therefore, the teacher implemented a change procedure. Before the learner performed the language activity, he went through Condition F. At Condition F, the learner sits at his desk and expresses each phrase from the blackboard-cleaning language unit (Level 5) in imitation of the teacher's verbal model. This practice session at Condition F immediately improved performance at Condition H^a. Progress is steady, and, when the learner performs at Condition H^a with no interventions, the practice session will be eliminated. It is hoped that progress will continue, without the additional language work before testing at Condition H^a.

The various charts presented illustrate the ways in which careful evaluation can serve as an invaluable aid in developing appropriate and specific objectives and in designing lessons to achieve those objectives. Evaluation may be done at the beginning of a lesson to determine performance before practice and to enable the teacher to gear the remainder of lesson time to specific errors. If errors are consistently the same, this information may also be written in on the chart and a change procedure designed to remediate the difficulty. For example (see Figure 9), one of my students consistently confused the written directions "in tub" and "on table" when reading and following directions ("Put (object) in/on/under (place)"). A change procedure was implemented in which the learner performed in response to ten direction cards, five of them "(object) in tub," and five, "(object) on table." This task was performed at the beginning of the lesson. Data were not recorded on these two sets of directions but, rather, on the regular lesson (a variety of ten directions including "(object) in tub," "(object) on table."). His improved performance reflects the effect of the "in tub," "on table" drill. Progress was slow but steady. Therefore the drill was continued until the learner performed with 100% accuracy. After several consecutive days with no incorrect responses, the pretesting drill was eliminated. There were initially one or two incorrect responses, but these errors were eliminated by the end of the week. The task was not made more difficult until the learner consistently performed correctly for another week, to ensure overlearning. At that time, another place ("in closet") was added to the lesson.

The teacher may determine how and when to evaluate performance. It may be more convenient or appropriate to the individual lesson to base an evaluation on the first 10 trials, a given amount of time, or on performance of a complete activity. Evaluation of a specific objective must be conducted in the same way, at the same time, however. Any changes in evaluation procedure must be noted on the data chart. For example, if a learner's performance indicates little improvement when tested on the first trial, you might test and record on the second or third trial (e.g., when performing a work activity). This must be noted on the chart, to determine the effect of practice and when the learner's performance can be recorded on the first trial. Any change in the order of lessons must be indicated on the chart. If a different teacher performs the lesson, this, also, should be noted. Changes, however minor, that may possibly affect performance must be accounted for in the evaluation to make it both valid and maximally informative.

MONITORING BEHAVIOR

The daily behavior charts may also be used to monitor behavior. As in recording lesson performance, any changes in responses to behavior, reinforcement, environment, medication, and so forth, must be noted on the chart. In this way, the teacher will have a valuable source of information regarding the learner/behaver. By using the same charting procedure for lesson performance and behavior, the teacher may compare the effects of behavior on learning. For example, you can monitor the effects of medication change on behavior and then compare these data with data on task performance. It is possible that changes that improve behavior (such as an increase in medication) may have an adverse effect on task performance. By having reliable records at hand, you can make informed decisions regarding an individual's complete program. People to whom you must report progress in learning and behavior will be less inclined to challenge clear data than opinion based on observation.

Keeping accurate data simplifies the task of reporting progress and determining "where to go from here." The teacher can identify specific problems in lack of achievement of an objective by referring to the data. For example, you can say that the learner can read and follow a set of ten directions, one direction per card (and specify the vocabulary involved), under a given set of conditions. Or you may report that the learner can identify numerals 1-5 when presented on cards, but makes two errors by confusing numerals "2" and "3." These data also allow you to identify appropriate objectives, because you can see where a learner is, how long it took him to get there, what the next steps should be, and what problems you may encounter (based on past data) in getting there.

Another benefit of ongoing evaluation is that it may serve to boost staff morale. When conducting the same lessons each day, or dealing with behavior problems, slow progress may not be readily apparent. A teacher may easily become discouraged or frustrated. A chart or graph of performance or behavior allows the teacher to actively and consistently implement and test various methods, and see the effects of each change procedure. A teacher does not tend to feel inadequate as long as he can exercise some control over the learning process. Keeping careful data enables the teacher to say, "Well, I tried this for two weeks and there isn't much improvement. Maybe if we try this. . . ." Unless the teacher reaches a point where he, and others, feel that every possible method and procedural change has been fairly tried without results, he can continue to find a rationale for his efforts. There are few, if any, cases where some change in some aspect of the learning situation does not affect performance. But if the teacher tries methods without recording an ongoing "picture" of the process, he may easily become impatient or discouraged. Some learners may demonstrate progress so slowly that it may appear as though they are not moving at all. But progress is, in fact, happening in many such cases. A teacher needs reinforcement of his efforts at least as much as the learner; seeing a "picture" of the learning process as it is altered can be a vital and rewarding part of effective teaching.

FORMAL REPORTING

The following report is an excerpt from a quarterly report from Benhaven submitted to parents and school boards. Each area of the school prepares a report on each student within that area (e.g., language, academics, readiness, gross motor, prevocational and vocational workshops). The reprinted section of the report is taken from the area of applied academics. The report includes previous objectives, statements on whether the objectives have been achieved, and comments on progress, and presents objectives for the next 3-month reporting period. (Included in the complete report is a section on social and behavioral objectives for each student. These objectives are worked on and monitored throughout the different areas of the student's school program.)

QUARTERLY REPORT

III. Applied Academics
Previous Objectives:
1. Work Activity: Learner will place table-setting objects in correct position on a table when given 2 placemats at angles to each other and the correct number of appropriate objects are on a shelf near the table.   ACHIEVING
2. Reading: Learner reads (signs) each of the following words from the table-setting activity when presented on word cards or on the black-

board: placemat, tub, in chair, plate, bowl, cup, napkin, fork, spoon, knife, get, on, table, drawer, closet, shelf, kitchen, go to.   ACHIEVED
3. Reading: Learner will demonstrate ability to follow a sequence of 2 written directions by reading a series of 6 cards (2 directions per card) and getting the correct objects from across the room (e.g., "get plate," "get fork").   ACHIEVING
4. Language: Learner will sign correctly in response to the following pictures from the Chicken Card Vocational Activity: chickens, water, sponge, scoop, feeder, feed barrel, egg table, eggs, refrigerator, egg carton, egg basket, pail, nest.   ACHIEVED
5. Reading: Learner reads (signs) the following words from the Chicken Card Vocational Activity when presented on word cards or on the blackboard: eggs, chickens, water, refrigerator, basket, pail.   ACHIEVED
6. Numbers: Learner will demonstrate one-to-one correspondence by counting out objects through sign when presented with objects and directed to count (1–8).   NOT ACHIEVED
7. Numbers: Learner will verbally (through sign) identify numerals printed on cards or on the blackboard (1–8).   ACHIEVING
8. Numbers: Learner will get correct number of objects in response to numerals (1–3) printed on cards, when objects are placed on the other side of the room.   NOT ACHIEVED

Progress:
1. G. makes 2–3 errors in placement of objects unless the teacher hands him each object.
3. G. makes 1–2 errors in getting objects in response to 12 written directions (6 directions, 2 on each card).
6. G. demonstrated much difficulty in differentiating numbers 7 and 8 when counting (5 errors in 10 trials).
7. G. makes 1–2 errors in identifying numerals 1–9 (within 8 trials).
8. G. gets 2 objects in response to the numeral 3 when he is not supervised directly.

New Objectives:
1. Work Activity: Learner will place table-setting objects in correct positions on a table when given 2 placemats at angles to each other and the correct number of objects are on a shelf near the table.
2. Reading: Learner expresses through sign (reads) each of the following 25 words from the table-setting unit when presented on word cards or on the blackboard: placemat, plate, bowl, cup, napkin, fork, knife, spoon, table, tub, chair, get, in, on, go to, kitchen, drawer, closet, shelf, *put, open, close, cupboard, dining room, set.*
3. Reading Comprehension: Learner demonstrates ability to follow a sequence of 3 written directions by reading a series of 5 cards (3 directions per card) and getting the correct objects from across the room (e.g., "get plate," "get fork," "get bowl").
4. Reading: Learner expresses through sign (reads) each of the following words from the Poultry Care Unit when presented with word cards or on the blackboard: eggs, chickens, water, refrigerator, pail, basket, *egg carton, egg table, barrel, scoop, nest, feeder, sponge, egg room, floor, chicken coop.*

5. Numbers: Learner will demonstrate one-to-one correspondence by counting out through sign a number of objects presented (1-7).
6. Numbers: Learner will identify through sign numerals (1-3) printed on cards or on the blackboard.
7. Numbers: Learner will get the correct number of objects in response to numerals (1-3) printed on cards when objects are on a table a few feet away.

14

DEVELOPING YOUR OWN CURRICULUM UNITS

The curriculum units presented in the appendices in Part IV are provided to serve as both comprehensive programs and as models for other possible curriculum units. The teacher may develop curriculum units that follow the structure, format, and methods provided here, based on a wide variety of activities.

First, an activity must be selected that can be taught within the teaching environment. It may be a self-care activity, a maintenance activity (e.g., washing windows, vacuuming a floor, loading a dishwasher), a daily living activity (e.g., food preparation), a vocational activity, or a recreational activity. It is also best to choose an activity rich in language skills and concepts that can be concretely demonstrated through the activity. However, an activity may be chosen to primarily teach the learner to perform a work activity adequately and independently, and then to teach the corresponding functional academic skills. Or an activity that the learner can perform adequately may be used as the basis for developing language, reading, and number skills.

Once an appropriate activity has been selected, it must be broken down into small, teachable steps, which will become the levels of performance. You may arrange these steps in sequential order (i.e., the order in which the steps of the activity are performed), in order from the simplest step to the most complex, or in some combination of sequential arrangement and progression from least to most complex steps. For example, the table-setting work activity is first broken down sequentially (Levels 1-3: teaching placement of objects under various conditions — on a template, on a placemat, when objects are several feet from the table to be set). The task is systematically complicated by increasing the number and arrangement of place settings (Levels 4-8), by varying the environmental conditions (e.g., objects provided, objects in drawers and cupboards), and by requiring the appropriate number and reading skills (Levels 11-12). The blackboard-cleaning work activity teaches the learner to adequately clean first a small, and then, a larger blackboard. Levels 3-5 involve getting and putting away materials, which may be performed at any level of the activity, but evaluated as part of performance only at those levels.

Once the teacher has broken down the work activity into levels of performance, he may determine the language involved in the activity. The language that will comprise the language program for each activity level may be based on verbal directions (e.g., "Cut the sandwich") and/or descriptions of each step of the activity (e.g., "I cut the sandwich"). Once these phrases or sentences have been identified, they may be broken down into the individual language components (vocabulary words). In addition, any concepts that relate to the activity (e.g., *big, little; clean, dirty*) may become supplementary skill areas. Any additional language that may be used within "Variations of the Language Program" may also be included in the language vocabulary.

The reading skills area of the curriculum unit is based primarily on the language skills area. Therefore, the vocabulary that has been identified as "language vocabulary" becomes the reading vocabulary as well. The phrases and sentences from the language units and from the variations of the language program serve as the directions that the learner must read and then read and follow (reading comprehension skills). As described in Chapters 7 and 8, the variations of the language program and variations in reading may be comprised of functional combinations of vocabulary from the curriculum unit plus any previously learned vocabulary.

The work activity chosen as the basis for the curriculum unit may not necessarily be well suited to the development of number skills. The teacher must determine whether materials can be used or adapted to teach counting and number/numeral/quantity association skills. If not, a more suitable unit (e.g., table setting) may be used to teach number skills. The teacher should also determine the applicability of number skills to the work activity itself. For example, some of the students at Benhaven School are taught to care for the poultry raised at Benhaven's farm as part of the vocational program. This activity involves gathering eggs, washing them, and placing them in egg cartons. A learner could be taught to count the eggs as well, a necessary part of monitoring egg production.

When the teacher has selected an activity, determined levels of performance for that activity, identified the corresponding language and reading material, and determined the suitability of the activity for work in the number skills area, he can begin preparing the necessary materials (Chapter 12) and can then implement the program.

Following is a list of suggested activities for curriculum unit development:

Washing hands	Loading and operating a dishwasher
Tying shoes	Table cleaning
Dressing	Sweeping
Operating washing machine, dryer	Vacuuming
Folding clothing, towels, etc.	Baking cookies, cakes
Washing dishes (by hand)	Preparing a simple meal
	Playing ping-pong

Individual needs and abilities will help identify the appropriateness of these activities for particular students. The teaching environment, as well, will help determine the suitability of a specific activity for curriculum unit development.

15
EVALUATION AND CONCLUSION

The value of any curriculum can be judged both in terms of its effectiveness as a teaching tool and by the factors involved in its implementation. The curriculum model presented in this book can be a meaningful and effective vehicle for achieving realistic gains and growth for severely handicapped learners. It has proved to be efficient in reducing paper work, simplifying reporting, and training staff members to carry out lessons. Student progress at Benhaven School/Community for Autistic and Neurologically Impaired Individuals, in New Haven, Connecticut, has supported the curriculum's effectiveness.

In discussing student progress, reference is made below both to general growth of the group as a whole and to achievements of specific students. A statistical analysis is not feasible at this time for several reasons. Benhaven has an ongoing enrollment, so students have been in my classroom under the curriculum for as short a period as 6 months and for as long as 3 years. Although several students are no longer at Benhaven, all are included in the general discussion of student progress. Statistical analysis is also precluded by the absence of a control group. It would be unethical for us, as educators, to deprive any students (the control group) of the best services we have to offer. Standardized measures of growth are inadequate because most of the students under the curriculum are either untestable or were untestable 3 years ago before the curriculum was instituted. The fact that some of those students are now testable is evidence of both academic and behavioral growth. Standardized measures of achievement and statistical analyses are not available at this time, but the need for further research into curriculum effectiveness is recognized.

The curriculum has been a part of 20 students' programs during the past 3 years. The period of time each student spends in the classroom has varied from several months to 3 years; some students are no longer attending Benhaven, having left for non-curriculum-related reasons (such as transfer to a program closer to home). The students are in the classroom for a minimum of 30 minutes, 5 days a week, to a maximum of 2 hours, 5 days a week. For most, this time in the classroom serves as the major portion of academic training, with the remaining periods of the school day spent in gross motor, self-care, language, prevocational, and vocational work. In addition, several students have one or more periods daily of more traditional (albeit special) academics, including reading, writing, and arithmetic. All the students have been diagnosed autistic or psychotic with functional retardation, and/or neurologically impaired. Two students are also deaf. Seven of the 20 students are nonverbal; that is, they demonstrate no oral language. All are between the ages of 13 and 22. Fifteen of them are either untestable or achieve age-equivalent scores under 3 years, 6 months on standardized tests (Peabody Picture Vocabulary Test, Illinois Test of Psycholinguistic Abilities). Sixteen of the 20 students demonstrate aggressive behavior toward others or themselves with varying intensity and frequency. All 20 had been rejected from other public and private educational institutions before entering Benhaven.

CURRICULUM EFFECTIVENESS

Changes in standardized test scores as a function of the curriculum alone are not available for most of the students. However, several students who were designated untestable in 1975 can now be tested with the Peabody Picture Vocabulary Test, with the Peabody Individual Achievement Test, and on some dimensions of the Illinois Test of Psycholinguistic Abilities. Their scores place them on pre-kindergarten grade levels and in mental age ranges between 2 years, 6 months and 3 years, 6 months. Most significant is their newly acquired ability to attend to the tester and test materials (both unfamiliar), to understand and carry out verbal and nonverbal directions, and to demonstrate appropriate work behaviors throughout the testing sessions.

Language Achievement

In terms of language achievement under the curriculum, all seven of the nonverbal students have learned to express at least three-word phrases through sign language. Six of them had never demonstrated the ability to express more than one word or a two-word phrase because of memory, attentional, sequencing, and other related problems. Six of them can sign an appropriate phrase describing each step of an activity taught within the curriculum, as they perform the activity. The 13 verbal students can also describe orally each step of an activity as they perform it, and eight students (two of them nonverbal) can describe the actions of another person performing the activity, in or out of the activity sequence, or instruct another person in how to perform an activity. Seventeen of the students can also suc-

Evaluation and Conclusion   217

cessfully carry out a variety of simple verbal directions composed of functional combinations of vocabulary from a given activity and previously learned vocabulary.

One of the most outstanding examples of achievement is H., whose spontaneous language was limited to requests to go to the bathroom. He has achieved all of the language objectives for more than six different activities (e.g., table setting, blackboard cleaning, table cleaning, assembling campaign buttons in the workshop, preparing a salad and sandwich, loading a dishwasher, and caring for the poultry at Benhaven's Farm), which means he can describe each step of the activities as he performs them, describe another person performing the steps of the activities out of sequence, direct another person to perform the activities, and follow directions involving concepts and vocabulary learned through the activities. In addition, H. has generalized these language skills so that he demonstrates them in nonstructured situations (e.g., on the playground, in other areas of the school, at home), and in any activity that he performs (if he has been verbally directed through that activity several times). He can also request any materials he needs to carry out an activity.

Another student is nonverbal and demonstrated no understanding of, or ability to express himself through, sign language when he came to Benhaven several years ago. He can now feed and water the chickens at the farm, gather and clean the eggs, and put them in egg cartons, in response to another student's signed directions.

In general, all of the students involved in the curriculum demonstrate improved language comprehension, probably because of the concreteness, repetition, and consistency within the structure of the curriculum. Students who never spontaneously expressed language other than a few requests (e.g., bathroom) now describe each step of an activity as they perform it when directed to "tell me how you _____." Needless to say, the students, teachers, parents, and others interacting with the students have benefited from this improved ability to understand and communicate.

Reading Progress

Reading is another area in which achievement is evident. Five students involved in the curriculum read phonetically but showed limited comprehension; nine demonstrated some word recognition skills, and six had no reading vocabulary and were engaged in readiness activities (e.g., matching shapes, letters, words) when they entered the classroom under the curriculum. Now, 19 students can read (16 read through whole-word recognition). Three students who entered Benhaven within the last year and had never demonstrated any word recognition skills are now learning to read words at a rate of one new word every week or so. Another student was unable to recognize any word other than his name, after 1 year of using conventional sight-word methods. Since he has been involved in the curriculum (almost 3 years), he has acquired a reading vocabulary of more than 50 words relating to several different activities. All but three of the students (including one who left Benhaven after 8 months) can read and follow a series of cards with a simple two- or three-word written direction, five can read and follow a sequence of two directions on each card in a series, and 12 can read and follow a sequence of more than three (up to 25) written directions on a series of cards. These skills have enabled nine students to perform various activities or parts of activities without direct supervision. That is, the teacher can give them a list of written directions involving going to areas of the school within and outside the classroom, and they can carry out these directions independently. Several other students demonstrate the ability to read and follow directions but are not ready to move out of the classroom without supervision because they have not yet developed appropriate work behaviors. For these students who lack the appropriate work behaviors but have acquired the necessary skills, improving the ability to work adequately and independently will become the primary goal. It is hoped that all of the students currently under the curriculum will achieve independence in some or all of the activities taught through the curriculum, and perhaps generalize these skills to any activity they perform.

Number Skills Acquisition

Number skills by their very nature are somewhat abstract and therefore more difficult to learn for some students. Eleven of the students can count out at least 10 objects in response to a verbal direction or written numeral. The other eight students still in the classroom are working on number concepts under 10. Those 11 students who have learned to use some number skills can therefore perform a wider range of activities. One of the students has the job of filling tubs with the correct number of appropriate objects for each of eight lunchrooms in the school. Several others use their number skills in the vocational workshop, filling orders for a specific number of items.

Work Activity Achievement

In terms of the curriculum unit activities, the students perform on a wide range of levels. For instance, 11 can complete at least one of the activities adequately and independently; no teacher interventions are necessary. Some of these 11 students can perform several of the curriculum unit activities satisfactorily and without direct supervision. The remaining students perform on varying levels of one or more activities, depending on their abilities, behavior problems, and the amount of time spent in the classroom each day. Most importantly, all are engaged in one or more work activity that requires learning specific skills, eliminating interfering behaviors, and developing appropriate work behaviors, such as perseverance, cooperation, speed, and independence.

Carryover

Another exciting effect of the curriculum has been carryover into other areas of the school and into the home. There has been a general improvement in student language comprehension and ability to communicate. Some of the reading and number skills are used in other areas of the school (e.g., setting the table when given written directions). Students demonstrate improved behavior and work skills in other areas of the school, and some parents have reported similar improvements in behavior at home and a willingness to engage in work tasks (e.g., making the bed, setting a table).

Affective Change

Another benefit of a well organized, highly structured, consistent curriculum, which can only be measured through observation, is affective changes. The curriculum allows each individual to proceed at his own pace, to work on a level just above his demonstrated level of ability, and to be repeatedly successful in attempts to perform a given learning task. Frustrations are limited, and opportunities for success and all the external and internal rewards of achievement are increased. The mood of the classroom is generally busy, active, and pleasant. Most of the students and teachers appear genuinely interested in whatever aspect of the curriculum they are working on. Many often smile and laugh as they perform the various tasks that give them and their teachers the satisfaction of accomplishment.

CURRICULUM IMPLEMENTATION

Identifying Goals and Objectives

The curriculum provides clear and explicit goals for each lesson and each student. This allows the teacher to direct energies toward achieving a specific goal, and efforts are usually rewarded with student achievement of that goal. Subsequent goals, and even the long range objectives, are spelled out so that everyone involved in a program knows where it is going. All that remains is reaching that point. Teaching experience and evaluations of each student's strengths and weaknesses can be used as the basis for determining specific procedures for achieving each goal. The initial amount of time spent in preparing materials for each curriculum unit can be less than 6 hours. These materials include performance objectives for each level of the specific activity, language and reading vocabulary lists, and phrases/sentences for the language unit of each activity level (see Chapter 12). The language teaching model conditions apply for any unit and need be written only once. Materials, such as word cards, number cards, and direction cards and lists, can be made up within a few minutes as needed for each student. In terms of lesson procedures, I have written up various procedures for teaching counting, numeral identification, object identification, word recognition, reading comprehension, and other skills with several different methods for teaching each skill (developed in response to individual student needs). The lesson procedures are written so that any of the specific content of the curriculum units can be "plugged in," without necessitating any changes in lesson procedures.

Teacher Training

Teacher training is simplified because both the goals and the methods for each curriculum unit follow the same structure and format; only the specific content changes according to the curriculum unit. If a teacher has been trained to teach word recognition skills using the table-setting curriculum unit, he can teach word recognition for any of the curriculum units. Any variations in teaching method are in response to individual students rather than the material being taught.

Record-Keeping

Recording data and monitoring progress are also relatively simple. As discussed in Chapter 13, precision teaching frequency charts are used at Benhaven, but any simple and appropriate record-keeping method can be used. It takes about 10 to 15 minutes to initially explain how to use the daily behavior chart, and everyone who conducts a lesson records data. Each lesson has an evaluation procedure, which may be to record correct and incorrect responses during a specific task, to record correct and incorrect responses for a given number of trials, or to record the number of teacher interventions necessary to perform a level of a task or complete a task (depending on the goal of the lesson). These data provide guidelines for modifying lessons, changing methods, and choosing appropriate goals for each student according to his style and pace of learning. Specific progress can thus be clearly communicated to other staff members, parents, and other interested parties.

Teaching Environment

The structure and staffing at Benhaven allow teaching on a one-to-one basis, as needed. However. it is also possible to teach two or more students in a group using the curriculum. Of course, some of the difficulties inherent in group teaching students with severe learning and behavior disorders will still be encountered. But the important factor to keep in mind is the level of ability of the students working together. The curriculum can be easily implemented in a group situation when students perform at similar levels on specific tasks and skills. It is not necessary, however, to teach only in groups of students who are at similar skill levels. For instance, it may be effective to pair a student who can express language with a student who can only follow verbal directions or imitate a verbal model. In addition to any academic gains made by the nonexpressive student, the student who can now play "teacher" gains a new sense of competence. Group lessons should also provide opportunities for social interaction and foster social behaviors, such as waiting, taking turns, and learning each others' names.

ADAPTATIONS TO CIRCUMVENT CURRICULUM LIMITATIONS

Limitations of the curriculum are primarily attributable to the setting in which it is implemented. The setting may restrict the types of activity that can be taught. If a teacher is restricted to the classroom, suitable activities must be chosen or appropriate materials brought into the classroom. For example, pictures of a student performing an activity outside the classroom (e.g., feeding the chickens at the farm) can be used as an aid in language and reading work. Work on that particular activity or a simulation of it within the classroom is not possible and must be left to the teachers in the appropriate area (e.g., vocational).

The curriculum may be difficult to implement within an institutional setting where staffing and other resources are relatively poor. These factors, regardless of setting, have an impact on effectiveness and usefulness of any curriculum. The severe learning and behavioral handicaps of the population for whom this curriculum has been designed demand adequate staffing in order for the programs to be carried out effectively.

Difficulties encountered within the curriculum may primarily be problems that arise generally in teaching the severely handicapped. Frustration, discouragement, and disappointment are likely to be felt in situations where progress is slow, the obstacles many, and the interference of behavior problems with learning frequent. At times, the teacher may feel inadequate, overburdened, anxious, and even angry. Working within a highly structured, systematic, and functional program, such as this curriculum, can help ease these feelings and eliminate much of the difficulty in questions of "What do I do now?", "Where do I go from here?", and, perhaps most importantly, "Am I teaching something worthwhile?" Seeing students busily engaged in work activities, attempting to communicate, and reading and following directions should make it relatively easy to justify and affirm your efforts.

Boredom, as a result of the repetitive nature of most activities and techniques, should be able to be stemmed by the step-by-step nature of the curriculum. Students are seldom bored by the activities because the tasks present new challenges to the learners and become systematically more varied and complex as each step in the progression of tasks is mastered. The boredom experienced from time to time by teachers can usually be counteracted by the progress (although it may be erratic and slow) demonstrated by the learner.

Frustration is usually a product of feeling as though there has been no progress or feeling as though one has tried everything without success. However, ongoing monitoring of performance enables the teacher to see progress and to recognize when to modify curriculum objectives and tasks so that the learner can perform successfully even at a very simplified level of any task. This should help to minimize teacher frustration, and, when objectives of a task are appropriate to a learner's abilities, the learner is challenged without feeling undue frustration.

SUMMARY

The development of appropriate objectives and educational opportunities is the primary rationale for this curriculum. It is designed to provide activities and objectives that meet the learner's educational needs and that, when mastered, will improve the individual's overall level of functioning and provide him with useful and usable skills. If you, as an educator, believe that individuals with severe learning and behavior disorders are entitled to an education, then you must also believe in their right to a proscriptive, individualized program, geared to their very special needs and abilities. The curriculum model presented here can help provide appropriate and effective educational programs. Well organized, efficient, and relatively easy to implement in both the school and home settings, it is a valuable tool for teaching a wide variety of worthwhile activities and skills. Although developed for persons with severe learning and behavior disorders, with further development to provide for higher level and more complex learning, the curriculum could also be used to teach less handicapped learners. Through implementation of the curriculum units, each day students can move one more step toward circumventing and overcoming their handicaps to become more productive, independent, competent, and happier individuals.

Part IV

Appendices
The Curriculum Units

Appendix A

TABLE-SETTING CURRICULUM

Work Activity Skill Area

Criterion for performance: Learner will proceed to next level of task after performing adequately and independently on given level three times consecutively.

Level 1 Learner visually matches table-setting objects (plate, bowl, cup, napkin, fork, spoon, knife) provided by teacher to correct positions *on a template.*

Level 2 Learner places table-setting objects provided by teacher in correct positions *on a placemat.*

Level 3 Learner places table-setting objects in correct positions on a placemat *when objects are on a shelf near the table.*

Level 4 Learner places table-setting objects in correct positions on placemats *when two placemats are side by side on the table* and the appropriate number of objects are on a shelf near the table.

Level 5 Learner places table-setting objects in correct positions on placemats *when two placemats are at angles to each other on the table* and the appropriate number of objects are on a shelf near the table.

Level 6 Learner places table-setting objects in correct positions on placemats *when two placemats are across from each other on the table* and the appropriate number of objects are on a shelf near the table.

Level 7 Learner places table-setting objects in correct positions on placemats *when three placemats are at angles and across from each other on the table* and the appropriate number of objects are on a shelf near the table.

Level 8 Learner sets a table correctly *with four or more place settings* when the correct number of appropriate objects are on a shelf near the table.

Level 9 Learner places table-setting objects in correct positions on placemats *when given a number of placemats and more than the appropriate number of objects* are on a shelf near the table.

Level 10 Learner places table-setting objects in correct positions on placemats *when given a number of placemats and objects are in a closet/cupboard and drawer in the same room as the table to be set.*

When learner demonstrates appropriate number skills:

Level 11 Learner gets correct number of table-setting objects from appropriate place (e.g., kitchen cupboards, drawers) and sets a table (in the kitchen or dining room) *in response to verbal directions.*

When learner demonstrates appropriate number and reading skills:

Level 12 Learner gets correct number of table-setting objects from appropriate place (e.g., kitchen cupboards, drawers) and sets a table (in the kitchen or dining room) *in response to written directions.*

Language Skills Area

1. **Receptive Identification:** Learner demonstrates reception of the following task-related objects, actions, areas of the environment, and descriptive words/phrases by selecting objects, performing actions, and going to areas of the environment in response to verbal directions:

placemat	tub	put
plate	table	set (the table)
bowl	closet/cupboard	open
cup	drawer	close
napkin	kitchen	in
fork	dining room	on
knife	get	
spoon	go (to)	

2. **Expressive Identification:** Learner verbally identifies the above-listed task-related objects, actions, and areas of the environment and uses the descriptive words/phrases appropriately.

3. **Language Program** *(a model for teaching language through an activity)*
   a. Language Units

   (Teacher direction: Set the table.)

Level (corresponds to Activity Level)	Basic	Expanded
1	plate on table	Put (the) plate on (the) table.
	bowl on table	Put (the) bowl on (the) table.
	cup on table	Put (the) cup on (the) table.
	napkin on table	Put (the) napkin on (the) table.
	fork on table	Put (the) fork on (the) table.
	knife on table	Put (the) knife on (the) table.
	spoon on table	Put (the) spoon on (the) table.
2	Same language as Level 1.	
3	get placemat	Get (the) placemat.
	placemat on table	Put (the) placemat on (the) table.
	get plate	Get (the) plate.
	plate on table	Put (the) plate on (the) table/placemat.
	get bowl	Get (the) bowl.
	bowl on table	Put (the) bowl on (the) table/placemat.
	get cup	Get (the) cup.
	cup on table	Put (the) cup on (the) table/placemat.
	get napkin	Get (the) napkin.
	napkin on table	Put (the) napkin on (the) table/placemat.
	get fork	Get (the) fork.
	fork on table	Put (the) fork on (the) table/placemat.

	get knife	Get (the) knife.
	knife on table	Put (the) knife on (the) table/placemat.
	get spoon	Get (the) spoon.
	spoon on table	Put (the) spoon on (the) table/placemat.
4	Same language as Level 3; may pluralize nouns.	
5	Same language as Level 3; may pluralize nouns.	
6	Same language as Level 3; may pluralize nouns.	
7	Same language as Level 3; may pluralize nouns.	
8	Same language as Level 3; may pluralize nouns.	
9	Same language as Level 3; may pluralize nouns.	
10	get tub	Get (the) tub.
	open closet/cupboard	Open (the) closet/cupboard.
	placemats in tub	Put (the) placemats in (the) tub.
	plates in tub	Put (the) plates in (the) tub.
	bowls in tub	Put (the) bowls in (the) tub.
	cups in tub	Put (the) cups in (the) tub.
	napkins in tub	Put (the) napkins in (the) tub.
	close closet/cupboard	Close (the) closet/cupboard.
	open drawer	Open (the) drawer.
	forks in tub	Put (the) forks in (the) tub.
	knives in tub	Put (the) knives in (the) tub.

	spoons in tub	Put (the) spoons in (the) tub.
	close drawer	Close (the) drawer.
	set table	Set (the) table.
	placemats on table	Put (the) placemats on (the) table.
	plates on table	Put (the) plates on (the) table/placemat.
	bowls on table	Put (the) bowls on (the) table/placemat.
	cups on table	Put (the) cups on (the) table/placemat.
	napkins on table	Put (the) napkins on (the) table/placemat.
	forks on table	Put (the) forks on (the) table/placemat.
	spoons on table	Put (the) spoons on (the) table/placemat.
11	get tub	Get (the) tub.
	go to kitchen	Go to (the) kitchen.
	open closet/cupboard	Open (the) closet/cupboard.
	# placemats in tub	Put # placemats in (the) tub.
	# plates in tub	Put # plates in (the) tub.
	# bowls in tub	Put # bowls in (the) tub.
	# cups in tub	Put # cups in (the) tub.
	# napkins in tub	Put # napkins in (the) tub.
	close closet/cupboard	Close (the) closet/cupboard.
	open drawer	Open (the) drawer.
	# forks in tub	Put # forks in (the) tub.
	# knives in tub	Put # knives in (the) tub.
	# spoons in tub	Put # spoons in (the) tub.
	close drawer	Close (the) drawer.

230   Appendix A

        spoons on table   Put (the) spoons on (the) table/placemat.

12   Follows written directions.

  b. *Language Conditions*

    <u>Reception</u>
    Condition A
      Teacher presents verbal commands (see Language Units, above) and puts learner through steps of table-setting activity.
    Condition B
      Teacher presents verbal commands and performs steps of table-setting activity for learner to imitate.
    Condition C
      Teacher presents verbal commands in sequence. Learner follows the commands and performs steps of table-setting activity.
    Condition D
      Teacher presents verbal commands out of sequence. Learner follows the commands and performs steps of table-setting activity out of sequence.
    <u>Imitation</u>
    Condition E
      Teacher provides verbal model (see Language Units, above) and puts learner through verbal behavior (at desk).
    Condition F
      Teacher provides verbal model for imitation (at desk).
    Condition G
      Teacher provides verbal model for imitation. Learner imitates verbal model and performs steps of table-setting activity.
    <u>Expression</u>
    Condition H[a]
      Teacher presents a verbal cue (e.g., "What do you get?" "Where do you put the _____?") in response to which the learner will produce the verbal behavior and perform steps of table-setting activity.

Condition H[b]
: Teacher provides a nonverbal cue (e.g., points to objects) in response to which the learner will produce the verbal behavior and perform steps of table-setting activity.

Condition I
: Teacher presents a situation in which the learner will produce the verbal behavior and perform steps of table-setting activity, such as setting the table for a meal.

Condition J
: Learner is in the activity situation. Learner must instruct another person/teacher in how to perform steps of table-setting activity.

Condition K
: Learner is in the activity situation. Learner must describe the steps of table-setting activity as another person/teacher performs them out of sequence.

4. **Variations of the Language Program:** Learner demonstrates reception of verbal phrases outside the context/structure of the activity situation and language units by following verbal directions consisting of functional combinations of the vocabulary listed in objective 1, above, and any previously learned vocabulary. For example:

Basic	Expanded
plate on shelf	Put (the) plate on (the) shelf.
get chair	Get (the) chair.
napkin in drawer	Put (the) napkin in (the) drawer.

5. **Supportive and Additional Language Skills:** Task-related materials and the activity situation may be used as a basis for supportive language work, such as speech articulation, and in teaching additional language concepts according to the needs and abilities of the individuals. Listed below are suggestions and examples of some language concepts and skills that may be taught with table-setting activity and materials as a basis.

Speech articulation
: Learner imitates phrases from table-setting language units.

Sequencing: Teacher instructs learner to get objects in the order he says/signs them (e.g., "plate, cup").
Visual memory: Teacher presents several objects (e.g., plate, napkin, cup). Teacher removes one or more objects and learner must indicate which object is missing.
Attributes — size: Teacher instructs learner to get the *big/ little* plate.
Attributes — color: Teacher instructs learner to get the *red* cup.
Adverbs: Teacher instructs learner to put the cup to the *right/left* of the plate.
Pronouns: Learner describes self/other performing steps of table-setting activity (e.g., "I get the placemat," "You get the placemat," "He/she gets the placemat").
Vocabulary additions and substitutions: Learner uses other vocabulary, such as *shelf, counter, tablecloth* (e.g., "Put the fork on the *counter*," "Fold the *tablecloth*").
Answering questions: Learner answers appropriately questions related to the activity (e.g., "Where do you put the plate?" "Where do you get?").
Generalization: Learner demonstrates understanding of task-related vocabulary by using words appropriately in sentences (related, unrelated to activity) (e.g., "I put the meat on my *plate*").
Verbal/written expression: Learner says/signs/writes sentences/stories when presented with one or more activity-related pictures and/or words.

Reading Skills Area

A. Word Recognition Skills
1. Learner demonstrates reception of the following task-related words by selecting/circling written words in response to verbal words:

placemat	tub	put
plate	table	set (the table)
bowl	closet/cupboard	open
cup	drawer	close
napkin	kitchen	in
fork	dining room	on
knife	get	
spoon	go (to)	

2. Learner verbally expresses (reads) each of the above-listed task-related words as presented (on cards, blackboard, paper).
3. Learner demonstrates reception of the following written phrases from the table-setting language units by selecting/circling each written phrase in response to a verbal phrase:*

Basic	Expanded
set table	Set (the) table.
get placemat	Get (the) placemat.
get plate	Get (the) plate.
get bowl	Get (the) bowl.
get cup	Get (the) cup.
get napkin	Get (the) napkin.
get fork	Get (the) fork.
get knife	Get (the) knife.
get spoon	Get (the) spoon.
get tub	Get (the) tub.
open closet/cupboard	Open (the) closet/cupboard.
open drawer	Open (the) drawer.
close closet/cupboard	Close (the) closet/cupboard.
close drawer	Close (the) drawer.
placemat on table	Put (the) placemat on (the) table.
plate on table	Put (the) plate on (the) table.
bowl on table	Put (the) bowl on (the) table.
cup on table	Put (the) cup on (the) table.
napkin on table	Put (the) napkin on (the) table.
fork on table	Put (the) fork on (the) table.
knife on table	Put (the) knife on (the) table.
spoon on table	Put (the) spoon on (the) table.
placemat in tub	Put (the) placemat in (the) tub.
plate in tub	Put (the) plate in (the) tub.
bowl in tub	Put (the) bowl in (the) tub.
cup in tub	Put (the) cup in (the) tub.
napkin in tub	Put (the) napkin in (the) tub.
fork in tub	Put (the) fork in (the) tub.
knife in tub	Put (the) knife in (the) tub.
spoon in tub	Put (the) spoon in (the) tub.
go to kitchen	Go to (the) kitchen.
go to dining room	Go to (the) dining room.

*Phrases are grouped by similarity in structure (all "get" phrases together, all "on table" phrases together, etc.) because this presentation should simplify the learner's task by limiting the amount of new material presented at one time. Eventually, the learner should read the phrases presented in any sequence, composed of functional combinations of the reading word vocabulary listed in objective A1.

4. Learner verbally expresses (reads) each of the above-listed phrases from the table-setting language units as presented (on cards, blackboard, paper).
5. Learner demonstrates reception of a sequence of written phrases from the table-setting language units by selecting/circling a sequence of written phrases in response to verbal phrases. For example:

Basic	Expanded
get placemat	Get (the) placemat.
get plate	Get (the) plate.
placemat on table	Put (the) placemat on (the) table.
plate on table	Put (the) plate on (the) table.
cup on table	Put (the) cup on (the) table.
get fork	Get (the) fork.
fork on table	Put (the) fork on (the) table.
get spoon	Get (the) spoon.
spoon on table	Put (the) spoon on (the) table.

6. Learner verbally expresses (reads) each phrase from the table-setting language units when a sequence of written phrases is presented (on cards, blackboard, paper). (Refer to examples under objective A5.)

B. *Reading Comprehension Skills*

1. Learner demonstrates understanding of the following task-related words by selecting the correct object/picture, performing the action, and going to area of the environment in response to written word:

placemat	tub	put
plate	table	set (the) table
bowl	closet/cupboard	open
cup	drawer	close
napkin	kitchen	in
fork	dining room	on
knife	get	
spoon	go (to)	

2. Learner demonstrates understanding of written phrases from the table-setting language units by following a simple written direction (on cards, blackboard, paper) from the following:

Table-Setting Curriculum 235

Basic	Expanded
get tub	Get (the) tub.
get placemat	Get (the) placemat.
get plate	Get (the) plate.
get bowl	Get (the) bowl.
get cup	Get (the) cup.
get napkin	Get (the) napkin.
get fork	Get (the) fork.
get knife	Get (the) knife.
get spoon	Get (the) spoon.
set table	Set (the) table.
open closet/cupboard	Open (the) closet/cupboard.
open drawer	Open (the) drawer.
close closet/cupboard	Close (the) closet/cupboard.
close drawer	Close (the) drawer.
placemat on table	Put (the) placemat on (the) table.
plate on table	Put (the) plate on (the) table.
bowl on table	Put (the) bowl on (the) table.
cup on table	Put (the) cup on (the) table.
napkin on table	Put (the) napkin on (the) table.
fork on table	Put (the) fork on (the) table.
knife on table	Put (the) knife on (the) table.
spoon on table	Put (the) spoon on (the) table.
placemat in tub	Put (the) placemat in (the) tub.
plate in tub	Put (the) plate in (the) tub.
bowl in tub	Put (the) bowl in (the) tub.
cup in tub	Put (the) cup in (the) tub.
napkin in tub	Put (the) napkin in (the) tub.
fork in tub	Put (the) fork in (the) tub.
knife in tub	Put (the) knife in (the) tub.
spoon in tub	Put (the) spoon in (the) tub.
go to kitchen	Go to (the) kitchen.
go to dining room	Go to (the) dining room.

3. Learner demonstrates understanding of a sequence of written phrases from the table-setting language units by following a sequence of simple written directions present in any order. For example:

Basic	Expanded
get placemat	Get (the) placemat.
get plate	Get (the) plate.
placemat on table	Put (the) placemat on (the) table.
plate on table	Put (the) plate on (the) table.
cup on table	Put (the) cup on (the) table.
open cupboard	Open (the) cupboard.
get plate	Get (the) plate.
plate in tub	Put (the) plate in (the) tub.
close cupboard	Close (the) cupboard.

(Activity and Language Unit Level 10)

get tub	Get (the) tub.
open closet/cupboard	Open (the) closet/cupboard.
get plates	Get (the) plates.
plates in tub	Put (the) plates in (the) tub.
get bowls	Get (the) bowls.
bowls in tub	Put (the) bowls in (the) tub.
get cups	Get (the) cups.
cups in tub	Put (the) cups in (the) tub.
get napkins	Get (the) napkins.
napkins in tub	Put (the) napkins in (the) tub.
close closet/cupboard	Close (the) closet/cupboard.
open drawer	Open (the) drawer.
get forks	Get (the) forks.
forks in tub	Put (the) forks in (the) tub.
get knives	Get (the) knives.
knives in tub	Put (the) knives in (the) tub.
get spoons	Get (the) spoons.
spoons in tub	Put (the) spoons in (the) tub.
close drawer	Close (the) drawer.
set table	Set (the) table.
plates on table	Put (the) plates on (the) table.
bowls on table	Put (the) bowls on (the) table.
cups on table	Put (the) cups on (the) table.
napkins on table	Put (the) napkins on (the) table.
forks on table	Put (the) forks on (the) table.
knives on table	Put (the) knives on (the) table.
spoons on table	Put (the) spoons on (the) table.

4. ***Variations in Reading:*** Learner demonstrates understanding of written phrases outside the context/structure of the activity situation by following written directions consisting of functional combinations of the vocabulary in objective A1 and any previously learned vocabulary. For example:

Basic	Expanded
plate on shelf	Put (the) plate on (the) shelf.
get chair	Get a chair.
napkin in drawer	Put (the) napkin in (the) drawer.

Learner demonstrates understanding of a sequence of written phrases outside the context/structure of the activity situation by following a sequence of simple written directions consisting of functional combinations of the vocabulary in objective A1 and any previously learned vocabulary. For example:

Basic	Expanded
get napkin	Get (a) napkin.
napkin on shelf	Put (the) napkin on (the) shelf.
go to kitchen	Go to (the) kitchen.
get chair	Get (a) chair.
chair in dining room	Put (the) chair in (the) dining room.

5. ***Supportive and Additional Reading Skills:*** Task-related materials and the activity situation may be used as a basis for supportive reading work, such as improving word recognition skills, and in teaching additional reading vocabulary. Any of the additional language skills suggested may be used as reading material, as appropriate. For example, attributes — size, color; adverbs — right/left.

    (*Note:* Before reading phrases, drills of the reading sequence — left/right, top/bottom — may be necessary.)

    Teacher may substitute or add vocabulary in language and reading. For example, shelf, counter, tablecloth, chair. ("Put the fork on the *counter*." "*Fold* the *tablecloth*.")

    Individuals with appropriate skills/needs may: 1) write vocabulary words in response to verbal words, and 2) write answers to questions related to the activity (e.g., "Where do you put the plate?").

Number Skills Area

1. ***Counting:*** Learner demonstrates one-to-one correspondence by counting out a number of task-related objects (forks, spoons, knives, plates, cups, etc.) presented.
2. ***Numeral Identification:*** Learner demonstrates recognition of numerals by selecting/circling numerals in response to verbal numbers.

    Learner verbally identifies numerals when presented (on cards, blackboard, paper).

3. ***Numeral/Quantity Association:*** Learner demonstrates association of verbal number and quantity by getting correct number of task-related objects in response to verbal number.

   Learner demonstrates association of numeral and quantity by selecting/circling appropriate numeral after counting out a group of objects.

   Learner demonstrates association of numeral and quantity by getting the correct number of task-related objects in response to numeral (on cards, blackboard, paper).

Reading and Number Comprehension Skills

Learner demonstrates reading and number skills by following written directions (one or more phrases) and getting the correct number of appropriate objects. For example:

Basic	Expanded
get 6 plates	
get 6 bowls	
get 4 spoons	
go to closet	Go to (the) closet.
get tub	Get (the) tub.
get 10 forks	Get 10 forks.
go to kitchen	Go to (the) kitchen.
get 5 plates	Get 5 plates.
plates on table	Put (the) plates on (the) table.
get 2 chairs	Get 2 chairs.

Activity Level 12 (see Language Unit for Activity Level 11).

Supplementary Skills Area

Fine Motor

Learner traces with finger numerals/letters/words on blackboard/paper.

Learner traces with chalk/pencil numerals/letters/words on blackboard/paper.

Learner copies numerals/letters/words on blackboard/paper.

Learner writes numerals/letters/words on blackboard/paper in response to verbal numbers/letters/words.

Learner writes correct numerals on blackboard/paper after counting out a number of objects.

Learner writes words on blackboard/paper in response to verbal words.

Learner writes words on blackboard/paper in response to objects.

Appendix B
BLACKBOARD-CLEANING CURRICULUM

Work Activity Skill Area

Criterion for performance: Learner will proceed to next level of task after performing appropriately and independently on given level three times consecutively.

Level 1 Learner cleans a small (9 sq. ft.) blackboard when provided with a wet sponge and a tub of warm water.
Level 2 Learner cleans a *larger blackboard* when provided with a wet sponge and a tub of warm water.
Level 3 Learner *will go to a sink, fill a tub with warm water when the tub and sponge are provided,* and clean a blackboard.
Level 4 Learner *will get a tub and sponge from appropriate place (e.g., closet),* go to a sink and fill the tub with warm water, and clean a blackboard.
Level 5 Learner will get a tub and sponge from appropriate place (e.g., closet), go to a sink and fill the tub with warm water, clean a blackboard, *empty the dirty water into the sink, and return sponge and tub to appropriate place.*

When learner demonstrates appropriate reading skills:

Level 6 Learner will get a tub and sponge from appropriate place (e.g., closet), go to a sink and fill the tub with warm water, clean a blackboard, empty the dirty water into the sink, and return sponge and tub to appropriate place *in response to written directions.*

Language Skills Area

1. ***Receptive Identification:*** Learner demonstrates reception of the following task-related objects, actions, areas of environment, and descriptive words/phrases by selecting objects, performing actions, and going to areas of the environment in response to verbal directions:

tub	get	put
sponge	go (to)	(put) down
sink	turn	pour
hot water	on	in
cold water	off	on
blackboard	wet	dirty (water)
kitchen/bathroom	squeeze	
closet	clean/wash	
classroom (any rooms where blackboards may be cleaned)		

2. ***Expressive Identification:*** Learner verbally identifies the above-listed task-related objects, actions, areas of the environment, and uses descriptive words/phrases appropriately.
3. ***Language Program*** *(a model for teaching language through an activity)*
   a. Language Units

   (Teacher direction: Clean/wash the blackboard.)

Level (corresponds to Activity Level)	Basic	Expanded
1	tub down	Put (the) tub down.
	wet sponge	Wet (the) sponge.
	squeeze sponge	Squeeze (the) sponge.
	clean/wash blackboard	Clean/wash (the) blackboard.
	sponge in tub	Put (the) sponge in (the) tub.
2	Same language as Level 1.	

Blackboard-Cleaning Curriculum 243

3		go to bathroom/ kitchen	Go to (the) bathroom/ kitchen.
		go to sink	Go to (the) sink.
		cold water on	Turn on (the) cold water.
		hot water on	Turn on (the) hot water.
		water in tub	Put (the) water in (the) tub.
		hot water off	Turn off (the) hot water.
		cold water off	Turn off (the) cold water.
		get tub	Get (the) tub.
		go to classroom	Go to (the) classroom.
		tub down	Put (the) tub down.
		wet sponge	Wet (the) sponge.
		squeeze sponge	Squeeze (the) sponge.
		clean/wash blackboard	Clean/wash (the) blackboard.
		sponge in tub	Put (the) sponge in (the) tub.
4		go to closet	Go to (the) closet.
		get tub	Get (the) tub.
		get sponge	Get (the) sponge.
		sponge in tub	Put (the) sponge in (the) tub.
		go to bathroom/ kitchen	Go to (the) bathroom/ kitchen.
		go to sink	Go to (the) sink.
		cold water on	Turn (on) (the) cold water.
		hot water on	Turn (on) (the) hot water.
		water in tub	Put (the) water in (the) tub.
		hot water off	Turn (off) (the) hot water.
		cold water off	Turn (off) (the) cold water.
		get tub	Get (the) tub.
		go to classroom	Go to (the) classroom.
		tub down	Put (the) tub down.
		wet sponge	Wet (the) sponge.
		squeeze sponge	Squeeze (the) sponge.

Appendix B

clean/wash blackboard	Clean/wash (the) blackboard.
sponge in tub	Put (the) sponge in (the) tub.

5   Same language as Level 4 with the following additions:

get tub	Get (the) tub.
go to bathroom/ kitchen	Go to (the) bathroom/ kitchen.
go to sink	Go to (the) sink.
dirty water in sink	Pour (the) dirty water in (the) sink.
sponge in tub	Put (the) sponge in (the) tub.
get tub	Get (the) tub.
go to classroom	Go to (the) classroom.
go to closet	Go to (the) closet.
tub in closet	Put (the) tub in (the) closet.

6   Follows written directions.

   b. *Language Conditions*

Reception

Condition A

Teacher presents verbal commands (see Language Units, above) and puts learner through steps of blackboard-cleaning activity.

Condition B

Teacher presents verbal commands and performs steps of blackboard-cleaning activity for learner to imitate.

Condition C

Teacher presents verbal commands in sequence. Learner follows the commands and performs steps of blackboard-cleaning activity.

Condition D

Teacher presents verbal commands out of sequence. Learner follows the commands and performs steps of blackboard-cleaning activity out of sequence.

Imitation

Condition E
> Teacher provides verbal model (see Language Units, above) and puts learner through verbal behavior (at desk).

Condition F
> Teacher provides verbal model for imitation (at desk).

Condition G
> Teacher provides verbal model for imitation. Learner imitates verbal model and performs steps of blackboard-cleaning activity.

Expression

Condition H[a]
> Teacher presents a verbal cue (e.g., "What do you get?" "Where do you put the _____?") in response to which the learner will produce the verbal behavior and perform steps of blackboard-cleaning activity.

Condition H[b]
> Teacher provides a nonverbal cue (e.g., points to objects) in response to which the learner will produce the verbal behavior and perform steps of blackboard-cleaning activity.

Condition I
> Teacher presents a situation in which the learner will produce the verbal behavior and perform steps of blackboard-cleaning activity, such as cleaning a dirty blackboard.

Condition J
> Learner is in the activity situation. Learner must instruct another person/teacher in how to perform steps of blackboard-cleaning activity.

Condition K
> Learner is in the activity situation. Learner must describe the steps of blackboard-cleaning activity as another person/teacher performs them out of sequence.

4. ***Variations of the Language Program:*** Learner demonstrates reception of verbal phrases outside the context/structure of the activity situation and language units by following verbal

directions consisting of functional combinations of the vocabulary listed in objective 1, above, and any previously learned vocabulary. For example:

Basic	Expanded
hot water in pot	Put hot water in (the) pot.
turn off light	Turn off (the) light.

5. ***Supportive and Additional Language Skills:*** Task-related materials and the activity situation may be used as a basis for supportive language work, such as speech articulation, and in teaching additional language concepts according to the needs and abilities of the individuals. Listed below are suggestions and examples of some language concepts and skills that may be taught with blackboard-cleaning activity and materials as a basis.

Speech articulation: Learner imitates phrases from blackboard-cleaning language units.

Sequencing: Teacher instructs learner to get objects in the order he says/signs them (e.g., "sponge/tub").

Visual memory: Teacher presents several objects (e.g., eraser, sponge, tub). Teacher removes one or more objects and learner must indicate which object is missing.

Concepts: clean/dirty

Pronouns: Learner describes self/other performing steps of blackboard-cleaning activity (e.g., "I get the sponge," "You get the sponge," "He/she gets the sponge").

Vocabulary additions and substitutions: Learner uses other vocabulary (e.g., "*Pick up* the tub," "*Fill* the tub *with* water," "*Pour* the water in the sink," "*Empty* the tub," "Put the tub *away*").

Answering questions: Learner answers appropriately questions related to activity (e.g., "Where do you pour the dirty water?" "Where do you put the tub?").

Generalization: Learner demonstrates understanding of task-related vocabulary by using words appropriately in sentences (related, unrelated to activity) (e.g., "I write on the *blackboard*," "I *clean* the counter").

Verbal/written expression: Learner says/signs/writes sentences/stories when presented with one or more activity-related pictures and/or words.

Reading Skills Area

A. *Word Recognition Skills*

1. Learner demonstrates reception of the following task-related words by selecting/circling written words in response to verbal words:

tub	get	put
sponge	go (to)	(put) down
sink	turn	pour
hot water	on	in
cold water	off	on
blackboard	wet	dirty (water)
kitchen/bathroom	squeeze	
closet	clean/wash	
classroom (any rooms where blackboards may be cleaned)		

2. Learner verbally expresses (reads) each of the above-listed task-related words as presented (on cards, blackboard, paper).
3. Learner demonstrates reception of the following written phrases from blackboard-cleaning language units by selecting/circling each written phrase in response to a verbal phrase:*

Basic	Expanded
clean blackboard	Clean (the) blackboard.
get tub	Get (the) tub.
get sponge	Get (the) sponge.
wet sponge	Wet (the) sponge.
squeeze sponge	Squeeze (the) sponge.
tub down	Put (the) tub down.
tub in closet	Put (the) tub in (the) closet.
sponge in tub	Put (the) sponge in (the) tub.
water in tub	Put (the) water in (the) tub.
dirty water in sink	Pour (the) dirty water in (the) sink.
cold water on	Turn on (the) cold water.
cold water off	Turn off (the) cold water.
hot water on	Turn on (the) hot water.
hot water off	Turn off (the) hot water.
go to closet	Go to (the) closet.
go to bathroom/ kitchen	Go to (the) bathroom/kitchen.
go to sink	Go to (the) sink.
go to classroom	Go to (the) classroom.

*Phrases are grouped by similarity in structure (all "in tub" phrases together, all "go to" phrases together, etc.) because this presentation should simplify the learner's task by limiting the amount of new material presented at one time. Eventually, the learner should read phrases presented in any sequence, composed of functional combinations of reading vocabulary listed in objective A1.

4. Learner verbally expresses (reads) each of the above-listed phrases from the blackboard-cleaning language units as presented (on cards, blackboard, paper).
5. Learner demonstrates reception of a sequence of written phrases from the blackboard-cleaning language units by selecting/circling a sequence of written phrases in response to verbal phrases. For example:

Basic	Expanded
get tub	Get (the) tub.
get sponge	Get (the) sponge.
go to closet	Go to (the) closet.
get tub	Get (the) tub.
get sponge	Get (the) sponge.
go to closet	Go to (the) closet.
get tub	Get (the) tub.
get sponge	Get (the) sponge.
sponge in tub	Put (the) sponge in (the) tub.

6. Learner verbally expresses (reads) each phrase from the blackboard-cleaning language units when a sequence of written phrases is presented (on cards, blackboard, paper). (Refer to examples under objective A5.)

B. Reading Comprehension Skills

1. Learner demonstrates understanding of the following task-related words by selecting the correct object/picture, performing the action, and going to area of the environment in response to written word:

tub	get	put
sponge	go (to)	(put) down
sink	turn	pour
hot water	on	in

cold water	off	on
blackboard	wet	dirty (water)
kitchen/bathroom	squeeze	
closet	clean	
classroom (any rooms where blackboards may be cleaned)		

2. Learner demonstrates understanding of written phrases from the blackboard-cleaning language units by following a simple written direction (on cards, blackboard, paper) from the following:

Basic	Expanded
clean blackboard	Clean (the) blackboard.
get tub	Get (the) tub.
get sponge	Get (the) sponge.
wet sponge	Wet (the) sponge.
squeeze sponge	Squeeze (the) sponge.
tub down	Put (the) tub down.
tub in closet	Put (the) tub in (the) closet.
sponge in tub	Put (the) sponge in (the) tub.
water in tub	Put (the) water in (the) tub.
dirty water in sink	Pour (the) dirty water in (the) sink.
cold water on	Turn on (the) cold water.
cold water off	Turn off (the) cold water.
hot water on	Turn on (the) hot water.
hot water off	Turn off (the) hot water.
go to closet	Go to (the) closet.
go to bathroom/ kitchen	Go to (the) bathroom/kitchen.
go to sink	Go to (the) sink.
go to classroom	Go to (the) classroom.

3. Learner demonstrates understanding of a sequence of written phrases from the blackboard-cleaning language units by following a sequence of simple written directions presented in any order. For example:

Basic	Expanded
get tub	Get (the) tub.
get sponge	Get (the) sponge.
go to closet	Go to (the) closet.
get tub	Get (the) tub.
get sponge	Get (the) sponge.

go to closet	Go to (the) closet.
get tub	Get (the) tub.
get sponge	Get (the) sponge.
sponge in tub	Put (the) sponge in (the) tub.

(Activity and Language Unit Level 6)

go to closet	Go to (the) closet.
get tub	Get (the) tub.
get sponge	Get (the) sponge.
sponge in tub	Put (the) sponge in (the) tub.
go to bathroom/ kitchen	Go to (the) bathroom/kitchen.
go to sink	Go to (the) sink.
cold water on	Turn on (the) cold water.
hot water on	Turn on (the) hot water.
water in tub	Put water in (the) tub.
hot water off	Turn off (the) hot water.
cold water off	Turn off (the) cold water.
get tub	Get (the) tub.
go to classroom	Go to (the) classroom.
tub down	Put (the) tub down.
wet sponge	Wet (the) sponge.
squeeze sponge	Squeeze (the) sponge.
clean blackboard	Clean (the) blackboard.
go to bathroom/ kitchen	Go to (the) bathroom/kitchen.
go to sink	Go to (the) sink.
dirty water in sink	Put (the) dirty water in (the) sink.
sponge in tub	Put (the) sponge in (the) tub.
get tub	Get (the) tub.
go to classroom	Go to (the) classroom.
go to closet	Go to (the) closet.
tub in closet	Put (the) tub in (the) closet.

4. ***Variations in Reading:*** Learner demonstrates understanding of written phrases outside the context/structure of the activity situation by following written directions consisting of functional combinations of the vocabulary in objective A1 and any previously learned vocabulary. For example:

Basic	Expanded
hot water in pot	Put hot water in (the) pot.
turn off light	Turn off (the) light.

Learner demonstrates understanding of a sequence of written phrases outside the context/structure of the activity situation by following a sequence of simple written directions consisting of functional combinations of the vocabulary in objective A1 and any previously learned vocabulary. For example:

Basic	Expanded
get washcloth	Get a washcloth.
wet washcloth	Wet (the) washcloth.
get washcloth	Get a washcloth.
wet washcloth	Wet (the) washcloth.
squeeze washcloth	Squeeze (the) washcloth.

5. *Supportive and Additional Reading Skills:* Task-related materials and the activity situation may be used as a basis for supportive reading work, such as improving word recognition skills, and in teaching additional reading vocabulary. Any of the additional language skills suggested may be used as reading material, as appropriate. (*Note:* Before reading phrases, drills of the reading sequence — left/right, top/bottom — may be necessary.)

Teacher may substitute or add vocabulary in language and reading. For example, "*Pick up* the tub," "*Fill* the tub *with* water," "*Empty* the *dirty* water *into* the sink," "*Empty* the tub," "Put the tub *away.*"

Individuals with appropriate skills/needs may: 1) write vocabulary words in response to verbal words, and 2) write answers to questions related to activity (e.g., "Where do you pour the dirty water?").

Number Skills Area

(*Note:* Blackboard cleaning is an activity that generates opportunities for development in language, reading, and work behaviors. It is not as readily adaptable as some other activities to work on number skills; counting may be limited to sponges or pictures of task-related objects (e.g., sinks, blackboards, tubs). The format is included here, but it is suggested that the reader refer to another activity better suited for developing number skills, such as the table-setting curriculum.)

1. **Counting:** Learner demonstrates one-to-one correspondence by counting out a number of task-related objects presented.
2. **Numeral Identification:** Learner demonstrates recognition of numerals by selecting/circling numerals in response to verbal numbers.
       Learner verbally identifies numerals when presented (on cards, blackboard, paper).
3. **Numeral/Quantity Association:** Learner demonstrates association of verbal number and quantity by getting correct number of task-related objects in response to verbal number.
       Learner demonstrates association of numeral and quantity by selecting/circling appropriate numeral after counting out a group of objects.
       Learner demonstrates association of numeral and quantity by getting correct number of task-related objects in response to numeral (on cards, blackboard, paper).

Reading and Number Comprehension Skills

Learner demonstrates reading and number skills by following written directions (one or more phrases) and getting the correct number of appropriate objects. For example:

Basic	Expanded
get 4 tubs	
get 2 tubs	
get 5 sponges	
go to closet	Go to (the) closet.
get 2 tubs	Get 2 tubs.
get 2 sponges	Get 2 sponges.
sponges in tubs	Put (the) sponges in (the) tubs.

Supplementary Skills Area

Fine Motor
Learner traces with finger numerals/letters/words on blackboard/paper.
    Learner traces with chalk/pencil numerals/letters/words on blackboard/paper.
    Learner copies numerals/letters/words on blackboard/paper.

Learner writes numerals/letters/words on blackboard/paper in response to verbal numbers/letters/words.

Learner writes correct numerals on blackboard/paper after counting out a number of objects.

Learner writes words on blackboard/paper in response to verbal words.

Learner writes words on blackboard/paper in response to objects.

Appendix C
BED-MAKING CURRICULUM

Work Activity Skill Area

Criterion for performance: Learner proceeds to next level of task after performing appropriately and independently on given level three times consecutively.

Level 1 Learner puts a bedspread properly on a bed that is otherwise made, when provided with the bedspread.

Level 2 *Learner puts a pillow and a bedspread properly on a bed* that is otherwise made, when provided with the pillow and bedspread.

Level 3 *Learner puts a pillow in a pillowcase,* puts the pillow on the bed, and puts the bedspread on the bed properly, when provided with the pillow, pillowcase, and bedspread.

Level 4 *Learner puts a blanket on the bed, tucks it in,* puts the pillow in the pillowcase and on the bed, and puts the bedspread on the bed properly, when provided with pillow, pillowcase, blanket, and bedspread.

Level 5 *Learner puts top sheet on the bed and tucks it in,* puts the blanket on the bed and tucks it in, puts the pillow in the pillowcase and on the bed, and puts the bedspread on the bed properly, when the top sheet, pillow, pillowcase, blanket, and bedspread are provided.

Level 6 *Learner puts the bottom sheet on the bed and tucks it in,* puts the top sheet on the bed and tucks it in, puts the blanket on the bed and tucks it in, puts the pillow in the pillowcase and on the bed, and puts the bedspread on the bed properly, when the bottom sheet, top sheet, pillow, pillowcase, blanket, and bedspread are provided.

Level 7 *Learner gets a bottom sheet, top sheet, pillowcase, pillow, blanket, and bedspread from a shelf near the bed* and makes the bed properly in response to verbal directions.

Level 8 *Learner goes to appropriate place (e.g., linen closet) and gets bottom sheet, top sheet, pillowcase, pillow, blanket, and bedspread and makes the bed properly.*

When learner demonstrates appropriate reading skills:

Level 9 *Learner goes to appropriate place (e.g., linen closet) and gets bottom sheet, top sheet, pillowcase, pillow, blanket, and bedspread and makes the bed properly, in response to written directions.*

Language Skills Area

1. **Receptive Identification:** Learner demonstrates reception of the following task-related objects, actions, areas of the environment, and descriptive words/phrases by selecting objects, performing actions, and going to areas of the environment in response to verbal directions:

bed	top (sheet)	get	over
bedspread	bottom (sheet)	put	in
pillow	sheet	pull	on
pillowcase	shelf	tuck	down
blanket	closet	make (the bed)	
everything			

2. **Expressive Identification:** Learner verbally identifies the above-listed task-related objects, actions, and areas of the environment, and uses descriptive words/phrases appropriately.
3. **Language Program** *(a model for teaching language through an activity)*
   a. Language Units

   (Teacher direction: Make the bed.)

Level (corresponds to Activity Level)	Basic	Expanded
1	bedspread on bed bedspread over pillow	Put (the) bedspread on (the) bed. Pull (the) bedspread over (the) pillow.

Bed-Making Curriculum 257

2	pillow on bed	Put (the) pillow on (the) bed.
	bedspread on bed	Put (the) bedspread on (the) bed.
	bedspread over pillow	Pull (the) bedspread over (the) pillow.
3	pillow in pillowcase	Put (the) pillow in (the) pillowcase.
	pillow on bed	Put (the) pillow on (the) bed.
	bedspread on bed	Put (the) bedspread on (the) bed.
	bedspread over pillow	Put (the) bedspread over (the) pillow.
4	blanket on bed	Put (the) blanket on (the) bed.
	tuck in blanket	Tuck in (the) blanket.
	pillow in pillowcase	Put (the) pillow in (the) pillowcase.
	pillow on bed	Put (the) pillow on (the) bed.
	bedspread on bed	Put (the) bedspread on (the) bed.
	bedspread over pillow	Pull (the) bedspread over (the) pillow.
5	top sheet on bed	Put (the) top sheet on (the) bed.
	tuck in sheet	Tuck in (the) sheet.
	blanket on bed	Put (the) blanket on (the) bed.
	tuck in blanket	Tuck in (the) blanket.
	pillow in pillowcase	Put (the) pillow in (the) pillowcase.
	pillow on bed	Put (the) pillow on (the) bed.
	bedspread on bed	Put (the) bedspread on (the) bed.
	bedspread over pillow	Pull (the) bedspread over (the) pillow.

Appendix C

6	bottom sheet on bed	Put (the) bottom sheet on (the) bed.
	tuck in sheet	Tuck in (the) sheet.
	top sheet on bed	Put (the) top sheet on (the) bed.
	tuck in sheet	Tuck in (the) sheet.
	blanket on bed	Put (the) blanket on (the) bed.
	tuck in blanket	Tuck in (the) blanket.
	pillow in pillow-case	Put (the) pillow in (the) pillowcase.
	pillow on bed	Put (the) pillow on (the) bed.
	bedspread on bed	Put (the) bedspread on (the) bed.
	bedspread over pillow	Pull (the) bedspread over (the) pillow.
7	go to shelf	Go to (the) shelf.
	get bottom sheet	Get (the) bottom sheet.
	get top sheet	Get (the) top sheet.
	get blanket	Get (the) blanket.
	get pillowcase	Get (the) pillowcase.
	get pillow	Get (the) pillow.
	get bedspread	Get (the) bedspread.
	put down	Put (everything) down.
	bottom sheet on bed	Put (the) bottom sheet on (the) bed.
	tuck in sheet	Tuck in (the) sheet.
	top sheet on bed	Put (the) top sheet on (the) bed.
	tuck in sheet	Tuck in (the) sheet.
	blanket on bed	Put (the) blanket on (the) bed.
	tuck in blanket	Tuck in (the) blanket.
	pillow in pillow-case	Put (the) pillow in (the) pillowcase.
	pillow on bed	Put (the) pillow on (the) bed.
	bedspread on bed	Put (the) bedspread on (the) bed.

Bed-Making Curriculum 259

	bedspread over pillow	Put (the) bedspread over (the) pillow.
8	go to closet	Go to (the) closet.
	go to shelf	Go to (the) shelf.
	get bottom sheet	Get (the) bottom sheet.
	get top sheet	Get (the) top sheet.
	get blanket	Get (the) blanket.
	get pillowcase	Get (the) pillowcase.
	get pillow	Get (the) pillow.
	get bedspread	Get (the) bedspread.
	put down	Put (everything) down.
	bottom sheet on bed	Put (the) bottom sheet on (the) bed.
	tuck in sheet	Tuck in (the) sheet.
	top sheet on bed	Put (the) top sheet on (the) bed.
	tuck in sheet	Tuck in (the) sheet.
	blanket on bed	Put (the) blanket on (the) bed.
	tuck in blanket	Tuck in (the) blanket.
	pillow in pillowcase	Put (the) pillow in (the) pillowcase.
	pillow on bed	Put (the) pillow on (the) bed.
	bedspread on bed	Put (the) bedspread on (the) bed.
	bedspread over pillow	Put (the) bedspread over (the) pillow.
9	Follows written directions.	

b. *Language Conditions*

Reception

Condition A

Teacher presents verbal commands (see Language Units, above) and puts learner through steps of bed-making activity.

Condition B
: Teacher presents verbal commands and performs steps of bed-making activity for learner to imitate.

Condition C
: Teacher presents verbal commands in sequence. Learner follows the commands and performs steps of bed-making activity.

Condition D
: Teacher presents verbal commands out of sequence. Learner follows the commands and performs steps of bed-making activity out of sequence.

<u>Imitation</u>

Condition E
: Teacher provides verbal model (see Language Units, above) and puts learner through verbal behavior (at desk).

Condition F
: Teacher provides verbal model for imitation (at desk).

Condition G
: Teacher provides verbal model for imitation. Learner imitates verbal model and performs steps of bed-making activity.

<u>Expression</u>

Condition H[a]
: Teacher presents a verbal cue (e.g., "What do you get?" "Where do you put the _____?") in response to which the learner will produce the verbal behavior and perform steps of bed-making activity.

Condition H[b]
: Teacher provides a nonverbal cue (e.g., points to objects) in response to which the learner will produce the verbal behavior and perform steps of bed-making activity.

Condition I
: Teacher presents a situation in which the learner will produce the verbal behavior and perform steps of bed-making activity, such as making an unmade bed.

Condition J
: Learner is in the activity situation. Learner must instruct another person/teacher in how to perform steps of bed-making activity.

Condition K
: Learner is in the activity situation. Learner must describe the steps of bed-making activity as another person/teacher performs them out of sequence.

4. ***Variations of the Language Program:*** Learner demonstrates reception of verbal phrases outside the context/structure of the activity situation and language units by following verbal directions consisting of functional combinations of the vocabulary listed in objective A1, above, and any previously learned vocabulary. For example:

Basic	Expanded
blanket on table	Put (the) blanket on (the) table.
pillow on chair	Put (the) pillow on (the) chair.

5. ***Supportive and Additional Language Skills:*** Task-related materials and the activity situation may be used as a basis for supportive language work, such as speech articulation, and in teaching additional language concepts according to the needs and abilities of the individuals. Listed below are suggestions and examples of some language concepts and skills that may be taught with bed-making activity and materials as a basis.

Speech articulation: Learner imitates phrases from bed-making language units.

Sequencing: Teacher instructs learner to get objects or pictures in the order he says/signs them (e.g., "bed, pillow").

Visual memory: Teacher presents several objects or pictures (e.g., bed, pillow, blanket). Teacher removes one or more objects and learner must indicate which object is missing.

Attributes — color: Teacher instructs learner to get the *red* blanket.

Pronouns: Learner describes self/other performing steps of bed-making activity (e.g., "I get the blanket," "You get the blanket," "He/she gets the blanket").

Vocabulary additions and substitutions: Learner uses other vocabulary (e.g., "*Move* the bed," "*Smooth* the sheets," "Fold the bedspread over (to make it neater over the pillow)," "*Cover* the bed *with* the bedspread").

Answering questions: Learner answers appropriately questions related to the activity (e.g., "What do you pull over the pillow?" "Where do you put the blanket?").
Generalizations: Learner demonstrates understanding of task-related vocabulary by using words appropriately in sentences (related, unrelated to activity) (e.g., "I sleep in the bed," "I put my head on the pillow").
Verbal/written expression: Learner says/signs/writes sentences/stories when presented with one or more activity-related pictures and/or words.

Reading Skills Area

A. *Word Recognition Skills*

1. Learner demonstrates reception of the following task-related words by selecting/circling written words in response to verbal words:

bed	top	get	over
bedspread	bottom	put	in
pillow	sheet	pull	on
pillowcase	shelf	tuck	down
blanket	closet	make	
everything			

2. Learner verbally expresses (reads) each of the above-listed task-related words as presented (on cards, blackboard, paper).
3. Learner demonstrates reception of the following written phrases from bed-making language units by selecting/circling each written phrase in response to a verbal phrase:*

Basic	Expanded
make bed	Make (the) bed.
get blanket	Get (the) blanket.
get bedspread	Get (the) bedspread.
get pillow	Get (the) pillow.
get pillowcase	Get (the) pillowcase.
get top sheet	Get (the) top sheet.
get bottom sheet	Get (the) bottom sheet.
put down	Put (everything) down.
go to shelf	Go to (the) shelf.
go to closet	Go to (the) closet.

tuck in blanket	Tuck in (the) blanket.
tuck in sheet	Tuck in (the) sheet.
pillow in pillowcase	Put (the) pillow in (the) pillowcase.
pillow on bed	Put (the) pillow on (the) bed.
bedspread on bed	Put (the) bedspread on (the) bed.
blanket on bed	Put (the) blanket on (the) bed.
top sheet on bed	Put (the) top sheet on (the) bed.
bottom sheet on bed	Put (the) bottom sheet on (the) bed.
bedspread over pillow	Pull (the) bedspread over (the) pillow.

*Phrases are grouped by similarity in structure (all "get" phrases together, all "on bed" phrases together, etc.) because this presentation should simplify the learner's task by limiting the amount of new material presented at one time. Eventually, the learner should read phrases presented in any sequence, composed of functional combinations of reading word vocabulary listed in objective A1.

4. Learner verbally expresses (reads) each of the above-listed phrases from the bed-making language units as presented (on cards, blackboard, paper).
5. Learner demonstrates reception of a sequence of written phrases from the bed-making language units by selecting/circling a sequence of written phrases in response to verbal phrases. For example:

Basic	Expanded
get blanket	Get (the) blanket.
get pillow	Get (the) pillow.
get blanket	Get (the) blanket.
get pillow	Get (the) pillow.
get pillowcase	Get (the) pillowcase.
get blanket	Get (the) blanket.
get pillow	Get (the) pillow.
get pillowcase	Get (the) pillowcase.
pillow in pillowcase	Put (the) pillow in (the) pillowcase.

6. Learner verbally expresses (reads) each phrase from the bed-making language units when a sequence of written phrases is presented (on cards, blackboard, paper). (Refer to examples under objective A5.)

B. Reading Comprehension Skills

1. Learner demonstrates understanding of the following task-related words by selecting the correct object/picture, performing the action, and going to area of the environment in response to written word:

bed	top (sheet)	get	over
bedspread	bottom (sheet)	put	in
pillow	sheet	pull	on
pillowcase	shelf	tuck	down
blanket	closet	make (the bed)	
everything			

2. Learner demonstrates understanding of written phrases from the bed-making language units by following a simple written direction (on cards, blackboard, paper) from the following:

Basic	Expanded
make bed	Make (the) bed.
get blanket	Get (the) blanket.
get bedspread	Get (the) bedspread.
get pillow	Get (the) pillow.
get pillowcase	Get (the) pillowcase.
get top sheet	Get (the) top sheet.
get bottom sheet	Get (the) bottom sheet.
put down	Put (everything) down.
go to shelf	Go to (the) shelf.
go to closet	Go to (the) closet.
tuck in blanket	Tuck in (the) blanket.
tuck in sheet	Tuck in (the) sheet.
pillow in pillowcase	Put (the) pillow in (the) pillowcase.
pillow on bed	Put (the) pillow on (the) bed.
bedspread on bed	Put (the) bedspread on (the) bed.
blanket on bed	Put (the) blanket on (the) bed.
top sheet on bed	Put (the) top sheet on (the) bed.
bottom sheet on bed	Put (the) bottom sheet on (the) bed.
bedspread over pillow	Pull (the) bedspread over (the) pillow.

3. Learner demonstrates understanding of a sequence of written phrases from the bed-making language units by following a sequence of simple written directions presented in any order. For example:

Basic	Expanded
get pillow	Get (the) pillow.
get pillowcase	Get (the) pillowcase.
go to closet	Go to (the) closet.
get pillow	Get (the) pillow.
get pillowcase	Get (the) pillowcase.
go to closet	Go to (the) closet.
get pillow	Get (the) pillow.
get pillowcase	Get (the) pillowcase.
pillow in pillowcase	Put (the) pillow in (the) pillowcase.

(Activity and Language Unit Level 9)

Basic	Expanded
go to closet	Go to (the) closet.
go to shelf	Go to (the) shelf.
get bottom sheet	Get (the) bottom sheet.
get top sheet	Get (the) top sheet.
get blanket	Get (the) blanket.
get pillowcase	Get (the) pillowcase.
get pillow	Get (the) pillow.
get bedspread	Get (the) bedspread.
put down	Put (everything) down.
bottom sheet on bed	Put (the) bottom sheet on (the) bed.
tuck in sheet	Tuck in (the) sheet.
top sheet on bed	Put (the) top sheet on (the) bed.
tuck in sheet	Tuck in (the) sheet.
blanket on bed	Put (the) blanket on (the) bed.
tuck in blanket	Tuck in (the) blanket.
pillow in pillowcase	Put (the) pillow in (the) pillowcase.
pillow on bed	Put (the) pillow on (the) bed.
bedspread on bed	Put (the) bedspread on (the) bed.
bedspread over pillow	Put (the) bedspread over (the) pillow.

4. ***Variations in Reading:*** Learner demonstrates understanding of written phrases outside the context/structure of the activity situation by following written directions consisting of functional combinations of the vocabulary in objective A1 and any previously learned vocabulary. For example:

Basic	Expanded
blanket on table	Put (the) blanket on (the) table.
pillow on chair	Put (the) pillow on (the) chair.

Learner demonstrates understanding of a sequence of written phrases outside the context/structure of the activity situation by following a sequence of simple written directions consisting of functional combinations of the vocabulary in objective A1 and any previously learned vocabulary. For example:

Basic	Expanded
get sheet	Get (the) sheet.
sheet in basket	Put (the) sheet in (the) basket.
get basket	Get (the) basket.
get blanket	Get (the) blanket.
blanket on shelf	Put (the) blanket on (the) shelf.

5. ***Supportive and Additional Reading Skills:*** Task-related materials and the activity situation may be used as a basis for supportive reading work, such as improving word recognition skills, and in teaching additional reading vocabulary. Any of the additional language skills suggested may be used as reading material, as appropriate. (*Note:* Before reading phrases, drills of the reading sequence — left/right, top/bottom — may be necessary.)

Teacher may substitute or add vocabulary (e.g., "*Smooth* the blanket").

Individuals with appropriate skills/needs may: 1) write vocabulary words in response to verbal words, and 2) write answers to questions related to activity (e.g., "Where do you put the blanket?").

Number Skills Area

(*Note:* Bed making is an activity that generates opportunities for development in language, reading, and work behaviors. It is not as readily adaptable as some other activities to work on number skills; counting may be limited to sheets, pillows, blankets, or pictures of task-related items. The format is included here, but it is suggested that the reader refer to another activity better suited for developing number skills, such as the table-setting curriculum.)

1. ***Counting:*** Learner demonstrates one-to-one correspondence by counting out a number of task-related objects presented (e.g., sheets, pillowcases).
2. ***Numeral Identification:*** Learner demonstrates recognition of numerals by selecting/circling numerals in response to verbal numbers.

    Learner verbally identifies numerals when presented (on cards, blackboard, paper).
3. ***Numeral/Quantity Association:*** Learner demonstrates association of verbal number and quantity by getting correct number of task-related objects in response to verbal number.

    Learner demonstrates association of numeral and quantity by selecting/circling appropriate numeral after counting out a group of objects.

    Learner demonstrates association of numeral and quantity by getting the correct number of task-related objects in response to numeral (on cards, blackboard, paper).

Reading and Number Comprehension Skills

Learner demonstrates reading and number skills by following written directions (one or more phrases) and getting the correct number of appropriate objects. For example:

Basic	Expanded
get 4 blankets	
get 4 blankets	
get 4 pillows	
go to closet	Go to (the) closet.
get 4 blankets	Get 4 blankets.
get 4 pillows	Get 4 pillows.
make bed	Make (the) bed.

Supplementary Skills Area

Fine Motor
Learner traces with finger numerals/letters/words on blackboard/paper.

Learner traces with chalk/pencil numerals/letters/words on blackboard/paper.

Learner copies numerals/letters/words on blackboard/paper.

Learner writes numerals/letters/words on blackboard/paper in response to verbal numbers/letters/words.

Learner writes correct numerals on blackboard/paper after counting out a number of objects.

Learner writes words on blackboard/paper in response to verbal words.

Learner writes words on blackboard/paper in response to objects.

Appendix D
TOOTHBRUSHING CURRICULUM

Work Activity Skill Area

Criterion for performance: Learner will proceed to next level of task after performing appropriately and independently on a given level three consecutive times.

Level 1 Learner turns on cold water, fills cup with water, wets toothbrush, and turns off water.

Level 2 Learner turns on cold water, fills cup with water, wets toothbrush, turns off water, *picks up tube of toothpaste, unscrews cap,* and *squeezes appropriate amount of toothpaste on the toothbrush.*

Level 3 Learner turns on cold water, fills cup with water, wets toothbrush, turns off water, picks up tube of toothpaste, unscrews cap, squeezes appropriate amount of toothpaste on toothbrush, and *brushes lower left/right teeth using proper brushing motion for 10 seconds.*

Level 4 Learner turns on cold water, fills cup with water, wets toothbrush, turns off water, picks up tube of toothpaste, unscrews cap, squeezes appropriate amount of toothpaste on toothbrush, brushes lower left/right teeth using proper brushing motion for 10 seconds, *and brushes lower right/left teeth using proper motion for 10 seconds.*

Level 5 Learner turns on cold water, fills cup with water, wets toothbrush, turns off water, picks up tube of toothpaste, unscrews cap, squeezes appropriate amount of toothpaste on toothbrush, brushes lower left/right teeth and lower right/left teeth using proper brushing motion for 10 seconds on each side *and spits into sink.*

Level 6 Learner turns on cold water, fills cup with water, wets toothbrush, turns off water, picks up toothpaste, unscrews cap, squeezes appropriate amount of toothpaste on toothbrush, brushes lower left/right teeth and lower right/left teeth using proper brushing motion for 10 seconds on each side, spits in sink, *and brushes upper left/right teeth using proper brushing motion for 10 seconds.*

Level 7 Learner turns on cold water, fills cup with water, wets toothbrush, turns off water, picks up tube of toothpaste, unscrews cap, squeezes appropriate amount of toothpaste on toothbrush, brushes lower left/right teeth and lower right/left teeth using proper brushing motion for 10 seconds each side, spits in sink, brushes upper left/right teeth, *and brushes upper right/left teeth using proper brushing motion for 10 seconds on each side.*

Level 8 Learner turns on cold water, fills cup with water, wets toothbrush, turns off water, picks up tube of toothpaste, unscrews cap, squeezes appropriate amount of toothpaste on toothbrush, brushes lower left/right teeth and lower right/left teeth, spits in sink, brushes upper left/right teeth and upper right/left teeth using proper brushing motion for 10 seconds on each side, *and spits in sink.*

Level 9 Learner turns on cold water, fills cup with water, wets toothbrush, turns off water, picks up tube of toothpaste, unscrews cap, squeezes appropriate amount of toothpaste on toothbrush, brushes lower left/right teeth and lower right/left teeth, spits in sink, brushes upper left/right teeth and upper right/left teeth using proper brushing motion for 10 seconds on each side, spits in sink, *and brushes upper front teeth using proper brushing motion for 10 seconds.*

Level 10 Learner turns on cold water, fills cup with water, wets toothbrush, turns off water, picks up tube of toothpaste, unscrews cap, squeezes appropriate amount of toothpaste on toothbrush, brushes lower left/right teeth and lower right/left teeth, spits in sink, brushes upper left/right teeth and upper right/left teeth, spits in sink, and brushes lower front teeth *and upper front teeth using proper brushing motion for 10 seconds on each side.*

Level 11 Learner turns on cold water, fills cup with water, wets toothbrush, turns off water, picks up tube of toothpaste, unscrews cap, squeezes appropriate amount of toothpaste on toothbrush, brushes lower left/right teeth and lower right/left teeth, spits in sink, brushes upper left/right teeth and upper right/left teeth, spits in sink, brushes lower front teeth and upper front teeth using proper brushing motion for 10 seconds on each side, *spits in sink, and rinses mouth with water.*

Level 12 Learner turns on cold water, fills cup with water, wets toothbrush, turns off water, picks up tube of toothpaste, unscrews cap, squeezes appropriate amount of toothpaste on toothbrush, brushes lower left/right teeth and lower right/left teeth, spits in sink, brushes upper left/right teeth and upper right/left teeth, spits in sink, brushes lower front teeth and upper front teeth using proper brushing motion for 10 seconds on each side, spits in sink, rinses mouth with water, *screws cap on tube of toothpaste, and puts toothbrush, toothpaste, and cup away in appropriate place (e.g., cabinet).*

Level 13 Learner goes to bathroom, gets toothbrush, toothpaste, and cup from appropriate place (e.g., cabinet), turns on cold water, fills cup with water, wets toothbrush, turns off water, picks up tube of toothpaste, unscrews cap, squeezes appropriate amount of toothpaste on toothbrush, brushes lower left/right teeth and lower right/left teeth, spits in sink, brushes upper left/right teeth and upper right/left teeth, spits in sink, brushes lower front teeth and upper front teeth using proper brushing motion for 10 seconds on each side, spits in sink, rinses mouth with water, screws cap on tube of toothpaste, and puts toothbrush, toothpaste, and cup away in appropriate place (e.g., cabinet).

Level 14 Learner goes to bathroom, gets toothbrush, toothpaste, and cup from appropriate place (e.g., cabinet), turns on cold water, fills cup with water, wets toothbrush, turns off water, picks up tube of toothpaste, unscrews cap, squeezes appropriate amount of toothpaste on toothbrush, brushes lower left/right teeth and lower right/left teeth, spits in sink, brushes upper left/right teeth and upper right/left teeth, spits in sink, brushes lower front teeth and upper front teeth using proper brushing motion for 10 seconds on each side, spits in sink, rinses mouth with water, screws cap on tube of toothpaste, and puts toothbrush, toothpaste, and cup away in appropriate place (e.g., cabinet), *in response to written directions.*

Language Skills Area

1. ***Receptive Identification:*** Learner demonstrates reception of the following task-related objects, actions, descriptive

words/phrases, and areas of the environment by selecting objects, performing actions, and going to areas of the environment in response to verbal directions:

toothbrush	pick up	spit
toothpaste	turn	rinse
cap	on	get
cup	off	go (to)
sink	put	open
cold	(take) off	close
water	squeeze	on
teeth	wet	in
mouth	brush	down
cabinet		
bathroom		

2. ***Expressive Identification:*** Learner verbally identifies the above-listed task-related objects, actions, and areas of the environment, and uses descriptive words/phrases appropriately.
3. ***Language Program*** *(a model for teaching language through an activity)*
   a. *Language Units*
   (Teacher direction: Brush (your) teeth.)

Level (corresponds to Activity Level)	Basic	Expanded
1	cold water on	Turn on (the) cold water.
	water in cup	Put water in (the) cup.
	cup down	Put (the) cup down.
	wet toothbrush	Wet (the) toothbrush.
	toothbrush down	Put (the) toothbrush down.
	water off	Turn off (the) water.
2	cold water on	Turn on (the) cold water.
	water in cup	Put water in (the) cup.
	cup down	Put (the) cup down.
	wet toothbrush	Wet (the) toothbrush.
	toothbrush down	Put (the) toothbrush down.
	water off	Turn off (the) water.
	pick up toothpaste	Pick up (the) toothpaste.

	cap off	Take off (the) cap.
	squeeze tooth-paste	Squeeze (the) tooth-paste.
	toothpaste on	Put toothpaste on (the) toothbrush.
3	cold water on	Turn on (the) cold water.
	water in cup	Put water in (the) cup.
	cup down	Put (the) cup down.
	wet toothbrush	Wet (the) toothbrush.
	toothbrush down	Put (the) toothbrush down.
	water off	Turn off (the) water.
	pick up toothpaste	Pick up (the) toothpaste.
	cap off	Take off (the) cap.
	squeeze toothpaste	Squeeze (the) toothpaste.
	toothpaste on toothbrush	Put toothpaste on (the) toothbrush.
	brush teeth	Brush my/your teeth.
4	Same language as Level 3.	
5	cold water on	Turn on (the) cold water.
	water in cup	Put water in (the) cup.
	cup down	Put (the) cup down.
	wet toothbrush	Wet (the) toothbrush.
	toothbrush down	Put (the) toothbrush down.
	water off	Turn off (the) water.
	pick up toothpaste	Pick up (the) toothpaste.
	cap off	Take off (the) cap.
	squeeze toothpaste	Squeeze (the) toothpaste.
	toothpaste on toothbrush	Put toothpaste on (the) toothbrush.
	brush teeth	Brush my/your teeth.
	spit	Spit in (the) sink.
6	cold water on	Turn on (the) cold water.
	water in cup	Put water in (the) cup.

	cup down	Put (the) cup down.
	wet toothbrush	Wet (the) toothbrush.
	toothbrush down	Put (the) toothbrush down.
	water off	Turn off (the) water.
	pick up toothpaste	Pick up (the) toothpaste.
	cap off	Take off (the) cap.
	squeeze toothpaste	Squeeze (the) toothpaste.
	toothpaste on toothbrush	Put toothpaste on (the) toothbrush.
	brush teeth	Brush my/your teeth.
	spit	Spit in (the) sink.
	brush teeth	Brush my/your teeth.
7	Same language as Level 6.	
8	cold water on	Turn on (the) cold water.
	water in cup	Put water in (the) cup.
	cup down	Put (the) cup down.
	wet toothbrush	Wet (the) toothbrush.
	toothbrush down	Put (the) toothbrush down.
	water off	Turn off (the) water.
	pick up toothpaste	Pick up (the) toothpaste.
	cap off	Take off (the) cap.
	squeeze toothpaste	Squeeze (the) toothpaste.
	toothpaste on toothbrush	Put (the) toothpaste on (the) toothbrush.
	brush teeth	Brush my/your teeth.
	spit	Spit in (the) sink.
	brush teeth	Brush my/your teeth.
	spit	Spit in (the) sink.
9	cold water on	Turn on (the) cold water.
	water in cup	Put water in (the) cup.
	cup down	Put (the) cup down.
	wet toothbrush	Wet (the) toothbrush.
	toothbrush down	Put (the) toothbrush down.

	water off pick up tooth- paste cap off squeeze tooth- paste toothpaste on toothbrush brush teeth spit brush teeth spit brush teeth	Turn off (the) water. Pick up (the) tooth- paste. Take off (the) cap. Squeeze (the) tooth- paste. Put toothpaste on (the) toothbrush. Brush my/your teeth. Spit in (the) sink. Brush my/your teeth. Spit in (the) sink. Brush my/your teeth.
10	Same language as Level 9.	
11	cold water on water in cup cup down wet toothbrush toothbrush down water off pick up tooth- paste cap off squeeze tooth- paste toothpaste on toothbrush brush teeth spit brush teeth spit brush teeth spit rinse mouth spit	Turn on (the) cold water. Put water in (the) cup. Put (the) cup down. Wet (the) toothbrush. Put (the) toothbrush down. Turn off (the) water. Pick up (the) tooth- paste. Take off (the) cap. Squeeze (the) tooth- paste. Put toothpaste on (the) toothbrush. Brush my/your teeth. Spit in (the) sink. Brush my/your teeth. Spit in (the) sink. Brush my/your teeth. Spit in (the) sink. Rinse my/your teeth. Spit in (the) sink.
12	Same language as Level 11 with the following additions: cap on open cabinet	Put (the) cap on. Open (the) cabinet.

	toothbrush in cabinet	Put (the) toothbrush in (the) cabinet.
	toothpaste in cabinet	Put (the) toothpaste in (the) cabinet.
	cup in cabinet	Put (the) cup in (the) cabinet.
	close cabinet	Close (the) cabinet.
13	go to bathroom	Go to (the) bathroom.
	go to sink	Go to (the) sink.
	get toothbrush	Get (the) toothbrush.
	get toothpaste	Get (the) toothpaste.
	get cup	Get (the) cup.
	close cabinet	Close (the) cabinet.
	cold water on	Turn on (the) cold water.
	water in cup	Put water in (the) cup.
	cup down	Put (the) cup down.
	wet toothbrush	Wet (the) toothbrush.
	toothbrush down	Put (the) toothbrush down.
	water off	Turn off (the) water.
	pick up toothpaste	Pick up (the) toothpaste.
	cap off	Take off (the) cap.
	squeeze toothpaste	Squeeze (the) toothpaste.
	toothpaste on toothbrush	Put toothpaste on (the) toothbrush.
	brush teeth	Brush my/your teeth.
	spit	Spit in (the) sink.
	brush teeth	Brush my/your teeth.
	spit	Spit in (the) sink.
	brush teeth	Brush my/your teeth.
	spit	Spit in (the) sink.
	rinse mouth	Rinse my/your mouth.
	spit	Spit in (the) sink.
	cap on	Put (the) cap on.
	open cabinet	Open (the) cabinet.
	toothbrush in cabinet	Put (the) toothbrush in (the) cabinet.

toothpaste in cabinet	Put (the) toothpaste in (the) cabinet.
cup in cabinet	Put (the) cup in (the) cabinet.
close cabinet	Close (the) cabinet.

b. *Language Conditions*

Reception

Condition A
   Teacher presents verbal commands (see Language Units, above) and puts learner through steps of toothbrushing activity.

Condition B
   Teacher presents verbal commands and performs steps of toothbrushing activity for learner to imitate.

Condition C
   Teacher presents verbal commands in sequence. Learner follows the commands and performs steps of toothbrushing activity.

Condition D
   Teacher presents verbal commands out of sequence. Learner follows the commands and performs steps of toothbrushing activity out of sequence.

Imitation

Condition E
   Teacher provides verbal model (see Language Units, above) and puts learner through verbal behavior (at desk).

Condition F
   Teacher provides verbal model for imitation (at desk).

Condition G
   Teacher provides verbal model for imitation. Learner imitates verbal model and performs steps of toothbrushing activity.

Expression

Condition H[a]
   Teacher presents a verbal cue (e.g., "What do you get?" "Where do you put the _____?") in response to which the learner will produce the verbal behavior and perform steps of toothbrushing activity.

Condition H[b]
: Teacher provides a nonverbal cue (e.g., points to objects) in response to which the learner will produce the verbal behavior and perform steps of toothbrushing activity.

Condition I
: Teacher presents a situation in which the learner will produce the verbal behavior and perform steps of toothbrushing activity, such as brushing dirty teeth after a meal.

Condition J
: Learner is in the activity situation. Learner must instruct another person/teacher in how to perform steps of toothbrushing activity.

Condition K
: Learner is in the activity situation. Learner must describe the steps of toothbrushing activity as another person/teacher performs them out of sequence.

4. **Variations of the Language Program:** Learner demonstrates reception of verbal phrases outside the context/structure of the activity situation and language units by following verbal directions consisting of functional combinations of the vocabulary listed in objective 1, above, and any previously learned vocabulary. For example:

Basic	Expanded
pick up hairbrush	Pick up (the) hairbrush.
hairbrush in cabinet	Put (the) hairbrush in (the) cabinet.

5. **Supportive and Additional Language Skills:** Task-related materials and the activity situation may be used as a basis for supportive language work, such as speech articulation, and in teaching additional language concepts according to the needs and abilities of the individuals. Listed below are suggestions and examples of some language concepts and skills that may be taught with toothbrushing activity and materials as a basis.

Speech articulation
: Learner imitates phrases from toothbrushing language units.

Sequencing
: Teacher instructs learner to get objects in the order he says/signs them (e.g., "toothbrush, cup").

Visual memory
: Teacher puts out several objects (e.g., toothbrush, toothpaste, cup). Teacher removes one or

more objects and learner must indicate which object is missing.

Pronouns: Learner describes self/other performing steps of toothbrushing activity (e.g., "I brush my teeth," "You brush your teeth," "He/she brushes his/her teeth").

Vocabulary additions and substitutions: Learner uses other vocabulary (e.g., "*Fill* the cup *with* water," "Put the toothbrush *away*").

Concepts: Lower, upper; front, back; right, left.

Answering questions: Learner answers appropriately questions related to the activity (e.g., "Where do you put the toothbrush?" "Where do you spit?").

Generalization: Learner demonstrates understanding of task-related vocabulary by using words appropriately in sentences (related, unrelated to activity) (e.g., "I put the plates in the *cabinet*," "I *turn on* the light").

Verbal/written expression: Learner says/signs/writes sentences/stories when presented with one or more activity-related pictures and/or words.

Reading Skills Area

A. Word Recognition Skills

1. Learner demonstrates reception of the following task-related words by selecting/circling written words in response to verbal words:

toothbrush	pick up	spit
toothpaste	turn	rinse
cap	on	get
cup	off	go (to)
sink	put	open
water (cold)	(take) off	close
teeth	squeeze	on
mouth	wet	in
cabinet	brush	
bathroom		

2. Learner verbally expresses (reads) each of the above-listed task-related words as presented (on cards, blackboard, paper).

3. Learner demonstrates reception of the following written phrases from the toothbrushing language units by se-

lecting/circling each written phrase in response to a verbal phrase:*

Basic	Expanded
spit	Spit in (the) sink.
get cup	Get (the) cup.
get toothbrush	Get (the) toothbrush.
get toothpaste	Get (the) toothpaste.
cup down	Put (the) cup down.
toothbrush down	Put (the) toothbrush down.
wet toothbrush	Wet (the) toothbrush.
water off	Turn off (the) water.
cold water on	Turn on (the) cold water.
cap on	Put on (the) cap.
cap off	Take off (the) cap.
brush teeth	Brush my/your teeth.
rinse mouth	Rinse my/your mouth.
open cabinet	Open (the) cabinet.
close cabinet	Close (the) cabinet.
squeeze toothpaste	Squeeze (the) toothpaste.
pick up toothpaste	Pick up (the) toothpaste.
go to bathroom	Go to (the) bathroom.
go to sink	Go to (the) sink.
water in cup	Put water in (the) cup.
toothpaste on toothbrush	Put toothpaste on (the) toothbrush.
toothpaste in cabinet	Put (the) toothpaste in (the) cabinet.
toothbrush in cabinet	Put (the) toothbrush in (the) cabinet.
cup in cabinet	Put (the) cup in (the) cabinet.

*Phrases are grouped by similarity in structure (all "get" phrases together, all "go to" phrases together, etc.) because this presentation should simplify the learner's task by limiting the amount of new material presented at one time. Eventually, the learner should read phrases presented in any sequence, composed of functional combinations of reading words vocabulary listed in objective A1.

4. Learner verbally expresses (reads) each of the above-listed phrases from the toothbrushing language units as presented (on cards, blackboard, paper).
5. Learner demonstrates reception of a sequence of written phrases from the toothbrushing language units by selecting/circling a sequence of written phrases in response to verbal phrases. For example:

Basic	Expanded
get toothbrush	Get (the) toothbrush.
get cup	Get (the) cup.
get toothbrush	Get (the) toothbrush.
get cup	Get (the) cup.
get toothpaste	Get (the) toothpaste.
open cabinet	Open (the) cabinet.
get toothbrush	Get (the) toothbrush.
get cup	Get (the) cup.
get toothpaste	Get (the) toothpaste.

6. Learner verbally expresses (reads) each phrase from the toothbrushing language units when a sequence of written phrases is presented (on cards, blackboard, paper). (Refer to examples under objective A5.)

B. Reading Comprehension Skills

1. Learner demonstrates understanding of the following task-related words by selecting the correct object/picture, performing the action, and going to area of the environment in response to written word:

toothbrush	pick up	spit
toothpaste	turn	rinse
cap	on	get
cup	off	go (to)
sink	put	open
water (cold)	(take) off	close
teeth	squeeze	on
mouth	wet	in
cabinet	brush	down
bathroom		

2. Learner demonstrates understanding of written phrases from the toothbrushing language units by following a simple written direction (on cards, blackboard, paper) from the following:

Basic	Expanded
spit	Spit in (the) sink.
get cup	Get (the) cup.
get toothbrush	Get (the) toothbrush.
get toothpaste	Get (the) toothpaste.
cup down	Put (the) cup down.
toothbrush down	Put (the) toothbrush down.

wet toothbrush	Wet (the) toothbrush.
water off	Turn off (the) water.
cold water on	Turn on (the) cold water.
cap on	Put (the) cap on.
cap off	Take off (the) cap.
brush teeth	Brush my/your teeth.
rinse mouth	Rinse my/your mouth.
open cabinet	Open (the) cabinet.
close cabinet	Close (the) cabinet.
squeeze toothpaste	Squeeze (the) toothpaste.
pick up toothpaste	Pick up (the) toothpaste.
go to bathroom	Go to (the) bathroom.
go to sink	Go to (the) sink.
water in cup	Put water in (the) cup.
toothpaste on toothbrush	Put toothpaste on (the) toothbrush.
toothpaste in cabinet	Put (the) toothpaste in (the) cabinet.
toothbrush in cabinet	Put (the) toothbrush in (the) cabinet.
cup in cabinet	Put (the) cup in (the) cabinet.

3. Learner demonstrates understanding of a sequence of written phrases from the toothbrushing language units by following a sequence of simple written directions presented in any order. For example:

Basic	Expanded
get toothbrush	Get (the) toothbrush.
get cup	Get (the) cup.
get toothbrush	Get (the) toothbrush.
get cup	Get (the) cup.
get toothpaste	Get (the) toothpaste.
open cabinet	Open (the) cabinet.
get toothbrush	Get (the) toothbrush.
get cup	Get (the) cup.
get toothpaste	Get (the) toothpaste.

(Activity and Language Unit Level 14)

go to bathroom	Go to (the) bathroom.
go to sink	Go to (the) sink.
open cabinet	Open (the) cabinet.
get toothbrush	Get (the) toothbrush.
get toothpaste	Get (the) toothpaste.
get cup	Get (the) cup.
close cabinet	Close (the) cabinet.
cold water on	Turn on (the) cold water.
water in cup	Put (the) water in (the) cup.
cup down	Put (the) cup down.

wet toothbrush	Wet (the) toothbrush.
toothbrush down	Put (the) toothbrush down.
water off	Turn off (the) water.
pick up toothpaste	Pick up (the) toothpaste.
cap off	Take off (the) cap.
squeeze toothpaste	Squeeze (the) toothpaste.
toothpaste on toothbrush	Put (the) toothpaste on (the) toothbrush.
brush teeth	Brush my/your teeth.
spit	Spit in (the) sink.
brush teeth	Brush my/your teeth.
spit	Spit in (the) sink.
brush teeth	Brush my/your teeth.
spit	Spit in (the) sink.
rinse mouth	Rinse my/your mouth.
spit	Spit in (the) sink.
cap on	Put (the) cap on.
open cabinet	Open (the) cabinet.
toothbrush in cabinet	Put (the) toothbrush in (the) cabinet.
toothpaste in cabinet	Put (the) toothpaste in (the) cabinet.
cup in cabinet	Put (the) cup in (the) cabinet.
close cabinet	Close (the) cabinet.

4. ***Variations in Reading:*** Learner demonstrates understanding of written phrases outside the context/structure of the activity situation by following written directions consisting of functional combinations of the vocabulary in objective A1 and any previously learned vocabulary. For example:

Basic	Expanded
pick up hairbrush	Pick up (the) hairbrush.
hairbrush in cabinet	Put (the) hairbrush in (the) cabinet.

Learner demonstrates understanding of a sequence of written phrases outside the context/structure of the activity situation by following a sequence of simple written directions consisting of functional combinations of the vocabulary in objective A1 and any previously learned vocabulary. For example:

Basic	Expanded
get plate	Get (the) plate.
plate in cabinet	Put (the) plate in (the) cabinet.

get plate	Get (the) plate.
plate in cabinet	Put (the) plate in (the) cabinet.
pick up cup	Pick up (the) cup.

5. ***Supportive and Additional Reading Skills:*** Task-related materials and the activity situation may be used as a basis for supportive reading work, such as improving word recognition skills, and in teaching additional reading vocabulary. Any of the additional language skills suggested may be used as reading material, as appropriate. (*Note:* Before reading phrases, drills of the reading sequence — left/right, top/bottom — may be necessary.)

    Teacher may substitute or add vocabulary in language and reading (e.g., "*Fill* the cup *with* water," "*Put* the cup *away*").

    Individuals with appropriate skills/needs may: 1) write vocabulary words in response to verbal words, and 2) write answers to questions related to the activity (e.g., "Where is the toothpaste?" "Where do you spit?").

Number Skills Area

1. ***Counting:*** Learner demonstrates one-to-one correspondence by counting out a number of task-related objects (toothbrushes, cups) or pictures of objects presented.
2. ***Numeral Identification:*** Learner demonstrates recognition of numerals by selecting/circling numerals in response to verbal numbers.

    Learner verbally identifies numerals when presented (on cards, blackboard, paper).
3. ***Numeral/Quantity Association:*** Learner demonstrates association of verbal number and quantity by getting correct number of task-related objects in response to verbal number.

    Learner demonstrates association of numeral and quantity by selecting/circling appropriate numeral after counting out a group of objects.

    Learner demonstrates association of numeral and quantity by getting the correct number of task-related objects in response to numeral (on cards, blackboard, papers).

Reading and Number Comprehension Skills

Learner demonstrates reading and number skills by following written directions (one or more phrases) and getting the correct number of appropriate objects. For example:

Basic	Expanded
get 4 cups	
get 4 cups get 2 toothbrushes	
go to cabinet get 4 cups get 2 toothbrushes get 2 toothpastes	Go to (the) cabinet. Get 4 cups. Get 2 toothbrushes. Get 2 toothpastes.

Supplementary Skills Area

Fine Motor

Learner traces with finger numerals/letters/words on blackboard/paper.

Learner traces with chalk/pencil numerals/letters/words on blackboard/paper.

Learner copies numerals/letters/words on blackboard/paper.

Learner writes numerals/letters/words on blackboard/paper in response to verbal numbers/letters/words.

Learner writes correct numerals on blackboard/paper after counting out a number of objects.

Learner writes words on blackboard/paper in response to verbal words.

Learner writes words on blackboard/paper in response to objects.

Appendix E
SANDWICH-MAKING CURRICULUM

Work Activity Skill Area

Criterion for performance: Learner proceeds to next level of task after performing appropriately and independently on given level three times consecutively.

Level 1 Learner spreads sandwich filling (e.g., peanut butter, jelly, tuna salad, egg salad) evenly on a slice of bread when given a slice of bread with sandwich filling on it and a knife.

Level 2 Learner puts proper amount of sandwich filling (e.g., 1 tablespoon) *on a slice of bread* and spreads it evenly when given a slice of bread, a container of sandwich filling, a spoon and a knife.

Level 3 Learner puts proper amount of sandwich filling on a slice of bread, spreads it evenly, *and covers it with a second slice of bread,* when given two slices of bread, a container of sandwich filling, a spoon, and a knife.

Level 4 Learner puts proper amount of sandwich filling on a slice of bread, spreads it evenly, covers it with a second slice of bread, and *cuts the sandwich in half,* when given two slices of bread, a container of sandwich filling, a spoon, and a knife.

Level 5 Learner *gets two slices of bread from a loaf,* puts proper amount of sandwich filling on a slice of bread, spreads it evenly, covers it with a second slice of bread, and cuts the sandwich in half, when given a loaf of bread, a container of sandwich filling, a spoon, and a knife.

Level 6 *Learner goes to appropriate place (e.g., drawer) and gets a spoon and knife,* gets two slices of bread from a loaf, puts the proper amount of sandwich filling on a slice of bread, spreads it evenly, covers it with a second slice of bread, and cuts the sandwich in half, when given a loaf of bread and a container of sandwich filling.

Level 7 *Learner goes to appropriate places (e.g., cupboard, refrigerator, drawer) and gets a loaf of bread,* a spoon, and a knife; gets two slices of bread from the loaf, puts the proper amount of sandwich filling on a slice of bread, spreads it evenly, covers it with a second slice of bread, and cuts the sandwich in half.

Level 8 Learner goes to appropriate places (e.g., cupboard, refrigerator, drawer) *and gets a container of sandwich filling,* a loaf of bread, a spoon, and a knife; gets two slices of bread from the loaf, puts the proper amount of sandwich filling on a slice of bread, spreads it evenly, covers it with a second slice of bread, and cuts the sandwich in half.

When learner demonstrates appropriate reading skills:

Level 9 Learner goes to appropriate places (e.g., cupboard, refrigerator, drawer) and gets a container of sandwich filling, a loaf of bread, a spoon, and a knife; gets two slices of bread from the loaf, puts the proper amount of sandwich filling on a slice of bread, spreads it evenly, covers it with a second slice of bread, and cuts the sandwich in half, *in response to written directions.*

Language Skills Area

1. **Receptive Identification:** Learner demonstrates reception of the following task-related objects, actions, areas of the environment, and descriptive words/phrases by selecting objects, performing actions, and going to areas of the environment in response to verbal directions:

bread (slice)		sandwich	put	on
peanut butter		knife	make	in
jelly	sandwich	spoon	spread	with
tuna fish	fillings	drawer	get	and
egg salad		cupboard	open	of
chopped ham		refrigerator	close	
		table	cover	
			cut	

Sandwich-Making Curriculum   289

2. ***Expressive Identification:*** Learner verbally identifies the above-listed task-related objects, actions, and areas of the environment and uses the descriptive words/phrases appropriately.
3. ***Language Program*** *(a model for teaching language through an activity)*
   a. Language Units
      (Teacher direction: Make a sandwich.)

Level (corresponds to Activity Level)	Basic	Expanded
1	spread (sandwich filling)	Spread (the) (sandwich filling).
2	get spoon/knife get (sandwich filling) (sandwich filling) on bread spread (sandwich filling)	Get (the) spoon/knife. Get (the) (sandwich filling). Put (the) (sandwich filling) on (the) bread. Spread (the) (sandwich filling).
3	get spoon/knife get (sandwich filling) (sandwich filling) on bread spread (sandwich filling) cover bread	Get (the) spoon/knife. Get (the) (sandwich filling). Put (the) (sandwich filling) on (the) bread. Spread (the) (sandwich filling). Cover (the) bread.
4	get spoon/knife get (sandwich filling) (sandwich filling) on bread spread (sandwich filling) cover bread get knife cut sandwich	Get (the) spoon/knife. Get (the) (sandwich filling). Put (the) (sandwich filling) on (the) bread. Spread (the) (sandwich filling). Cover (the) bread. Get (the) knife. Cut (the) sandwich.

290   Appendix E

5   get 2 breads   Get 2 slices (of bread).
     get spoon/knife   Get (the) spoon/knife.
     get (sandwich   Get (the) (sandwich fill-
       filling)   ing).
     (sandwich filling)   Put (the) (sandwich fill-
       on bread   ing) on bread.
     spread (sandwich   Spread (the) (sandwich
       filling)   filling).
     cover bread   Cover (the) bread.
     get knife   Get (the) knife.
     cut sandwich   Cut (the) sandwich.

6   open drawer   Open (the) drawer.
     get spoon   Get (the) spoon.
     get knife   Get (the) knife.
     close drawer   Close (the) drawer.
     spoon on table   Put (the) spoon on (the)
                                 table.
     knife on table   Put (the) knife on (the)
                                 table.
     get 2 breads   Get 2 slices (of bread).
     get spoon/knife   Get (the) spoon/knife.
     get (sandwich   Get (the) (sandwich fill-
       filling)   ing).
     (sandwich filling)   Put (the) (sandwich fill-
       on bread   ing) on (the) bread.
     spread (sandwich   Spread (the) (sandwich
       filling)   filling).
     cover bread   Cover (the) bread.
     get knife   Get (the) knife.
     cut sandwich   Cut (the) sandwich.

7   open refrigerator/   Open (the) refrigerator/
       cupboard   cupboard.
     get bread   Get (the) bread.
     close refriger-   Close (the) refrigerator/
       ator/cupboard   cupboard.
     bread on table   Put (the) bread on (the)
                                 table.
     open drawer   Open (the) drawer.
     get spoon   Get (the) spoon.
     get knife   Get (the) knife.

Sandwich-Making Curriculum

	close drawer	Close (the) drawer.
	spoon on table	Put (the) spoon on (the) table.
	knife on table	Put (the) knife on (the) table.
	get 2 breads	Get 2 slices (of bread).
	get spoon/knife	Get (the) spoon/knife.
	get (<u>sandwich filling</u>)	Get (the) (<u>sandwich filling</u>).
	(<u>sandwich filling</u>) on bread	Put (the) (<u>sandwich filling</u>) on (the) bread.
	spread (<u>sandwich filling</u>)	Spread (the) (<u>sandwich filling</u>).
	cover bread	Cover (the) bread.
	get knife	Get (the) knife.
	cut sandwich	Cut (the) sandwich.
8	open refrigerator/ cupboard	Open (the) refrigerator/ cupboard.
	get (<u>sandwich filling</u>)	Get (the) (<u>sandwich filling</u>).
	close refrigerator/cupboard	Close (the) refrigerator/ cupboard.
	(<u>sandwich filling</u>) on table	Put (the) (<u>sandwich filling</u>) on (the) table.
	open refrigerator/ cupboard	Open (the) refrigerator/ cupboard.
	get bread	Get (the) bread.
	close refrigerator/cupboard	Close (the) refrigerator/ cupboard.
	bread on table	Put (the) bread on (the) table.
	open drawer	Open (the) drawer.
	get spoon	Get (the) spoon.
	get knife	Get (the) knife.
	close drawer	Close (the) drawer.
	spoon on table	Put (the) spoon on (the) table.
	knife on table	Put (the) knife on (the) table.
	get 2 breads	Get 2 slices.

Appendix E

get spoon/knife	Get (the) spoon/knife.
get (<u>sandwich filling</u>)	Get (the) (<u>sandwich filling</u>).
(<u>sandwich filling</u>) on bread	Put (the) (<u>sandwich filling</u>) on (the) bread.
spread (<u>sandwich filling</u>)	Spread (the) (<u>sandwich filling</u>).
cover bread	Cover (the) bread.
get knife	Get (the) knife.
cut sandwich	Cut (the) sandwich.

9   Follows written directions.

    b. Language Conditions

<u>Reception</u>

Condition A

    Teacher presents verbal commands (see Language Units, above) and puts learner through steps of sandwich-making activity.

Condition B

    Teacher presents verbal commands and performs steps of sandwich-making activity for learner to imitate.

Condition C

    Teacher presents verbal commands in sequence. Learner follows the commands and performs steps of sandwich-making activity.

Condition D

    Teacher presents verbal commands out of sequence. Learner follows the commands and performs steps of sandwich-making activity out of sequence.

<u>Imitation</u>

Condition E

    Teacher provides verbal model (see Language Units, above) and puts learner through verbal behavior (at desk).

Condition F

    Teacher provides verbal model for imitation (at desk).

Condition G

    Teacher provides verbal model for imitation. Learner imitates verbal model and performs steps of sandwich-making activity.

Expression
Condition H[a]
  Teacher presents a verbal cue (e.g., "What do you get?" "Where do you put the _____?") in response to which the learner will produce the verbal behavior and perform steps of sandwich-making activity.
Condition H[b]
  Teacher provides a nonverbal cue (e.g., points to objects) in response to which the learner will produce the verbal behavior and perform steps of sandwich-making activity.
Condition I
  Teacher presents a situation in which the learner will produce the verbal behavior and performs steps of sandwich-making activity, such as preparing sandwiches for lunchtime.
Condition J
  Learner is in the activity situation. Learner must instruct another person/teacher in how to perform steps of sandwich-making activity.
Condition K
  Learner is in the activity situation. Learner must describe the steps of sandwich-making activity as another person/teacher performs them out of sequence.

4. ***Variations of the Language Program:*** Learner demonstrates reception of verbal phrases outside the context/structure of the activity situation and language units by following verbal directions consisting of functional combinations of the vocabulary listed in objective 1, above, and any previously learned vocabulary. For example:

Basic	Expanded
tuna fish on plate	Put (the) tuna fish on (the) plate.
cut meat	Cut (the) meat.

5. ***Supportive and Additional Language Skills:*** Task-related materials and the activity situation may be used as a basis for supportive language work, such as speech articulation, and in teaching additional language concepts according to the needs and abilities of the individuals. Listed below are sug-

gestions and examples of some language concepts and skills that may be taught with sandwich-making activity and materials as a basis.

Speech articulation: Learner imitates phrases from sandwich-making language units.

Sequencing: Teacher instructs learner to get objects in the order he says/signs them (e.g., "knife, bread").

Pronouns: Learner describes self/other performing steps of sandwich-making activity. (e.g., "I get the bread," "He/she gets the bread," "You get the bread").

Conjunctions: Learner uses conjunctions, such as *and, with* (e.g., "Get the spoon *and* knife," "Cut the sandwich *with* a knife").

Prepositions: Learner uses prepositions, such as *in, on, under* (e.g., "Bread *on* the refrigerator," "Bread *in* the refrigerator," "Spoon *on* the table," "Knife *under* the table").

Vocabulary additions and substitutions: Learner uses other vocabulary, such as various sandwich fillings, *container, jar, loaf* (e.g., "Get the spoon and *jar*," "Put the spoon and *container* on the table").

Answering questions: Learner answers appropriately questions related to the activity (e.g., "Where is the bread?" "What is in the jar?").

Generalization: Learner demonstrates understanding of task-related vocabulary by using words appropriately in sentences (related, unrelated to activity) (e.g., "I eat my *sandwich*," "I *cut* my meat.").

Verbal/written expression: Learner says/signs/writes sentences/stories when presented with activity-related pictures and/or words.

Reading Skills Area

A. *Word Recognition Skills*
1. Learner demonstrates reception of the following task-related words by selecting/circling written words in response to verbal words:

bread (slice)		sandwich	put	on
peanut butter		knife	make	in
jelly		spoon	spread	with
tuna fish	sandwich	drawer	get	and
egg salad	fillings	cupboard	open	of
chopped ham		refrigerator	close	
		table	cover	
			cut	

2. Learner verbally expresses (reads) each of the above-listed task-related words as presented (on cards, blackboard, paper).
3. Learner demonstrates reception of the following written phrases from the sandwich-making language units by selecting/circling each written phrase in response to a verbal phrase:*

Basic	Expanded
get (sandwich filling)	Get (the) (sandwich filling).
get bread	Get (the) bread.
get 2 breads	Get 2 slices (of bread).
get spoon	Get (the) spoon.
get knife	Get (the) knife.
open refrigerator/cupboard	Open (the) refrigerator/cupboard.
open drawer	Open (the) drawer.
close refrigerator/cupboard	Close (the) refrigerator/cupboard.
close drawer	Close (the) drawer.
spread (sandwich filling)	Spread (the) (sandwich filling).
cover bread	Cover (the) bread.
cut sandwich	Cut (the) sandwich.
(sandwich filling) on bread	Put (the) (sandwich filling) on (the) bread.
(sandwich filling) on table	Put (the) (sandwich filling) on (the) table.
spoon on table	Put (the) spoon on (the) table.
knife on table	Put (the) knife on (the) table.

*Phrases are grouped by similarity in structure (all "get" phrases together, all noun-verb phrases together, etc.), because this presentation should simplify the learner's task by limiting the amount of new material presented at one time. Eventually, the learner should read the phrases

presented in any sequence, composed of functional combinations of the reading word vocabulary listed in objective A1.
4. Learner verbally expresses (reads) each of the above-listed phrases from the sandwich-making language units as presented (on cards, blackboard, paper).
5. Learner demonstrates reception of a sequence of written phrases from the sandwich-making language units by selecting/circling a sequence of written phrases in response to verbal phrases:

Basic	Expanded
get bread	Get (the) bread.
get knife	Get (the) knife.
open drawer	Open (the) drawer.
get spoon	Get (the) spoon.
close drawer	Close (the) drawer.
get (sandwich filling)	Get (the) (sandwich filling).
spread (sandwich filling)	Spread (the) (sandwich filling).
cover bread	Cover (the) bread.
cut sandwich	Cut (the) sandwich.

6. Learner verbally expresses (reads) each phrase from the sandwich-making language units when a sequence of written phrases is presented (on cards, blackboard, paper). (Refer to examples under objective A5.)

B. *Reading Comprehension Skills*
1. Learner demonstrates understanding of the following task-related words by selecting correct object/picture, performing action, and going to area of the environment, in response to written word:

bread (slice)		sandwich	put	on
peanut butter		knife	make	in
jelly		spoon	spread	with
tuna fish	sandwich	drawer	get	and
egg salad	fillings	cupboard	open	of
chopped ham		refrigerator	close	
		table	cover	
			cut	

2. Learner demonstrates understanding of written phrases from the sandwich-making language units by following a simple written direction (on cards, blackboard, paper) from the following:

Sandwich-Making Curriculum 297

Basic	Expanded
get (sandwich filling)	Get (the) (sandwich filling).
get bread	Get (the) bread.
get 2 breads	Get 2 slices (of bread).
get spoon	Get (the) spoon.
get knife	Get (the) knife.
open refrigerator/cupboard	Open (the) refrigerator/cupboard.
open drawer	Open (the) drawer.
close refrigerator/cupboard	Close (the) refrigerator/cupboard.
close drawer	Close (the) drawer.
spread (sandwich filling)	Spread (the) (sandwich filling).
cover bread	Cover (the) bread.
cut sandwich	Cut (the) sandwich.
(sandwich filling) on bread	Put (the) (sandwich filling) on (the) bread.
(sandwich filling) on table	Put (the) (sandwich filling) on (the) table.
bread on table	Put (the) bread on (the) table.
spoon on table	Put (the) spoon on (the) table.
knife on table	Put (the) knife on (the) table.

3. Learner demonstrates understanding of a sequence of written phrases from the sandwich-making language units by following a sequence of simple written directions presented in any order. For example:

Basic	Expanded
get bread	Get (the) bread.
get knife	Get (the) knife.
open refrigerator	Open (the) refrigerator.
get (sandwich filling)	Get (the) (sandwich filling).
close refrigerator	Close (the) refrigerator.
open drawer	Open (the) drawer.
get knife	Get (the) knife.
open cupboard	Open (the) cupboard.
get bread	Get (the) bread.

(Activity and Language Unit Level 9)

open refrigerator/cupboard	Open (the) refrigerator/cupboard.
get (sandwich filling)	Get (the) (sandwich filling).
close refrigerator/cupboard	Close (the) refrigerator/cupboard.
(sandwich filling) on table	Put (the) (sandwich filling) on the table.
open refrigerator/cupboard	Open (the) refrigerator/cupboard.
get bread	Get (the) bread.
close refrigerator/cupboard	Close (the) refrigerator/cupboard.
bread on table	Put (the) bread on (the) table.

open drawer	Open (the) drawer.
get spoon	Get (the) spoon.
get knife	Get (the) knife.
close drawer	Close (the) drawer.
spoon on table	Put (the) spoon on (the) table.
knife on table	Put (the) knife on (the) table.
get 2 breads	Get 2 slices (of bread).
get spoon/knife	Get (the) spoon/knife.
get (sandwich filling)	Get (the) (sandwich filling).
(sandwich filling) on bread	Put (the) (sandwich filling) on (the) bread.
spread (sandwich filling)	Spread (the) (sandwich filling) on (the) bread.
cover bread	Cover (the) bread.
get knife	Get (the) knife.
cut sandwich	Cut (the) sandwich.

4. ***Variations in Reading:*** Learner demonstrates understanding of written phrases outside the context/structure of the activity situation by following written directions consisting of functional combinations of the vocabulary in objective A1 and any previously learned vocabulary. For example:

Basic	Expanded
tuna fish on plate	Put (the) tuna fish on (the) plate.
cut meat	Cut (the) meat.

Learner demonstrates understanding of a sequence of written phrases outside the context/structure of the activity situation by following a sequence of simple written directions consisting of functional combinations of the vocabulary in objective A1 and any previously learned vocabulary. For example:

Basic	Expanded
open refrigerator	Open (the) refrigerator.
get milk	Get (the) milk.
open cupboard	Open (the) cupboard.
get crackers	Get (the) crackers.
get peanut butter	Get (the) peanut butter.

5. ***Supportive and Additional Reading Skills:*** Task-related materials and the activity situation may be used as a basis for supportive reading work, such as improving word recognition skills, and in teaching additional reading vocabulary. Any of the additional language skills sug-

gested may be used as reading material, as appropriate. (*Note:* Before reading phrases, drills of the reading sequence — left/right, top/bottom — may be necessary.)

Teacher may substitute or add vocabulary in language and reading. For example, various sandwich fillings, prepositions, *container, jar, loaf* (e.g., "Cut the sandwich *with* a knife," "Get 2 slices *of* bread").

Individuals with appropriate skills/needs may: 1) write vocabulary words in response to verbal words, and 2) write answers to questions related to the activity (e.g., "Where is the bread?" "What do you spread?").

Number Skills Area

1. ***Counting:*** Learner demonstrates one-to-one correspondence by counting out a number of task-related objects (spoons, knives) or pictures of objects (slices of bread, jars or containers of sandwich filling) presented.
2. ***Numeral Identification:*** Learner demonstrates recognition of numerals by selecting/circling numerals in response to verbal numbers.

    Learner verbally identifies numerals when presented (on cards, blackboard, paper).
3. ***Numeral/Quantity Association:*** Learner demonstrates association of verbal number and quantity by getting correct number of task-related objects in response to verbal number.

    Learner demonstrates association of numeral and quantity by selecting/circling appropriate numeral after counting out a group of objects.

    Learner demonstrates association of numeral and quantity by getting correct number of task-related objects in response to numeral (on cards, blackboard, paper).

Reading and Number Comprehension Skills

Learner demonstrates reading and number skills by following written directions (one or more phrases) and getting the correct number of appropriate objects. For example:

Basic	Expanded
get 5 spoons	
open drawer	Open (the) drawer.
get 6 knives	Get 6 knives.
open drawer	Open (the) drawer.
get 6 knives	Get 6 knives.
get 5 spoons	Get 5 spoons.
open drawer	Open (the) drawer.
get 6 knives	Get 6 knives.
get 5 spoons	Get 5 spoons.
close drawer	Close (the) drawer.

Supplementary Skills Area

Fine Motor

Learner traces with finger numerals/letters/words on blackboard/paper.

Learner traces with chalk/pencil numerals/letters/words on blackboard/paper.

Learner copies numerals/letters/words on blackboard/paper.

Learner writes numerals/letters/words on blackboard/paper in response to verbal numbers/letters/words.

Learner writes correct numerals on blackboard/paper after counting out a number of objects.

Learner writes words on blackboard/paper in response to verbal words.

Learner writes words on blackboard/paper in response to objects.

REFERENCES

Axline, V. 1964. Dibbs: In Search of Self. Houghton Mifflin Co., Boston.
Axline, V. 1969. Play Therapy. Houghton Mifflin Co., Boston.
Baker, B., Brightman, A., Heifetz, L., and Murphy, D. 1976. Steps to Independence Series: A Skills Training Series for Children with Special Needs. Research Press, Champaign, Ill.
Bateman, B. 1964. Learning disabilities: Yesterday, today, and tomorrow. Except. Child. 31:167-177.
Bateman, B. 1971. The Essentials of Teaching. Adapt Press, Sioux Falls, S.D.
Bender, M., and Valletutti, P. 1976. Teaching the Moderately and Severely Handicapped: Curriculum Objectives, Strategies, and Activities. University Park Press, Baltimore.
Bettelheim, B. 1950. Love Is Not Enough: The Treatment of Disturbed Children. The Free Press, Glencoe, Ill.
Bettelheim, B. 1967. The Empty Fortress. The Free Press, New York.
Bettelheim, B. 1974. A Home for the Heart. Alfred A. Knopf, New York.
Bijou, S. W., and Baer, D. M. 1967. Child Development: Readings in Experimental Analysis. Appleton-Century-Crofts, New York.
Bornstein, H., Hamilter, L., Saulnier, K., and Roy, H. L. (eds.). 1975. The Signed English Dictionary for Preschool and Elementary Levels. Gallaudet College Press, Washington, D.C.
Bugelski, B. R. 1964. The Psychology of Learning Applied to Teaching. Bobbs-Merrill Company, Indianapolis.
Churchill, D. 1972. The relation of infantile autism and early childhood schizophrenia to developmental language disorders of childhood. J. Autism Child. Schizo. 2:182-197.
Cohen, D. 1975. Childhood autism and physical development. Tardoff Memorial Lecture, University of Utah School of Medicine, April, Salt Lake City.
Cohen, D. 1976. The diagnostic process in child psychiatry. Psychiatr. Ann. 6:404-416.
Cohen, D., and Caparulo, B. 1975. Childhood autism. Children Today. 4:2-6.
Cohen, D. J., Shaywitz, B. A., Johnson, W. T.,. Bowers, M., Jr. 1974. Biogenic amines in autistic and atypical children: Cerebrospinal fluid measures of homovanillic acid and 5-hydroxyindoleacetic acid. Arch. Gen. Psychiatry 31:845-853.
Connor, F., and Talbot, M. 1964. An Experimental Curriculum for Young Retarded Children. 1957-1961 (Mental Retardation Project). Teachers College Press, New York.
Delacato, C. 1974. The Ultimate Stranger: The Autistic Child. Doubleday & Co., New York.
Ebersole, M., Kephart, N., and Ebersole, J. 1968. Steps to Achievement for the Slow Learner. Charles E. Merrill Publishing Co., Columbus, Oh.
Fant, L. J. 1964. Say It with Hands. Gallaudet College Press, Washington, D.C.
Fenichel, C. 1966. Psycho-educational approaches for seriously disturbed children in the classroom. In: Intervention Approaches in Educating Emotionally Disturbed Children. Syracuse Division of Special Education and Rehabilitation, Syracuse University, Syracuse, N.Y.

Ferster, C. B. 1961. Positive reinforcement and behavioral deficits of autistic children. Child Dev. 32:437-456.
Frank, A. R. 1973. Breaking down learning tasks: A sequence approach. Teach. Except. Child. 6:16-22.
Freschi, D. 1973. An Experimental Prevocational Training Project for Autistic and Neurologically Impaired Children. Connecticut State Department of Education, Division of Vocational Education, Research and Planning Unit, Hartford, Conn.
Frostig, M. 1972. Visual perception, integrative functions, and academic learning. J. Learn. Disabil. 5:5-19.
Furth, H., and Wachs, H. 1974. Thinking Goes to School: Piaget's Theory in Practice. Oxford University Press, New York.
Gallistel, E. 1971. Classification of reading materials on the basis of the principles used to teach the phonetic code and to determine the order in which words are introduced. Unpublished paper, Southern Connecticut State College, New Haven, Conn.
Gallistel, E. 1972. The relation of visual and auditory aptitudes to first grade low readers' achievement under sight-word and systematic phonic instructions. R and D Center in Education of Handicapped Children, Minneapolis, Minn. pp. 1-4.
Graziano, A. M. 1970. A group treatment approach to multiple problem behaviors of autistic children. Except. Child. 36:765-770.
Greenfeld, J. 1973. A Child Called Noah. Warner Books, New York.
Gustason, G., Pfetzing, D., and Zawalkow, E. 1972. Signing Exact English: Seeing Instead of Hearing. Modern Signs Press, Rossmoor, Cal.
Hammill, D. 1972. Training visual perceptual processes. J. Learn. Disabil. 5:552-559.
Hammill, D., and Larsen, S. C. 1974. The effectiveness of psycholinguistic training. Except. Child. 41:5-14.
Hewett, F. M. 1968. The Emotionally Disturbed Child in the Classroom. Allyn & Bacon, Boston.
Himwich, H., Jenkins, R., Masamoto, F., Narasimhachari, M., and Ebersole, M. 1972. A biochemical study of early infantile autism. J. Autism Child. Schizo. 2:114-126.
Holt, J. 1964. How Children Fail. Pitman Publishing Co., New York.
Holt, J. 1967. How Children Learn. Pitman Publishing Company, New York.
Hunt, N. 1967. The World of Nigel Hunt: The Diary of a Mongoloid Youth. Garrett Publications, New York.
Kanner, L. 1973. Childhood Psychosis: Initial Studies and New Insights. Winston and Sons, Washington, D.C.
Lerner, J. 1971. Learning Disabilities: Theories, Diagnosis, and Teaching Strategies. Houghton Mifflin Co., Boston.
Lettick, A. 1972. Benhaven's Way. Printed privately by author, New Haven, Conn.
Lettick, A. 1973. On structuring a lesson. J. Learn. Disabil. 6:11-15.
Lettick, A. 1974. My lesson was a flop! Academ. Ther. 9:289-300.
Longstreth, L. E. 1968. Psychological Development of the Child. Ronald Press Company, New York.
Lovaas, O. I. 1966. A program for the establishment of speech in psychotic children. In: Wing, J. K. (ed.), Early Childhood Autism: Clinical, Educational, and Social Aspects, pp. 115-144. Pergamon Press, Oxford.
Lovaas, O. I., Koegel, R., Simmons, J. Q., and Stevens, J. 1973. Some generaliza-

tion and follow-up measures on autistic children in behavior therapy. J. Appl. Behav. Anal. 6:131-166.
MacCracken, M. 1973. Circle of Children. J. B. Lippincott Co., Philadelphia.
Mager, R. 1962. Preparing Instructional Objectives. Fearon Publishers, Belmont, Cal.
Mussen, P. 1973. Psychological Development of the Child. 2nd Ed. Prentice-Hall, Englewood Cliffs, N.J.
Myklebust, H., and Johnson, D. 1967. Learning Disabilities: Educational Principles and Practices. Grune & Stratton, New York.
Nolen, P. A., Kunzelmann, H. P., and Haring, N. G. 1967. Behavioral modification in a junior high learning disabilities classroom. Except. Child. 34:163-168.
Oppenheim, R. 1974. Effective Teaching Methods for Autistic Children. Charles C Thomas, Springfield, Ill.
Ornitz, E. M. 1973. Childhood autism: A review of the clinical and experimental literature. California Medicine: The Western Journal of Medicine 118:21-47.
Quay, H. 1968. Children's Behavior Disorders: Selected Readings. Van Nostrand Reinhold Co., New York.
READ Project Staff. 1973a. Beginning Speech. Behavioral Education Projects, Inc., Cambridge, Mass.
READ Project Staff. 1973b. Speech and Language. Behavioral Education Projects, Inc., Cambridge, Mass.
Rimland, B. 1964. Infantile Autism: The Syndrome and Its Implications for a Neutral Theory of Behavior. Appleton-Century-Crofts, New York.
Risley, T. R., and Wolf, M. M. 1964. Experimental manipulation of autistic behaviors and generalization into the home. Paper presented at the annual meeting of the American Psychological Association, Los Angeles.
Rumanoff, L. 1978. Developing group games for children with severe learning and behavior disorders. Teach. Except. Child. 10:51-53.
Sarason, S., and Doris, J. 1969. Psychological Problems in Mental Deficiency. Harper & Row, New York.
Schopler, E. 1973. Current approaches to the autistic child. Unpublished paper. Grant #15539-4, Department of Psychiatry, University of North Carolina, Chapel Hill.
Schopler, E., and Rutter, M. (eds.). 1976. J. Autism Child. Schizo. 1976 volumes.
Stock, C. 1969. Minimal Brain Dysfunction Child: Some Clinical Manifestations, Definitions, Descriptions, and Remediation Approaches. Pruett Press, Boulder, Col.
Strauss, A., and Lehtinen, L. 1947. Psychopathology and the Education of the Brain-Injured Child. Grune & Stratton, New York.
Teaching Research Infant and Child Center. (staff). 1976. The Teaching Curriculum for Moderately and Severely Handicapped. Charles C Thomas, Springfield, Ill.
Valett, R. 1970. Effective Teaching: A Guide to Diagnostic Prescriptive Task Analysis. Fearon Publishers, Belmont, Cal.
Wilson, P., Goodman, L., and Wood, R. 1975. Manual Language for the Child Without Language: A Behavioral Approach for Teaching the Exceptional Child. Department of Mental Retardation, Hartford, Conn.
Wing, J. K. (ed.). 1966. Early Childhood Autism: Clinical, Educational and Social Aspects. Pergamon Press, Oxford.
Wing, L. 1972. Autistic Children. Brunner/Mazel, New York.

INDEX

Academic skills area of curriculum unit, 20-21
Affective change, curriculum effectiveness for, 219
Autism, 3-10
  causes of, 5-7
  characteristics of, 3-5
  curriculum model for, *see* Curriculum, model of
  facts and theories of, 3-10
  treatment of, 7-10

Bed-making curriculum, 255-268
  language skills area in, 256-262
  number skills area in, 266-267
  reading and number comprehension in, 267
  reading skills area in, 262-266
  sample lessons in, 63-64
  supplementary skills area, 267-268
  work activity skill area in, 255-256
Behavior
  in curriculum unit selection and adaptation, 42
  interfering, control of
    in implementation of work activity area, 55-57
    use of curriculum area in, 26
  modification of, in treatment of autism, 8
  monitoring of, charts for, 206-207
  problems with, in learning situation, behavioral approach to, 15-18
  work, and reading comprehension, 129-130
Behavioral approach in education for severely handicapped learner, 15-18
Bettleheim's theory on causes of autism, 5-6
Blackboard-cleaning curriculum, 241-253
  language skills area in, 242-246
  number skills area in, 251-252
  reading and number comprehension skills in, 252
  reading skills area in, 247-251
  sample lessons, 61-62
  supplementary skills area in, 252-253
  work activity skill area in, 241

Carryover, curriculum effectiveness for, 219
Cohen's theory on causes of autism, 6, 7
Communication, total, in development of language skills in severely handicapped learner, 68
Comprehension
  of phrases, 119-120
  reading, *see* Reading, comprehension of
Conditions in language program, 72-74
  case example of, 74-83
  use of
    at expressive level, 80-83
    at imitative level, 78-80
    at receptive level, 75-78
  student progress in, 83
Counseling, parental, in treatment of autism, 8
Counting, teaching of, 145-149
  sample lessons for, 162
Curriculum
  age of student in selection of appropriate, 23-24
  application of, 21-22
  bed-making, 63-64
    see also Bed-making curriculum
  blackboard-cleaning, 61-62
    see also Blackboard-cleaning curriculum
  comprehensive or remedial use of, 25-27
  design of, 18-21
  evaluation of, 215-222
  functional
    appropriate, selection of, 23-25
    use of, considerations in, 23-27
  implementation of, 219-221

306 Index

Curriculum — *continued*
   evaluating and recording, 189-206
   teacher training for, 179-180
   limitations of, adaptations to circumvent, 221-222
   model of
      behavioral approach in, 15-18
      developing individual educational program within, 43-47
      educational credibility of, 11-12
      introduction to, 1-37
      overview of, 11-22
      preparation and assessment in, 175-222
   principles and theories behind, 12-15
   sandwich-making, 65-66
      see also Sandwich-making curriculum
   table-setting, 59-60
      see also Table-setting curriculum
   toothbrushing, 269-285
      see also Toothbrushing curriculum
   units of
      development of, 211-213
      implementation of, 39-174
      integrating, 175-176
      language skills area of, implementation of, 67-104
      number skills area of, implementation of, 145-172
      reading skills area of, implementation of, 105-144
      selection of, 41-47
      supplementary skills area of, implementation of, 173-174
      work activity area of, implementation of, 49-66

Echolalia in autism, 4
Education, remedial, in treatment of autism, 9
Educational needs in selection of appropriate curriculum, 24
Educational programs, individual, development of, within curriculum model, 43-47
Environment
   for effective teaching, 29-31
   teaching, for curriculum implementation, 220-221
Evaluation
   ongoing, of effectiveness of teaching, 37
   of performance, 189-206
Expression
   as reading readiness skill, development of, 113-116
   sample lessons for, 139-141
   and reception
      of longer phrases, 121-123
      of sequence of phrases, 123-125
      of simple phrases, 118-119
Expressive identification
   in implementation of language skills area of curriculum unit, 71-72
   of numerals, 152-154
   sample lessons for, 166, 168
   relation of, to language program, 84-85
Expressive level of language program, use of language conditions in, 80-83

Fine motor skills, development of, supplementary skills for, 173-174
Formal reporting, format for, 207-209
Functioning, student's level of, in selection of appropriate curriculum, 23-24

Goals, identification of, in curriculum implementation, 219-220
Guthrie, learning theories of, 13

Hebb, learning theories of, 13
Hull, learning theories of, 12

Identification
   expressive, *see* Expressive identification
   receptive, *see* Receptive identification
Imitative level of language program, use of language conditions in, 78-80

Index   307

Independence, relation of reading skills to, 122, 127-130
Instruction, length of time needed for, 125-127

Kanner's theory on causes of autism, 5

Label, object, teaching of, 68-71
Language, achievement in, curriculum effectiveness for, 216-217
Language conditions, use of, in implementation of language skills area of curriculum unit, 74-83
  see also Conditions in language program
Language program
  in implementation of language skills area of curriculum unit, 72-74
  relation of receptive and expressive identification to, 84-85
  sample lessons in, 92-104
  units of, relation of work activity level to, 85-86
  variations of, 86-88
    sample lessons in, 97
Language skills area of curriculum unit, 21
  for bed-making, 256-262
  for blackboard-cleaning, 242-246
  development of supportive and additional skills in, 90-91
  sample lessons in, 98-104
  implementation of, 67-104
    expressive identification in, 71-72
    language program in, 72-74
    receptive identification in, 68-71
    using language conditions in, 74-83
  objectives for, examples of, for individual students, 88-90
  relation of
    to reading skills, 117-127
    to work activity, 160-161
  for sandwich-making, 288-294
  for table-setting, 226-232
  for toothbrushing, 271-279
Learning, theories of, behind curriculum model, 12-13

Lesson(s)
  appropriate, designing of, in implementation of work activity area in curriculum unit, 49-55
  pace of, for effective teaching, 35
  presentation of, for effective teaching, 33-35

Matching, visual, as reading readiness skill, development of, 106-108
  sample lessons for, 136
Materials, preparation of, for curriculum implementation, 180-188
Model, curriculum, introduction to, 1-37
  see also Curriculum, model of
Modification of behavior, in treatment of autism, 8
Monitoring of behaviors, charts for, 206-207
Motor skills, fine, development of, supplementary skills area for, 173-174

Number skills, acquisition of, curriculum effectiveness for, 218
Number skills area of curriculum unit, 21
  for bed-making, 266-267
  for blackboard-cleaning, 251-252
  counting in, 145-149
  implementation of, 145-172
  numeral identification of, 149-154
  numeral/quantity association of, 154-159
  and reading skills, combining, 159-160
  for sandwich-making, 298-299
  for table-setting, 237-238
  for toothbrushing, 284-285
  and work activity, relation between, 160-161
Numerals
  identification of
    expressive, 152-154
    receptive, 149-157
    sample lessons in, 163-168
  teaching of, 149-154

Numerals — *continued*
   and quantity, association between demonstration of, 157-159
   sample lessons in, 169-172
   teaching of, 154-159

Objectives
   appropriate, determination of, 49-55
   identification of, in curriculum implementation, 219-220
Ornitz's theory on causes of autism, 6

Pace of lesson for effective teaching, 35
Parents, counseling of, in treatment of autism, 8
Performance
   evaluating and recording, 189-206
   level of, evaluation of, in implementing work activity area, 49-51
Phrases
   comprehension of, 119-120
   longer, reception and expression of, 121-123
   sequence of, reception and expression of, 123-125
   simple, reception and expression of, 118-119
Piaget, learning theories of, 13

Quantity
   and numerals, association between demonstration of, 157-159
   sample lessons in, 169-172
   teaching of, 154-159
   and verbal number, association between, teaching of, 155-156

Reading
   progress in, curriculum effectiveness for, 217-218
   readiness skills for, development of, 106-116
   sample lessons for, 135-140

Reading comprehension, relation of, to work activity, 127-130
Reading skills
   in bed-making curriculum, 267
   in blackboard-cleaning curriculum, 252
   development of, 116-117, 143-145
   in sandwich-making curriculum, 299
   in table-setting curriculum, 238
   in toothbrushing curriculum, 285
   and work behaviors, 129-130
Reading skills area of curriculum unit, 21
   for bed-making, 262-266
   for blackboard-cleaning, 247-251
   development of supportive and additional skills in, 130
   implementation of, 105-146
   and number skills, combining, 159-160
   objectives for, examples of, for individual students, 131-133
   relation of
     to language units, 117-127
     to work activity, 160-161
   sample lessons in, 135-144
   for sandwich-making, 294-298
   for table-setting, 232-237
   for toothbrushing, 279-284
Reception
   and expression
     of longer phrases, 121-123
     of sequence of phrases, 123-125
     of simple phrases, 118-119
   as reading readiness skill, development of, 108-113
   sample lessons for, 136-138
Receptive identification
   in implementation of language skills area of curriculum unit, 68-71
   of numerals, 149-152
   sample lessons for, 167
   relation of, to language program, 84-85
Receptive level of language program, use of language conditions in, 75-78
Record-keeping for curriculum implementation, 220

Recording of performance evaluations, 189–206
  uses of, 206–207
Reinforcement for effective teaching, 35–37
Reporting, formal, format for, 207–209

Sandwich-making curriculum, 287–299
  language skills area in, 289–294
  number skills area in, 298–299
  reading and number comprehension skills in, 299
  reading skills area in, 294–298
  sample lessons in, 65–66
  supplementary skills area in, 299
  work activity skill area in, 287–288
Seating for effective teaching, 30
Skills
  academic, area of curriculum unit, 20–21
  as focus of curriculum, disadvantages of, 19
  language, supportive and additional development of, 90–91
  reading comprehension, *see* Reading skills
  reading, supportive and additional development of, 130
  word recognition, 106–116
  work activity, generalization of, 57
Skinner, learning theories of, 12–13
Student(s)
  examples of language objectives for, 88–90
  examples of reading objectives for, 131–133
  interests of, in curriculum unit selection and adaptation, 42
  progress of, in language program, 83
  strengths and weaknesses of, in curriculum unit selection and adaptation, 42
Supplementary skills area of curriculum unit
  for bed-making, 267–268
  for blackboard-cleaning, 252–253
  implementation of, 173–174
  for sandwich-making, 299
  for table-setting, 238–239
  for toothbrushing, 285

Table-setting curriculum, 225–239
  language skills area in, 226–232
  number skills area in, 237–238
  reading and number comprehension skills in, 238
  reading skills area in, 232–237
  sample lessons in, 225–226
  supplementary skills area in, 238–239
  work activity skill area in, 225–226
Task(s)
  as focus of curriculum, 19–20
  modification of, in implementation of work activity area, 49–55
  sequence of, in implementation of work activity area, 54–55
  simplification of, in implementation of work activity area, 52–53
Teacher
  in control of learning situation, 14, 19
  preparation of, for effective teaching, 31–33
  training of, for curriculum implementation, 179–181, 220
Teaching
  effective
    environment for, 29–31
    ongoing evaluation of, 37
    presentation of lesson in, 33–35
    principles of, 29–37
    reinforcement in, 35–37
    teacher preparation for, 31–33
  environment for, for curriculum implementation, 220–221
  task analysis approach to, 14–15, 19
Thorndike, learning theories of, 12
Toothbrushing curriculum, 269–285
  language skills area in, 272–279
  number skills area in, 284–285
  reading and number comprehension skills in, 285
  reading skills area, 279–284

Toothbrushing curriculum — *continued*
  supplementary skills area in, 285
  work activity skill area in, 269-272
Training
  of teachers for curriculum implementation, 179-180, 220
  vocational, in treatment of autism, 9

Verbal language, definition of, 67
Verbal number and quantity, association between, teaching, 155-156
Visual matching as reading readiness skill, development of, 106-108
  sample lessons for, 135
Vitamins in treatment of autism, 9
Vocational training in treatment of autism, 9-10
Voice, tone of, for effective teaching, 34

Words, recognition of, skills for, 106-116

Work activity skill area of curriculum unit, 20
  for bed-making, 255-256
  for blackboard-cleaning, 241
  implementation of, 49-66
    behavioral considerations in, 55-57
    performance level evaluation in, 49-51
    task modification in, 51-55
  relation of
    to number, language, and reading skills to, 160-161
    to reading comprehension, 125-129
    to units of language program, 85-86
  sample lesson procedures in, 57-66
  for sandwich-making, 287-288
  for table-setting, 225-226
  for toothbrushing, 269-272
Work activity skills
  achievement in, curriculum effectiveness for, 218-219
  generalization of, 57
Work behaviors and reading comprehension, 129-130